REFLEXIVE MODERNIZATION

Reflexive Modernization

*Politics, Tradition and Aesthetics in the
Modern Social Order*

Ulrich Beck, Anthony Giddens and Scott Lash

POLITY PRESS

First published in 1994 by Polity Press in association with Blackwell Publishers.

Editorial office:
Polity Press
65 Bridge Street
Cambridge CB2 1UR, UK

Marketing and production:
Blackwell Publishers
108 Cowley Road
Oxford OX4 1JF, UK

ISBN 0 7456 1277 6
ISBN 0 7456 1278 4 (pbk)

British Library Cataloguing-in-Publication Data
A CIP catalogue record for this book is available from the British Library.

Typeset in 10^1/$_2$ on 12 pt Palatino by Best-set Typesetter Ltd., Hong Kong
Printed in Great Britain by Hartnolls Ltd, Bodmin, Cornwall
This book is printed on acid-free paper.

Contents

Preface

The idea of this book was originally suggested by Ulrich Beck. Scott Lash taught for some while in Germany and Lash and Beck came to see common threads in each other's work. Giddens and Beck gained a proper grasp of each other's writings only at a somewhat later date. Once this three-way interchange was established, however, a number of striking convergences emerged between what were originally separate bodies of work. These cluster around several dominant themes. Reflexivity – although understood in rather different ways by each of the three authors – is one of the most significant. For all of us, the protracted debate about modernity versus postmodernity has become wearisome and like so many such debates in the end has produced rather little. The idea of reflexive modernization, regardless of whether or not one uses that term as such, breaks the stranglehold which these debates have tended to place upon conceptual innovation.

The notion of detraditionalization, appropriately understood, is a second common theme. To speak of detraditionalization in the present day at first seems odd, particularly given the emphasis of some forms of postmodern thinking upon the revival of tradition. To speak of detraditionalization, however, is not to talk of a society without traditions – far from it. Rather, the concept refers to a social order in which tradition changes its status. In a context of global cosmopolitanism, traditions are today called upon to defend themselves: they are routinely subject to interrogation. Particularly important in this respect, the 'hidden substratum' of modernity, involving traditions affecting gender, the family, local communities and other aspects of day-to-day social life, becomes exposed to view and subject to public debate. The implications are both profound and worldwide in scope.

A concern with issues of ecology is a third common focus. Although again there are some differences between us here, we agree that ecological questions cannot simply be reduced to a preoccupation with the 'environment'. The 'environment' sounds like an external context of human action. But ecological issues have come to the fore only because the 'environment' is in fact no longer external to human social life but thoroughly penetrated and reordered by it. If human beings once knew what 'nature' was, they do so no longer. What is 'natural' is now so thoroughly entangled with what is 'social' that there can be nothing taken for granted about it any more. In common with many aspects of life governed by tradition, 'nature' becomes transformed into areas of action where human beings have to make practical and ethical decisions. The 'ecological crisis' opens up a host of issues concerned essentially with the plasticity of human life today – the retreat of 'fate' in so many areas of our lives.

The paradoxes of human knowledge that have so nourished postmodern views – where they are often connected to the demise of epistemology – can now be understood in more mundane, sociological terms. The social and natural worlds today are thoroughly infused with reflexive human knowledge; but this does not lead to a situation in which collectively we are the masters of our destiny. Rather to the contrary: the future looks less like the past than ever before and has in some basic ways become very threatening. As a species we are no longer guaranteed survival, even in the short term – and this is a consequence of our own doings, as collective humanity. The notion of 'risk' is central to modern culture today precisely because so much of our thinking has to be of 'as-if' kind. In most aspects of our lives, individual and collective, we have regularly to construct potential futures, knowing that such very construction may in fact prevent them coming about. New areas of unpredictability are created quite often by the very attempts that seek to control them.

In these circumstances major transitions occur in everyday life, in the character of social organization and in the structuring of global systems. Tendencies towards the intensifying of globalization interact with, and causally condition, changes in everyday life. Many of the changes or policy-making decisions most influential upon our lives today do not derive from the orthodox sphere of decision-making: the formal political system. Instead, they shape and help redefine the character of the orthodox political order.

Practical political consequences flow from the analysis of these issues. We differ among ourselves in our various diagnoses of what these political ramifications might be. However, we all refuse the paralysis of the political will apparent in the work of so many authors who, following the dissolution of socialism, see no place for active political programmes any longer. Something like the contrary is actually the case. The world of developed reflexivity, where the interrogation of social forms becomes commonplace, is one that in many circumstances stimulates active critique.

The format of the book is as follows. Each of us has independently written a substantial essay upon aspects of reflexive modernization. The three essays have been guided by the common perspectives mentioned above, although we have not sought to conceal our differences with one another. Each of us then subsequently wrote critical responses to the contributions of the other two. These appear towards the end of the book in the same sequence as the original statements.

The contributions by Ulrich Beck were translated from the German by Mark Ritter.

Ulrich Beck
Anthony Giddens
Scott Lash

1   The Reinvention of Politics: Towards a Theory of Reflexive Modernization

Ulrich Beck

Introduction: what does reflexive modernization mean?

The year 1989 will go down in history, it seems fair to predict, as the symbolic date of the end of an epoch. As we are very aware today, 1989 was the year in which the communist world, quite unexpectedly, fell apart. But is this what will be remembered in fifty years' time? Or will the collapse of the communist nation-states of Eastern and Central Europe then be interpreted akin to Prinzip's shot at Sarajevo? Despite its apparent stability and its self-indulgent stand, it is already clear that the West was not left unaffected by the collapse of the East. 'Institutions founder on their own success', Montesquieu argued. An enigmatic yet exceptionally topical contention. The West is confronted by questions that challenge the fundamental premises of its own social and political system. The key question we are now confronting is whether the historical symbiosis between capitalism and democracy that characterized the West can be generalized on a global scale without exhausting its physical, cultural and social foundations. Should we not see the return of nationalism and racism in Europe precisely as a reaction to the processes of global unification? And should we not, after the end of the cold war and the rediscovery of the bitter realities of 'conventional' warfare, come to the conclusion that we have to rethink, indeed reinvent, our industrial civilization, now the old system of industrialized society is breaking down in the course of its own success? Are not new social contracts waiting to be born?

'Reflexive modernization' means the possibility of a creative (self-)destruction for an entire epoch: that of industrial society.[1] The 'subject' of this creative destruction is not the revolution, not the crisis, but the victory of Western modernization.

> The bourgeoisie cannot exist without continually revolutionizing the instruments of production, that is, the relations of production, hence all social relationships. Unchanged maintenance of the old mode of production, by contrast, was the primary condition for the existence of all previous industrial classes. Constant revolutionizing of production, uninterrupted disturbance of all social relations, everlasting uncertainty and agitation, distinguish the bourgeois epoch from all earlier times. All fixed, fast-frozen relationships, with their train of venerable ideas and views, are swept away, all new ones become obsolete before they can ossify. All that is solid melts into Air, all that is holy is profaned, and the people are at last forced to face with sober senses the real conditions of their lives and their relations with their fellows.[2]

If simple (or orthodox) modernization means, at bottom, first the disembedding and second the re-embedding of traditional social forms by industrial social forms, then reflexive modernization means first the disembedding and second the re-embedding of industrial social forms by another modernity.

Thus, by virtue of its inherent dynamism, modern society is undercutting its formations of class, stratum, occupation, sex roles, nuclear family, plant, business sectors and of course also the prerequisites and continuing forms of natural techno-economic progress. This new stage, in which progress can turn into self-destruction, in which one kind of modernization undercuts and changes another, is what I call the stage of reflexive modernization.

The idea that the dynamism of industrial society undercuts its own foundations recalls the message of Karl Marx that capitalism is its own gravedigger, but it means something quite different. First, it is not the crises, but, I repeat, the victories of capitalism which produce the new social form. This means, second, that it is not the class struggle but rather normal modernization and further modernization which are dissolving the contours of industrial society. The constellation that is coming into being as a result of this also has nothing in common with the by now failed utopias of a socialistic society. What is asserted instead is that high-speed industrial dynamism is sliding into a new society without the primeval explosion of a revolution, bypassing political debates and decisions in parliaments and governments.

Reflexive modernization, then, is supposed to mean that a change of industrial society which occurs surreptitiously and unplanned in the wake of normal, autonomized modernization and with an unchanged, intact political and economic order implies the following: a *radicalization* of modernity, which breaks up the premises and contours of industrial society and opens paths to another modernity.

What is asserted is exactly what is considered out of the question in unanimous antagonism by the two main authorities of simple modernization, Marxists and functionalists, namely that there will not be a revolution but there will be a new society. The taboo that we are breaking in this way is the tacit equation of latency and immanence in social change. The idea that the transition from one social epoch to another could take place unintended and unpolitically, bypassing all the forums for political decisions, the lines of conflict and the partisan controversies, contradicts the democratic self-understanding of this society just as much as it does the fundamental convictions of its sociology.

In the conventional view, it is above all collapses and bitter experiences which signal social upheavals. That need not be the case, however. The new society is not always born in pain. Not just growing poverty, but growing wealth as well, and the loss of an Eastern rival, produce an axial change in the types of problems, the scope of relevance and the quality of the political. Not only indicators of collapse, but also strong economic growth, rapid technification and high employment security can unleash the storm that will sail or float industrial society into a new epoch.

More participation by women in work outside the home, for instance, is welcomed and encouraged by all political parties, at least on the level of lip service, but it also leads to an upheaval in the snail's pace of the conventional occupational, political and private order of things. Temporal and contractual flexibilization of wage labour is striven for and advanced by many, but in sum it breaks up the old boundary lines drawn between work and non-work. Precisely *because* such small measures with large cumulative effects do not arrive with fanfares, controversial votes in parliament, programatic political antagonisms or under the flag of revolutionary change, the reflexive modernization of industrial society occurs on cats' paws, as it were, unnoticed by sociologists, who unquestioningly continue gathering data in the old categories. The insignificance, familiarity and often the desirability of the changes conceal their society-changing scope. More of the same, so people believe, cannot produce anything qualitatively new.

The desired + *the familiar* = *new modernity*. This formula sounds and seems paradoxical and suspicious.

Reflexive modernization, as a broad-scale, loose-knit and structure changing modernization, deserves more than philanthropic curiosity as a kind of 'new creature'. Politically as well, this modernization of modernization is a major phenomenon which requires the greatest attentiveness. For one thing, it implies difficult-to-delimit deep insecurities of an entire society, with factional struggles on all levels that are equally difficult to delimit. At the same time, reflexive modernization encompasses only one developmental dynamism, which by itself, although against a different background, can have precisely opposite consequences. In various cultural groups and continents this is joined by nationalism, mass poverty, religious fundamentalism of various factions and faiths, economic crises, ecological crises, possibly wars and revolutions, not forgetting the states of emergency produced by great catastrophic accidents – that is, the conflict dynamism of risk society in the narrower sense.

Reflexive modernization must of course be analytically distinguished from the conventional categories of social change – crisis, social transformation and revolutions – but it can also coincide with these traditional conceptualizations, favouring, overlapping and intensifying them. Thus one would have to ask:

First, under what conditions does reflexive modernization turn into what kind of social crises?

Second, what political challenges are connected to reflexive challenges, and what answers to them are conceivable in principle?

Third, what is the meaning and the implication of superpositions of reflexive modernization with antagonistic developments – prosperity and social security, crisis and mass unemployment, nationalism, world poverty, wars or new migratory movements? How then should reflexive modernizations be decoded in contradictory constellations in an international and intercultural comparison?

Does modernity, when applied to itself, contain a key to its self-control and self-limitation? Or does that approach simply set loose one more whirl in a whirl of events where there is no longer any control?

Self-criticism of risk society

Anyone who conceives of modernization as a process of autonomized innovation must count on even industrial society becoming obsolete. The other side of the obsolescence of the industrial society is the emergence of the risk society. This concept designates a developmental phase of modern society in which the social, political, economic and individual risks increasingly tend to escape the institutions for monitoring and protection in industrial society.

Two phases can be distinguished here: first, a stage in which the effects and self-threats are systematically produced but do not become public issues or the centre of political conflicts. Here the self-concept of industrial society still predominates, both multiplying and 'legitimating' the threats produced by decision-making as 'residual risks' (the 'residual risk society').

Second, a completely different situation arises when the dangers of industrial society begin to dominate public, political and private debates and conflicts. Here the institutions of industrial society become the producers and legitimators of threats they cannot control. What happens here is that certain features of industrial society become *socially* and *politically* problematic. On the one hand, society still makes decisions and takes actions according to the pattern of the old industrial society, but, on the other, the interest organizations, the judicial system and politics are clouded over by debates and conflicts that stem from the dynamism of risk society.

Reflection and reflexivity

In light of these two stages, the concept of 'reflexive modernization' can be differentiated against a fundamental misunderstanding. This concept does not imply (as the adjective 'reflexive' might suggest) *reflection*, but (first) *self-confrontation*. The transition from the industrial to the risk period of modernity occurs undesired, unseen and compulsively in the wake of the autonomized dynamism of modernization, following the pattern of latent side effects. One can virtually say that the constellations of risk society are produced because the certitudes of industrial society (the consensus for progress or the abstraction of ecological effects and hazards) dominate the thought and action of people and institutions in industrial society. Risk society is not an option that one can choose or reject in the course of political disputes. It arises in the continuity of autonomized modernization processes which are blind and deaf to their own effects and threats. Cumulatively and latently, the latter produce threats which call into question and eventually destroy the foundations of industrial society.

This type of confrontation of the bases of modernization with the consequences of modernization should be clearly distinguished from the increase of knowledge and scientization in the sense of self-reflection on modernization. Let us call the autonomous, undesired and unseen, transition from industrial to risk society *reflexivity* (to differentiate it from and contrast it with *reflection*). Then 'reflexive modernization' means self-confrontation with the effects of risk society that cannot be dealt with and assimilated in the system of industrial society – as measured by the latter's institutionalized standards.[3] The fact that this very constellation may later, in a second stage, in turn become the object of (public, political and scientific) reflection must not obscure the unreflected, quasi-autonomous mechanism of the transition: it is precisely abstraction which produces and gives reality to risk society.

With the advent of risk society, the distributional conflicts over 'goods' (income, jobs, social security), which constituted the basic conflict of classical industrial society and led to attempted solutions in the relevant institutions, are covered over by the distributional conflicts over 'bads'. These can be decoded as conflicts of distributive responsibility. They erupt over how the risks accompanying goods production (nuclear and chemical mega-technology, genetic research, the threat to the environment, overmilitarization and the increasing emiseration outside of Western industrial society) can be distributed, prevented, controlled and legitimized.

In the sense of a social theory and a diagnosis of culture, the concept of risk society designates a stage of modernity in which the threats produced so far on the path of industrial society begin to predominate. This raises the issue of the self-limitation of that development as well as the task of redetermining the standards (of responsibility, safety, monitoring, damage limitation and distribution of the consequences of damage) attained so far with attention to the potential threats. The problem here is, however, that the latter not only escape sensory perception and exceed our imaginative abilities: they also cannot be determined by science. The definition of danger is always a *cognitive* and *social* construct. Modern societies are thus confronted with the bases and limits of their own model to precisely the degree they do not change, do not reflect on their effects and continue a policy of more of the same. The concept of risk society brings up the epochal and systemic transformation in three areas of reference.

First, there is the relationship of modern industrial society to the resources of nature and culture, on the existence of which it is constructed but which are being dissipated in the wake of a fully established modernization. This applies to nonhuman nature and general human culture, as well as to specific cultural ways of life (for example the nuclear family and the gender order), and social labour resources (for example housework, which has convention-ally not been recognized as labour at all, even though it was what made the husband's wage labour possible in the first place).[4]

Second, there is the relationship of society to the threats and problems produced by it, which for their part exceed the foun-dations of social ideas of safety. For that reason, they are apt to shake the fundamental assumptions of the conventional social or-der as soon as people become conscious of them. This applies to components of society, such as business, law or science, but it becomes a particular problem in the area of political action and decision-making.

Third, collective and group-specific sources of meaning (for in-stance, class consciousness or faith in progress) in industrial society culture are suffering from exhaustion, break-up and disenchant-ment. These had supported Western democracies and economic societies well into the twentieth century and their loss leads to the imposition of all definition effort upon the individuals; that is what the concept of the 'individualization process' means. Yet individu-alization now has a rather different meaning. The difference, to Georg Simmel, Emile Durkheim and Max Weber, who theoretically shaped this process and illuminated it in various stages early in the twentieth century, lies in the fact that today people are not being 'released' from feudal and religious-transcendental certainties into the world of industrial society, but rather from industrial society into the turbulence of the global risk society. They are being ex-pected to live with a broad variety of different, mutually contradic-tory, global and personal risks.

At the same time, at least in the highly developed industrial states of the West, this liberation is taking place under the general conditions of the welfare state, that is to say, against the background of the expansion of education, strong demands for mobility in the labour market and a far advanced juridification of labour relation-ships. These make the individual as an individual – or, more exactly, only as an individual – the subject of entitlements (and obligations). Opportunities, threats, ambivalences of the biography, which it was previously possible to overcome in a family group, in the village community or by recourse to a social class or group, must increasingly be perceived, interpreted and handled by individuals themselves. To be sure, families are still to be found, but the nuclear family has become an ever more rare institution. There are increasing inequalities, but class inequalities and class-consciousness have lost their central position in society. And even the self is no longer just the unequivocal self but has become fragmented into contradictory discourses of the self. Individuals are now expected to master these 'risky opportunities',[5] without being able, owing to the complexity of modern society, to make the necessary decisions on a well-founded and responsible basis, that is to say, considering the possible consequences.

The return of uncertainty

In this context we should also reconsider the essence of today's 'ecological crisis'. The metamorphosis of unseen side-effects of industrial production into foci of global ecological crises no longer appears as a problem of the world surrounding us – a so-called 'environmental problem' – but a profound institutional crisis of industrial society itself. As long as these developments are seen against the conceptual horizon of industrial society, then, as negative effects of apparently responsible and calculable action, their system-destroying effects go unrecognized. Their systemic consequences appear only within the concepts and in the perspective of risk society, and only then do they make us aware of the necessity of a new reflexive self-determination. In the risk society, the recognition of the unpredictability of the threats provoked by techno-industrial development necessitates self-reflection on the foundations of social cohesion and the examination of prevailing conventions and foundations of 'rationality'. In the self-concept of risk society, society becomes reflexive (in the narrower sense of the word), which is to say it becomes a theme and a problem for itself.

The core of these irritations is what could be characterized as the 'return of uncertainty to society'. 'Return of uncertainty to society' means here first of all that more and more social conflicts are no longer treated as problems of order but as problems of risk. Such risk problems are characterized by having no unambiguous solutions; rather, they are distinguished by a fundamental ambivalence, which can usually be grasped by calculations of probability, but not removed that way. Their fundamental ambivalence is what distinguishes risk problems from problems of order, which by definition are oriented towards clarity and decidability. In the face of growing lack of clarity – and this is an intensifying development – the faith in the technical feasibility of society disappears almost by necessity.[6]

The category of risk stands for a type of social thought and action that was not perceived at all by Max Weber. It is post-traditional, and in some sense post-rational, at least in the sense of being no longer instrumentally rational (*post-zweckrational*). And yet risks arise precisely from the triumph of the instrumentally rational order. Only upon normalization, whether of an industrial development beyond the bounds of insurance or of the inquiry and perceptual form of risk, does it become recognizable that and to what extent risk issues cancel and break up issues of order from the inside out by their own means. Risks flaunt and boast with mathematics. These are always just probabilities, and nothing more, however, which rule nothing out. It is possible to chase away critics with a risk approaching zero today, only to bemoan the stupidity of the public tomorrow, after the catastrophe has happened, for misunderstanding probability statements. Risks are infinitely reproducible, for they reproduce themselves along with the decisions and the viewpoints with which one can and must assess decisions in pluralistic society. For example, how are the risks of enterprises, jobs, health and the environment (which in turn break down into global and local, or major and minor risks) to be related to one another, compared and put in hierarchical order?

In risk issues, no one is an expert, or everyone is an expert, because the experts presume what they are supposed to make possible and produce: cultural acceptance. The Germans see the world perishing along with their forests. The Britons are shocked by their toxic breakfast eggs: this is where and how their ecological conversion starts.

The decisive point, however, is that the horizon dims as risks grow. For risks tell us what should not be done but not what should be done. With risks, avoidance imperatives dominate. Someone who depicts the world as risk will ultimately become incapable of action. The salient point here is that the expansion and heightening of the intention of control ultimately ends up producing the opposite.

That means, however, that risks not only presume decisions, they ultimately also free up decisions, individually but also in a fundamental sense. Risk issues cannot be converted into issues of order, because the latter suffocate, so to speak, from the immanent pluralism of risk issues and metamorphose surreptitiously behind the façades of statistics into moral issues, power issues and pure decisionism. Turning it another way, it also means that the risk issues necessitate, or, more cautiously, appeal for, the 'recognition of ambivalence' (Zygmunt Bauman).[7]

In his review of *Risk Society*,[8] Bauman criticized the 'optimism' – some would say the illusion – which is also a basis of my diagnosis. This critique is based, as can be said from my perspective, on the widespread misunderstanding that risk issues are issues of order, or can at least be treated as such. That is what they are, but that is also precisely what they are not. Instead they are the form in which the instrumentally rational logic of control and order leads itself by virtue of its own dynamism *ad absurdum* (understood in the sense of 'reflexivity', that is, unseen and undesired, not necessarily in the sense of 'reflection'; see above). This implies that a breach is beginning here, a conflict inside modernity over the foundations of rationality and the self-concept of industrial society, and this is occurring in the very centre of industrial modernization itself (and not in its marginal zones or those which overlap with private life-worlds).

Industrial society, the civil social order and, particularly, the welfare state and the insurance state[9] are subject to the demand to make human living situations controllable by instrumental rationality, manufacturable, available and (individually and legally) accountable. On the other hand, in risk society the unforeseeable side and after-effects of this demand for control, in turn, lead to what had been considered overcome, the realm of the uncertain, of ambivalence, in short, of alienation. Now, however, this is also the basis of a multiple-voiced self-criticism of society.[10]

It can be shown that not only organizational forms and measures but also ethical and legal principles and categories, such as responsibility, guilt and the polluter-pays principle (for tracing damage, for instance) as well as political decision procedures (such as the majority principle) are not suited to comprehend or legitimate this return of uncertainty and uncontrollability. Analogously, it is true that social science categories and methods fail in the face of the vastness and ambivalence of the facts that must be presented and comprehended.

Not only decisions have to be taken here; instead, it is vital to re-establish the rules and bases for decisions, validity relations and criticism of unforeseeable and irresponsible consequences (conceptualized from the control claim). The reflexivity and uncontrollability of social development thus encroaches upon the individual subregions, breaking up regional, class-specific, national, political and scientific jurisdictions and boundaries. In the extreme case, facing the consequences of a nuclear catastrophe, there are no longer any non-participants. Conversely, this also implies that everyone under this threat is needed as a participant and affected party, and can appear equally self-responsible.

In other words, risk society is by tendency also a self-critical society. Insurance experts (involuntarily) contradict safety engineers. While the latter diagnose zero risk, the former decide: uninsurable. Experts are undercut or deposed by opposing experts. Politicians encounter the resistance of citizens' groups, and industrial management encounters morally and politically motivated organized consumer boycotts. Administrations are criticized by self-help groups. Ultimately, even polluter sectors (for instance, the chemical industry in the case of sea pollution) must count upon resistance from affected sectors (in this case the fishing industry and the sectors living from seashore tourism). The latter can be called into question by the former, monitored and perhaps even corrected. Indeed, the risk issue splits families, occupational groups from skilled chemical workers all the way up to the management,[11] often enough even individuals themselves. What the head wants and the tongue says might not be what the hand (eventually) does.

We are not talking here about those ultimately diffuse multiple antagonisms, ambivalent and grumbling in their overall political tendency and effect, which practised critics of criticism can and will dismiss as 'superficial' and not affecting the 'logic' of social development. Rather, a fundamental conflict reveals itself behind this, one which promises to become characteristic of the risk epoch. This conflict is already undermining and hollowing out the political coordinates of the old industrial society, that is, the ideological, cultural, economic and political antagonisms that group around the dichotomy safe/unsafe and attempt to distinguish themselves against each other. In a political and existential sense, the fundamental question and decision that opens up here is, will the new manufactured incalculability and disorder be opposed according to the pattern of instrumental rational control, that is by recourse to the old offerings of industrial society (more technology, market, government and so on)? Or is a rethinking and a new way of acting beginning here, which accepts and affirms the ambivalence – but then with far-reaching consequences for all areas of social action? Corresponding to the theoretical axis, one could call the former *linear* and the latter *reflexive*. Alongside the analytical and empirical interpretation of this distinction, the 'politically empirical' and 'normative philosophical' interpretation of these twin terms is becoming possible and necessary (but that goes beyond the purpose of this essay).

This social, political and theoretical meta-theoretical constellation arises and intensifies with reflexive modernization. Only in the redefinition of the present do the dams of the old order burst and the irreducible ambivalences, the new disorder of risk civilization, openly appear. Thus there are fewer and fewer social forms (role patterns) that produce binding orders and security fictions which are relevant to action. This crisis of industrial society's security fictions implies that opportunities and compulsions for action open up, between which one must permanently decide, without any claim to definitive solutions – a requirement through which living and acting in uncertainty becomes a kind of basic experience. Who can do this and learn this, how and why, or why not, becomes in turn a key biographical and political question of the current era.

There are many who say that the collapse of real existing socialism has pulled the rug out from under any social criticism. The opposite is true: the context for criticism, even for radical criticism, has never been so favourable. The petrification of criticism, which was one meaning of the predominance of Marxian theory among the critical intelligentsia for more than a century, is gone. The allpowerful father is dead. In fact social critique can now catch new breath, as well as opening and sharpening its eyes.

Many candidates for the position of subject have entered and exited the stage of world and intellectual history: the working class, the critical intelligentsia, the public sphere, social movements of the most varied tendencies and composition, women, subcultures, youth and alternative experts. In the theory of reflexive modernization, the basis for criticism is conceived of as in some sense autonomous. There is no clearly definable subject. By virtue of its independent dynamic and its successes, industrial society is skidding into the no man's land of uninsured threats. Uncertainty returns and proliferates everywhere. Non-Marxist critique of modernization, small and concrete, but large and fundamental as well, is becoming an everyday phenomenon inside and between the systems and organizations (not only on the margins and the zones of overlap between private life-worlds). Lines of conflict are coming into being over the what and how of progress, and they are becoming capable of organization and of building coalitions.[12]

Sub-politics – individuals return to society

'Individualization'[13] does not mean a lot of the things that many people think it means in order to be able to think it means nothing at all. It does not mean atomization, isolation, loneliness, the end of all kinds of society, or unconnectedness. One also often hears the refutable claim that it means emancipation or the revival of bourgeois individuals after their demise. But if all these are expedient misunderstandings, then what might be a consensus on the meaning of the term?

'Individualization' means, first, the disembedding and, second, the re-embedding of industrial society ways of life by new ones, in which the individuals must produce, stage and cobble together their biographies themselves. Thus the name 'individualization'. Disembedding and re-embedding (in Giddens's words) do not occur by chance, nor individually, nor voluntarily, nor through diverse types of historical conditions, but rather all at once and under the general conditions of the welfare state in developed industrial labour society, as they have developed since the 1960s in many Western industrial countries.

Individualization as social form

In the image of classical industrial society, collective ways of living are understood to resemble Russian dolls nested inside one another. Class presumes the nuclear family, which presumes sex roles, which presume the division of labour between men and women, which presumes marriage. Classes are also conceived of as the sum of nuclear familial situations, which resemble one another and are differentiated from other class-typical 'familial situations' (those of the upper class, for instance).

Even the empirical-operational definition of the class concept makes use of the family income, that is, the income of the 'head of household', an inclusive word, but one that clearly bears masculine features in practice. That means that women's labour participation either does not 'register' at all in class analysis or is 'averaged away'.[14] Turned the other way around: anyone who takes male income and female income separately as the basis must draw the image of a split social structure, which can never be put back together again into a single image. These are only examples of how the industrial society categories of life situations and life conduct presume one another in a certain way. Just as certainly, they are being systematically disembedded and re-embedded – that is the import of individualization theory.

They are being replaced not by a void (that is precisely the target of most refutations of individualization theory) but rather by a new type of conducting and arranging life – no longer obligatory and 'embedded' (Giddens) in traditional models, but based on welfare state regulations. The latter, however, presume the individual as actor, designer, juggler and stage director of his or her own biography, identity, social networks, commitments and convictions. Put in plain terms, 'individualization' means the disintegration of the certainties of industrial society as well as the compulsion to find and invent new certainties for oneself and others without them. But it also means new interdependences, even global ones. Individualization and globalization are in fact two sides of the same process of reflexive modernization.[15]

To put it yet another way, the complaining about individualization which is now in fashion – the invocation of 'we feelings', the disassociation from foreigners, the tendency to pamper family and feelings of solidarity, turned into a modern theory, communitarianism – all this is propagated against a background of established individualization. These are mostly reactions to experienced intolerable aspects of individualization, which is taking on anomalous traits.

Once again, individualization is not based on the free decision of individuals. To use Sartre's term, people are condemned to individualization. Individualization is a compulsion, but a compulsion for the manufacture, self-design and self-staging of not just one's own biography but also its commitments and networks as preferences and life phases change, but, of course, under the overall conditions and models of the welfare state, such as the educational system (acquiring certificates), the labour market, labour and social law, the housing market and so on. Even the traditions of marriage and the family are becoming dependent on decision-making, and with all their contradictions must be experienced as personal risks.

'Individualization' therefore means that the standard biography becomes a chosen biography, a 'do-it-yourself biography' (Ronald Hitzler), or, as Giddens says, a 'reflexive biography'.[16] Whatever a man or woman was and is, whatever he or she thinks or does, constitutes the individuality of the individual. That does not necessarily have anything to do with civil courage or personality, but rather with diverging options and the compulsion to present and produce these 'bastard children' of one's own and others' decisions as a 'unity'.

Now, how should one conceive of the connection between individualization and the welfare state, between individualization and the legally protected labour market more precisely? An example might clarify this, the work biography: for men it is taken for granted, but for women it is controversial. None the less, half the women (at least) work outside the home in all industrial countries, increasingly even those who are mothers. Surveys document that for the coming generation of women a career and motherhood are taken for granted as part of their life plans. If the movement towards two-career families continues, then two individual biographies – education, job, career – will have to be pursued together and held together in the form of the nuclear family.

Previously, status-based marriage rules dominated, as imperatives (the indissolubility of marriage, the duties of motherhood and the like). These constricted the scope of action, to be sure, but they also obligated and forced the individuals into togetherness. By contrast, there are no models today, but rather a number of models, specifically those that are negative: models that require women to build up and maintain educational and professional careers of their own as women, because otherwise they face ruin in case of divorce and remain dependent upon their husbands' money in marriage – with all the other symbolic and real dependencies this brings for them. These models do not weld people together but break apart the togetherness and multiply the questions. Thus they force every man and woman, both inside and outside marriage, to operate and persist as individual agent and designer of his or her own biography.

Social rights are individual rights. Families cannot lay claim to them, only individuals, more exactly working individuals (or those who are unemployed but willing to work). Participation in the material protections and benefits of the welfare state presupposes labour participation in the greatest majority of cases. This is confirmed by the debate over the exceptions, among other things:

wages for housework or a pension for housewives. Participation in work in turn presupposes participation in education and both presuppose mobility and the readiness to be mobile. All these are requirements which do not command anything but call upon the individual kindly to constitute herself or himself as an individual, to plan, understand, design and act – or to suffer the consequences which will have been self-inflicted in case of failure.

Here, too, the same picture: decisions, possibly undecidable decisions, certainly not free ones, but forced by others and wrested out of oneself, under models that lead into dilemmas. These are also decisions which put the individual as an individual into the centre of things and disincentivize traditional ways of life and interaction. Perhaps against its will, the welfare state is an experimental arrangement for conditioning ego-centred ways of life. One can inject the common good into the hearts of people as a compulsory vaccination. This litany of lost community remains two-faced and morally ambivalent as long as the mechanics of individualization remain intact, and no one really calls them seriously into question, neither wants to nor is able to.

Politics and sub-politics

This type of individualization does not remain private: it becomes political in a definite, new sense: the individualized individuals, the tinkerers with themselves and their world, are no longer the 'role players' of simple, classical industrial society, as assumed by functionalism. Individuals are constructed through a complex discursive interplay which is much more open-ended than the functionalist role model would assume. On the contrary, the fact is that the institutions are becoming unreal in their programmes and foundations, and therefore dependent on individuals. Nuclear power plants that can destroy or contaminate an entire millennium are assessed as *risks* and 'legitimated' by comparison to cigarette smoking, which is statistically riskier. There is beginning to be a search in the institutions for the lost class-consciousness of 'up there' and 'down here', because trade unions, political parties and others have built up their programmes, their membership and their power upon that. The dissolving post-familial pluralism of families is being poured into the old conceptual bottles, corked up and stored away. In short, a double world is coming into existence, one part of which cannot be depicted in the other: a chaotic world of conflicts, power games, instruments and arenas which belong to two different epochs, that of 'unambiguous' and that of 'ambivalent' modernity. On the one hand, a political vacuity of the institutions is evolving and, on the other hand, a non-institutional renaissance of the political. The individual subject returns to the institutions of society.

At first sight more or less everything seems to argue against this. The issues that are disputed in the political arenas – or, one would be tempted to say, whose antagonisms are simulated there – scarcely still offer any explosives that could yield sparks of the political. Accordingly, it is becoming less and less possible all the time to derive decisions from the party-political and corporatist superstructure. Conversely, the organizations of the parties, the trade unions and similar interest groups make use of the freely available masses of issues to hammer together the programatic prerequisites for their continued existence. Internally and externally, so it seems, the political is losing both its polarizing and its creative, utopian quality.

This diagnosis rests, in my view, upon a category error, the equation of politics and state, of politics with the political system; the correction of that error does not deprive the diagnosis of its elements of truth, but it does none the less turn it into its opposite.[17] People expect to find politics in the arenas prescribed for it, and performed by the duly authorized agents: parliament, political parties, trade unions and so on. If the clocks of politics stop here, the political as a whole has stopped ticking, in that view. That overlooks two things.

First, the immobility of the governmental apparatus and its subsidiary agencies is perfectly capable of accompanying mobility of the agents on all possible levels of society, that is to say, the petering out of politics with the activation of sub-politics. Anyone who stares at politics from above and waits for results is overlooking the self-organization of the political, which – potentially at least – can set many or even all fields of society into motion 'sub-politically'.

Second, the political monopoly of the political institutions and agents, which the latter demand from the political constellation of classical industrial society, is incorporated into views and judgements. This continues to ignore the fact that the political system and the historically political constellation can have the same relation to one another as the realities of two different epochs. For instance, the increase of welfare and the increase of hazards mutually condition one another. To the extent that this becomes (publicly) conscious, the defenders of security are no longer sitting in the same boat with the planners and producers of economic wealth. The coalition of technology and economy becomes shaky, because technology can increase productivity, but at the same time it puts legitimacy at risk. The judicial order no longer fosters social peace, because it sanctions and legitimates disadvantages along with the threats, and so on.

In other words, the political breaks open and erupts beyond the formal responsibilities and hierarchies. This is misunderstood particularly by those who unambiguously equate politics to the state, the political system, formal responsibilities and full-time political careers. An ambivalent, multilevel 'expressionistic concept of politics' (Jürgen Habermas), which permits us to posit the social form and the political as mutually variable, is being introduced here for a very simple reason. That is that it opens the possibility in thought which we increasingly confront today: the political constellation of industrial society is becoming unpolitical, while what was unpolitical in industrialism is becoming political. This is a category transformation of the political with unchanged institutions, and with intact power elites that have not been replaced by new ones.[18]

We thus look for the political in the wrong place, on the wrong floors and on the wrong pages of the newspapers. Those decision-making areas which had been protected by the political in industrial capitalism – the private sector, business, science, towns, everyday life and so on – are caught in the storms of political conflicts in reflexive modernity. An important point here is that how far this process goes, what it means and where it leads, is in turn dependent upon political decisions, which cannot simply be taken but must be formed, programatically filled out and transformed into possibilities for action. Politics determines politics, opening it up and empowering it. These possibilities of a *politics of politics*, a *(re)invention* of the political after its demonstrated demise, are what we must open up and illuminate.

The socially most astonishing and surprising – and perhaps the least understood – phenomenon of the 1980s was the unexpected renaissance of a political subjectivity, outside and inside the institutions. In this sense, it is no exaggeration to say that citizen-initiative groups have taken power politically. They were the ones who put the issue of an endangered world on the agenda, against the resistance of the established parties. Nowhere is this so clear as in the spectre of the new 'lip service morality' that is haunting Europe.

The compulsion to engage in the ecological salvation and renewal of the world has by now become universal. It unites the conservatives with the socialists and the chemical industry with its Green arch-critics. One almost has to fear that the chemical concerns will follow up on their full-page advertisements and re-establish themselves as a conservation association.

Admittedly, this is all just packaging, programatic opportunism, and now and then perhaps really intentional rethinking. The actions and the points of origin of the facts are largely untouched by it. Yet it remains true: the themes of the future, which are now on everyone's lips, have not originated from the farsightedness of the rulers or from the struggle in parliament – and certainly not from the cathedrals of power in business, science and the state. They have been put on the social agenda against the concentrated resistance of this institutionalized ignorance by entangled, moralizing groups and splinter groups fighting each other over the proper way, split and plagued by doubts. Sub-politics has won a quite improbable thematic victory.

This applies not only to the West, but also to the eastern part of Europe. There the citizens' groups – contrary to the entire social science intelligentsia – started from zero with no organization, in a system of surveilled conformity, and yet, with no copying machines or telephones, were able to force the ruling group to retreat and collapse just by assembling in a square. This rebellion of the real existing individuals against a 'system' that allegedly dominated them all the way into the capillaries of day-to-day existence is inexplicable and inconceivable in the prevailing categories and theories. But it is not only the planned economy which is bankrupt. Systems theory, which conceives of society as independent of the subject, has also been thoroughly refuted. In a society without consensus, devoid of a legitimating core, it is evident that even a single gust of wind, caused by the cry for freedom, can bring down the whole house of cards of power.

The differences between exuberant citizens in East and West are obvious and have often been discussed, but that is much less the case for their quite considerable common ground: both are grass-roots-oriented, extra-parliamentary, not tied to classes or parties, organizationally and programatically diffuse and feuding. The same goes for their rags-to-riches careers on both sides: criminalized, opposed, ridiculed, but later part of party programmes and government declarations or even the overthrow of a government.

Of course one could say, *tempi passati*. The insight might be difficult for many people, but even the extreme right-wing headhunters
who have been mobilizing in the streets of Germany since the
summer of 1992 against 'foreigners' (and whoever they consider to
be such), as well as the covert and unnerving support they find all
the way to the top of politics – the modification of the fundamental
constitutional right to asylum was supported by a two-thirds majority in Parliament in May 1993 – yes, even this mob is using and
acting out the opportunities of sub-politics. This contains a bitter
lesson. Sub-politics is always available to the opposite side or the
opposing party for their opposing goals.

What appeared to be 'an unpolitical retreat to private life', 'new
inwardness' or 'caring for emotional wounds' in the old understanding of politics can, when seen from the other side, represent
the struggle for a new dimension of the political.

The still prevailing impression that social awareness and consensus 'evaporates' in the 'heat' of individualization processes, is not
entirely false, certainly, but also not completely correct. It ignores
the compulsions and possibilities of manufacturing social commitments and obligations, no matter how tentative (the staging of the
new general consensus on the ecological issues, for instance). These
can take the place of the old categories, but cannot be expressed and
comprehended in them.

It makes sense to distinguish between different contexts and
forms of individualization. In some states, particularly in Sweden,
Switzerland, the Netherlands and western Germany, we are dealing
with an 'all-risk individualization'. That is to say, individualization
processes arise here from and in a milieu of prosperity and social
security (not for everyone, but for most people). On the other hand,
conditions in the eastern part of Germany, and especially in the
formerly communist countries and the Third World, lead to unrest
of a quite different dimension.

The individualized everyday culture of the West is simply a
culture of built-up knowledge and self-confidence: more and higher
education, as well as better jobs and opportunities to earn money, in
which people no longer just obey. Individuals still communicate in
and play along with the old forms and institutions, but they also
withdraw from them, with at least part of their existence, their
identity, their commitment and their courage. Their withdrawal,
however, is not just a withdrawal but at the same time an emi-
gration to new niches of activity and identity. The latter seem so
unclear and inconsistent not least because this inner immigration

often takes place half-heartedly, with one foot, so to speak, while the foot is still firmly planted in the old order.

People leave the 'nest' of their 'political home' step by step and issue by issue. But that means that in one place people are on the side of the revolution while in another they are supporting reaction, in one place they are dropping out while in another they are getting involved. All of that no longer fits into one design of an order upon which the surveying specialists of the political map can base their analyses. Here too, the 'end of clarity' (Bauman) applies. The forms of political involvement, protest and retreat blur together in an ambivalence that defies the old categories of political clarity.

The individualization of political conflicts and interests thus does not mean disengagement, not the 'opinion poll democracy' and not weariness of politics. But a contradictory multiple engagement arises, which mixes and combines the classical poles of politics so that, if we think things through to their logical conclusion, everyone thinks and acts as a right-winger and left-winger, radically and conservatively, democratically and undemocratically, ecologically and anti-ecologically, politically and unpolitically, all at the same time. Everyone is a pessimist, a passivist, an idealist and an activist in partial aspects of his or her self. That only means, however, that the current clarities of politics – right and left, conservative and socialistic, retreat and participation – are no longer correct or effective.

For this type of practice, which can be more easily comprehended negatively than positively – not instrumental, not dominating, not executing, not role-determined, not instrumentally rational – there are only faded and blurred direct concepts, which boast and mock almost slanderously with words like 'communal' and 'holistic'. All the non-labels can succeed only in denying and missing the state of affairs, not in getting rid of it. Beneath and behind the façades of the old industrial order, which are sometimes still brilliantly polished, radical changes and new departures are taking place, not completely unconsciously, but not fully consciously and in a focused way either. They rather resemble a collective blind person without a cane or a dog but with a nose for what is personally right and important and, if scaled up to the level of generality, cannot be totally false. This centipede-like non-revolution is under way. It is expressed in the background noise of the quarrelling on every level and in all issues and discussion groups, in the fact, for instance, that nothing 'goes without saying' any longer; everything must be inspected, chopped to bits, discussed and debated to death until finally, with the blessing of general dissatisfaction, it takes this particular 'turn' no one wants, perhaps only because otherwise there is the risk of a general paralysis. Such are the birth pangs of a new action society, a self-creation society, which must 'invent' everything, except that it does not know how, why, with whom and with whom absolutely not.

Political science has opened up and elaborated its concept of politics into three aspects. First, it inquires into the institutional constitution of the political community with which society organizes itself (the *polity*); second, into the substance of political programmes for shaping social circumstances (*policy*); and, third, into the process of political conflict over power-sharing and power positions (*politics*). Here it is not the individual who is considered fit for politics; rather the questions are directed at corporatist, that is, collective, agents.

Sub-politics is distinguished from 'politics' first, in that, agents *outside* the political or corporatist system are allowed to appear on the stage of social design (this group includes professional and occupational groups, the technical intelligentsia in plants, research institutions and management, skilled workers, citizens' initiatives, the public sphere and so on), and second, in that not only social and collective agents but individuals as well compete with the latter and each other for the emerging shaping power of the political.

If one transfers the distinction between polity, policy and politics to sub-politics (this is equivalent to the inquiry into the multivarious structure-changing practices of modernity), then the following questions come up:

First, how is the *sub-polity* constituted and organized institutionally? What are the sources of its power, its resistance possibilities and its potential for strategic action? Where are its switchpoints and what are the limits of its influence? How does the scope and power to shape things emerge in the wake of reflexive modernization?

Second, with what goals, content and programmes is *sub-policy* conducted, and in what areas of action (occupations, professions, plants, trade unions, parties and so on)? How is sub-policy objectified, restricted, conducted and implemented into non-policy? Which strategies – for example 'health precautions', 'social security', or 'technical necessities' – are applied for this purpose, how and by whom?

Third, what organizational forms and forums of *sub-politics* are emerging and can be observed? What power positions are opened up, solidified and shifted here, and how? Are there internal conflicts over the policy of an enterprise or a group (labour, technology or product policy)? Are there informal or formalizing coalitions for or against certain strategic options? Are specialist, ecological and feminist circles or working groups separating out inside occupational groups or plant labour relations? What degree and quality of organization do the latter exhibit (informal contacts, discussion meetings, by-laws, special journals, focused publicity work, congresses or code of ethics)?

Sub-politics, then, means shaping society *from below*. Viewed from above, this results in the loss of implementation power, the shrinkage and minimization of politics. In the wake of sub-politicization, there are growing opportunities to have a voice and a share in the arrangement of society for groups hitherto uninvolved in the substantive technification and industrialization process: citizens, the public sphere, social movements, expert groups, working people on site; there are even opportunities for courageous individuals to 'move mountains' in the nerve centres of development. Politicization thus implies a decrease of the central rule approach; it means that processes which had heretofore always run friction-free fizzle out in the resistance of contradictory objectives.

These are conditions where the various groups and levels of decision-making and participation mobilize the means of the constitutional state against one another. That occurs not just in the confrontation of institutions and citizens' groups but also in the conflicts of national and local politics, between a Green-motivated administration and the old industrial management, and so on. No side gets its way, neither the opponents of power nor power itself, where these concepts become as relative in actuality as they ought to be in thought. A general 'relative paralysis' comes into being (and it goes without saying that citizens' groups are affected too), which is the back side of sub-political activation. But the very fizzling out of the implementation process of industrialization, which used to be so well lubricated by consensus, which now produces losers on all levels, can slow the process, and can be a precursor of an unregulated anarchic self-limitation and self-control. Perhaps 'anything goes' means 'rien ne va plus', nothing goes any more?

The 'instrument of power' in sub-politics is 'congestion' (in the direct and the figurative sense) as the modernized form of the involuntary strike. The phrase that Munich motorists can read at a typically congested location, 'You're not in a jam, you are the jam', clarifies this parallel between strike and congestion.

Paths to a new modernity

A paradoxical situation has arisen with the end of the cold war. What had been completely unexpected, in fact had been proved to be out of the question – the political renaissance of Europe – has not led to a revival of Europe's ideas, to a purgatory and paradise of questioning, but rather to a general paralysis. Sometimes positively, sometimes negatively, one type of fatalism contradicts and corroborates another. Thus, despite all of Europe's inclination to realism, scepticism and nihilism, people misunderstand and cast aside the very thing that constitutes Europe's vitality: being able to renew itself through radical self-criticism and creative destruction. Enlightenment is the exception where the vanquished wins through defeat. Optimistic and pessimistic fatalism agree in one respect: that there is only one shape of modernity, that of industrial society, whose compulsion produces that beneficent mixture of the consumer society and democracy one time, and the next accelerates the general decline. *Tertium non datur. Tertium datur!* Many modernities are possible; that is the reply of reflexive modernization. According to the old formula of the Enlightenment, the latter counts on modernization to overcome modernization. How can that be conceptualized, methodologically and theoretically?

Sociology – or, let us say more precisely, the ageing sociology of modernization – must become a bit of art, that is, a bit playful, in order to liberate itself from its own intellectual blockades. One could call this the chemistry of premises; oppose pseudo-eternal verities, rub them together, agitate them against one another and fuse them together until the intellectual test tube starts giving off sparks and smoking, smelling and sputtering.

How does the image of 'functionally differentiated' industrial society change when one applies the premises of 'functional differentiation' to it? Why do the varieties of sociological functionalism always paint an image of the differentiated society in the sense of a final differentiation, while further differentiations of industrial society operating right now are possibly opening up paths to new types of modernity?

Why should modernity be exhausted in autonomization and culminate, of all things, in 'self-referentiality' as Luhmann argues? And why should it not find new and fertile grounds in focusing on the opposite, i.e. specialization on interrelationships, on contextual understandings and on cross-boundary communication? Perhaps the autonomy premise of modern systems theory, raised to the level of virtual autism, is only the basic multiplication table, while decimal arithmetic starts only where one autonomy is cross-linked with another, where negotiating institutions come into being, and so on? Does reflexive modernization perhaps begin where the logic of differentiation and dissection ends and is combined and opposed with a logic of mediation and self-limitation?

Is it not somewhat boring – all right, that is not a scientific category, so let us say, somewhat insufficiently complex – always to trace the disintegration of the old world in 'binary codes'? Is it not time to break this great sociological simplification taboo and, for instance, inquire into code syntheses, to search for where and how these are already being produced today? Is the combination of art and science, of technology and ecology, of economics and politics with the result of something neither–nor, some third entity, as yet unknown and yet to be discovered, really out of the question simply because the basic multiplication table of functionalism considers it out of the question? Why must science itself, which changes everything, be conceived of and conducted as unchangeable? Or is it perhaps possible that the way in which a change in the framework of science is considered and rejected pushes out of sight the very possibility of self-limitation and change which is available to and incumbent upon the sciences? This would be the *self-opening of the monopoly on truth* that is becoming possible and necessary in and along with the methodological doubts to which science itself pays homage.

No doubt the fatalism has its good sides. It prevents, for instance, the activism of a modernization of modernity which would open Pandora's box. But it also acts as brain surgery for sociologists, who, in their awareness of the autonomy of modernity, forbid themselves from even raising and discussing the issue of alternative modernities in any systematic way. Self-application was the magic word which is supposed to loosen and overcome these old cognitive blockades. In spelling out this thinking we intend to proceed methodically and name the respective principle of industrial modernity which is to be applied to industrial society itself (in the thought experiment). Then we shall inquire what face of modernity results if what is unavoidable becomes true, namely that modernization overruns even industrial society.[19]

Anyone who inquires into the 'functional differentiation' of 'functionally differentiated' society is raising, first, the issue of the (revolutionary) further differentiation of industrial society. If one uses the key concept of 'functional autonomy' as a basis, then two questions of reflexive modernity can be obtained: externally, second, the issue of the intersystemic mediation and negotiation institutions and internally, third, the inquiry into the conditions that make 'code syntheses' possible. These very different signposts into alternative modernities will be cognitively approached and pursued only for a few steps.

Further differentiation of industrial society

The door to industrial modernity was blown open by the French Revolution, which disembedded the question of power from its feudal–religious ascriptions and proscriptions. Contrary to all the professions of impossibility and against conservative rhetoric, the 'plebs' became sovereign – at least in terms of demand and process. This sets the standards for the political grounding of power, to which even dictators have had to subject themselves, at least verbally, to this day.

The industrial revolution also leads into industrial modernity. It permanently gave the owners of capital, the business middle class, the right to permanent innovation. Change, unstoppable and uncontrollable, something that appeared completely inconceivable, even blasphemous, to earlier periods, now comes to be taken for granted, a certainty that always deserves to be questioned; it becomes the law of modernity to which everyone must submit at the risk of political demise.

This reminder that 'functional systemic differentiation' is another word for revolution is sorely needed. Only then can it be understood what is meant when people ask what functional systemic differentiations might lead out of industrial society. Two such are becoming clear today, the earthquake of the feminist revolution on the one hand, and the systemic differentiation of nature 'in the age of its technical reproducibility', in Böhme's phrase.[20] An additional one can at least be thrown into the arena of possibilities as a hypothesis that makes the unthinkable thinkable: technology that wishes to escape the fate of its 'mediocrity', its yoke of economic and military utility and to become or be nothing but pure technology.

The revolt of women, unlike the explosion of the French Revolution, is a creeping revolution, a sub-revolution proceeding like a cat: on cat's paws but always with claws. Wherever it touches it changes industrial society's sensitive underside, the private sphere, and reaches from there (and back?) into the peaks of male domination and certainty. The sub-revolution of women, which directly cuts up the nervous system of the everyday order of society, despite setbacks, can certainly give society a different face. One need only venture this thought experiment: a society in which men and women were really equal (whatever that might imply in detail) would without a doubt be a new modernity. The fact that walls to prevent this are built from nature, anthropology and ideas of family and maternal happiness with the deliberate co-operation of women is another matter. It is not the least of all the shocks precipitated by the failure, in the view of many women, of the permanent feminist revolution which serve as a measure of the changes that will face us from its success. As social science studies show, the broad variety of fundamentalisms are patriarchal reactions, attempts to reordain the masculine 'laws of gravity'.

It is already becoming recognizable that nature, the great constant of the industrial epoch, is losing its pre-ordained character, it is becoming a product, the integral, shapable 'inner nature' of (in this sense) post-industrial society. The abstraction of nature leads into industrial society. The integration of nature into society leads beyond industrial society. 'Nature' becomes a social project, a utopia that is to be reconstructed, shaped and transformed. *Re*naturalization means *de*naturalization. Here the claim of modernity to shape things has been perfected under the banner of nature. Nature becomes politics. In the extreme case which can already be observed today, it becomes the field for genetic engineering solutions to social problems (environment, social and technical security, and so on). That means, however, that society and nature fuse into a 'social nature', either by nature becoming societalized or by society becoming naturalized. That only means, however, that both concepts – nature and society – lose and change their meaning.

What directions are taken here can be determined in advance only by prophecy – and by some application of the principles of production: industrial systems that are converted to natural production are transformed into natural systems which make social changes permanent. Manufactured 'nature' (in the non-symbolic, materialized meaning of this word), 'decided nature', makes the production of matters and bodies of fact possible. Here a policy of creation produces a world of living creatures which can conceal the manufacturing character it creates and represents.

The ecological issue and movement, which appear to be calling for the salvation of nature, accelerate and perfect this consumption process. It is not without penalty that the word 'ecology' is so ambivalent that everything from back-to-the-land sentiments to hypertechnologism can find a place and a rank in it.

The removal of technology from its contexts of military and economic utility, its functional deintegration and establishment as an autonomous subsystem (see p. 26 above) would be comparable to the abolition of the divinely ordained feudal order inside industrial society. The unconstrained rule of technology and technicians in the grey zone between law and politics would be broken up and crushed and give way to a second separation of powers, now between technology development and technology utilization. Yes and no to technology, on the one hand, and to the utilization of technology on the other, would be functionally separated and thus made possible in the first place: fantastic constructivism, self-doubt and technology pluralism, on one side; on the other, new negotiating and mediating institutions and democratic co-determination, where economic considerations rank below others. This would be possible only, if one wished to bring the project out of the clouds and back down to earth, if technology were declared an official concern – as has happened with education in the twentieth century – and financed from public means. Out of the question? It is conceivable in any case and thus a proof that technology – the quintessence of modernity – is organized in an antiquated way.

On dealing with ambivalence: the 'round table' model

Anyone who no longer wishes to accept the 'fate' of the production of side-effects and hazards, and thus wishes to force the associated loss of legitimation for techno-industrial development, must consider how the 'new ambivalence' can be made acceptable and capable of forming a consensus. The answer is intersystemic mediating institutions. These exist in rudimentary form in the various 'round table' models or in investigative, ethical and risk commissions. The theories of simple modernization conceive of modernization autistically, while the theories of reflexive modernization conceive of it as cross-linked, specifically, according to the model of specialization in the context. While simple modernization conceives of functional differentiation *post hoc* and 'naturally', reflexive modernization conceives of functional differentiation in the sense of a substantive 'dividing process', in which the boundaries between subsystems may be planned differently or collaboratively, that is to say, co-operatively. In other words, the question of system formations that are multivalent, permitting and making possible ambivalences and transcending borders is now becoming central.[21]

In risk society, new expressways, rubbish incinerator plants, chemical, nuclear or biotechnical factories and research institutes encounter the resistance of the immediately affected population groups. That, and not (as in early industrialization) rejoicing at this progress, is what has come to be predictable. Administrations on all levels find themselves confronted with the fact that what they plan to be a benefit to all is felt to be a curse by some and opposed. Accordingly, they and the experts in industrial plants and research institutes have lost their orientation. They are convinced that they have worked out these plans 'rationally', to the best of their knowledge and abilities, in accordance with 'the public good'. In this, however, they miss the onset of ambivalence.[22] They struggle against ambivalence with the old means of non-ambiguity.

First, the benefits and burdens of more or less dangerous and burdensome production or infrastructure plans can never be 'justly' distributed. Second, the conventional instrument of political consultation, the expert opinion, fails accordingly. Even the interplay between opinion and counter-opinion does not resolve the conflicts but only hardens the fronts. There are beginning to be cries for an 'ecological trade union' in many plants that deal with and in hazardous materials or products. It is the same everywhere: the demand is for forms and forums of consensus-building co-operation among industry, politics, science and the populace. For that to happen, however, the model of unambiguous instrumental rationality must be abolished.

First, people must say farewell to the notion that administrations and experts always know exactly, or at least better, what is right and good for everyone: demonopolization of expertise.

Second, the circle of groups to be allowed to participate can no longer be closed according to considerations internal to specialists, but must instead be opened up according to *social* standards of relevance: informalization of jurisdiction.

Third, all participants must be aware that the decisions have not already been made and now need only be 'sold' or implemented externally: opening the structure of decision-making.

Fourth, negotiating between experts and decision-makers behind closed doors must be transferred to and transformed into a public dialogue between the broadest variety of agents, with the result of additional uncontrollability: creation of a partial publicity.

Fifth, norms for this process – modes of discussion, protocols, debates, evaluations of interviews, forms of voting and approving – must be agreed on and sanctioned: self-legislation and self-obligation.

Negotiation and mediation institutions of this type must experiment with novel procedures, decision-making structures, overlaps of competence and incompetence and multiple jurisdictions. They can no more be had without breaking up monopolies and delegating power than with the old demands and models of efficient non-ambiguity. Everyone, the involved authorities and companies, as well as the trade unions and the political representatives, must be prepared to jump over their own shadows, just as, conversely, radical opponents must be willing and able to make compromises. This is more likely to be attained and amplified the more the old, instrumentally rational order, according to which the task is for specialists to 'enlighten' laypeople, is not even brought up.

Negotiation forums are certainly not consensus production machines with a guarantee of success. They can abolish neither conflict nor the uncontrolled dangers of industrial production. They can, however, urge prevention and precaution and work towards a symmetry of unavoidable sacrifices. And they can practice and integrate ambivalences, as well as revealing winners and losers, making them public and thereby improving the preconditions for political action.

In risk civilization, everyday life is culturally blinded;[23] the senses announce normalcy where – possibly – threats lurk. To put it another way, risks deepen the dependency on experts. A different way of handling ambivalence thus presumes that *experience* is once again made possible and justified in society – also and particularly against science. Science has long ceased to be based on experience; it is much rather a science of data, procedures and manufacturing.

In this context it is useful to distinguish two types of science which are beginning to diverge in the civilization of threat. On the one hand, there is the old, flourishing laboratory science, which penetrates and opens up the world mathematically and technically but devoid of experience and encapsulated in a myth of precision; on the other, there is a public discursivity of experience which brings objectives and means, constraints and methods, controversially into view. Both types have their particular perspective, shortcomings, constraints and methods. Laboratory science is systematically more or less blind to the consequences which accompany and threaten its successes. The public discussion – and illustration – of threats, on the other hand, is related to everyday life, drenched with experience and plays with cultural symbols. It is also media-dependent, manipulable, sometimes hysterical and in any case devoid of a laboratory, dependent in that sense upon research and argumentation, so that it needs an accompanying science (classical task of the universities). It is thus based more on a kind of science of questions than on one of answers. It can also subject objectives and norms to a public test in the purgatory of oppositional opinion, and in just this way it can stir up repressed doubts, which are chronically excluded in standard science, with its blindness to threats and consequences.

In both cases we are concerned with a completely different type of knowledge: on the one hand, specialized, complex, dependent on methodology, and, on the other, oriented towards fundamentals and fundamental errors (for instance in the setting of maximal acceptable levels, which cannot be corrected in an individual case). The goal ought to be to play the narrow-minded precision of laboratory science off against the narrow-mindedness of everyday consciousness and the mass media and vice versa (in Popper's sense). For that, one requires stages or forums, perhaps a kind of 'Upper House' or 'Technology Court' that would guarantee the division of powers between technology development and technology implementation.

Rationality reform: code syntheses

The 'acrobatic gospel of art as the last European metaphysics' (Benn) or Nietzsche's dictum that 'nihilism is a feeling of happiness' has by now reached and penetrated advertising, business, politics and everyday life, that is to say, it has been understood and is becoming a cliché. After nihilism we do not end up with emptiness, but with aestheticism. In post-traditional society, people walk a tightrope between art and artificiality. That was how boundaries, assignments and commitments formed and determined themselves in tightly woven networks; on the one hand, these make choice, accountability and commitments possible, as well as, on the other hand, mass production, design, sales and fashions. Gerhard Schulze forged the concept of 'sensation society' from and for this (and here he has probably – dare one say? – artfully and artificially overstylized an important and accurate partial aspect). Scott Lash built up this thought into a theory of aesthetic reflexivity.[24] He connects the inquiry into the limits of reflexivity with it, because he assigns aesthetic reflexivity to practical, 'emotional reason' (if such a connection of words is permitted). Here he confuses reflection (knowledge) with reflexivity (self-application). Of course, I have not dealt with the idea of aestheticization as a post-traditional ligature formation that connects mass production, mass consumption and self and social stylization.

I would like to take an essential further step, however. The aesthetic dimension of reflexive modernization, of which Scott Lash speaks, covers and describes only one special case from the large box of, using a somewhat dated phrase, realistic utopias (critics would say: horror visions) at the turn of the twenty-first century. The rigid theory of simple modernity, which conceives of system codes as exclusive and assigns each code to one and only one subsystem, blocks out the horizon of future possibilities, the ability to shape and delimit oneself, in short the art of making yourself at home in the maelstrom, as Marshall Berman put it so nicely.

This reservoir is discovered and opened up only when code combinations, code alloys and code syntheses are imagined, understood, invented and tried out. The 'aesthetics laboratory' that society has long since turned into is only one example for this. The question runs (in classic terms): how can truth be combined with beauty, technology with art, business with politics and so on? What realities and rationalities become possible and actually come into being when the communicative codes are applied to one another and fused together and a neither–nor results, some new third entity, which makes new things possible and permanent?

The problem can be explained with a parallel between the genetic and the communicative codes. The genetic code opens up the generative centre of nature (human nature as well), while the communicative code opens up the centre from which originate the designs of reality and the opportunities for reality of the subsystems. We are concerned here with the autonomized sub-rationalities which delimit and exclude the systemically frozen opportunities for action in modernity. This is where the analogy ends. There is no communicative code engineering (in the sense of genetic engineering), no way of opening and manipulating the codes of the sub-rationalities technically (like genetic codes). What is possible, and has to some extent already been done, is to bring the only apparently 'self-referential' sub-rationalities into relation with one another and apply one to another in a meta-rational thought experiment: in the sense not of 'anything goes', but of a focused regrounding, a creation or, more cautiously, a correction of system rationalities that have become obsolete and historically irrational. For instance, doesn't the recognition of the ambivalence forced upon us by the civilization of threat require a different 'type', that is, rationality of science (logic of research, rules of procedure, methodology of experiment and theory and a rethinking of the subsystemic procedure of peer review)?[25]

Doubt, for instance, which not only serves science but now, applied reflexively, disrupts and destroys the latter's false and fragile clarities and pseudo-certainties, could become the standard for a new modernity which starts from the principles of precaution and reversibility. Contrary to a widespread mistake, doubt makes everything – science, knowledge, criticism or morality – possible once again, only different, a couple of sizes smaller, more tentative, personal, colourful and open to social learning. Hence it is also more curious, more open to things that are contrary, unsuspected and incompatible, and all this with the tolerance that is based in the ultimate final certainty of error.

In other words, reflexive modernization also and essentially means a 'rationality reform' which does justice to the historical *a priori* of ambivalence in a modernity which is abolishing its own ordering categories. Of course, this is the sort of theme that cannot be dealt with in a few paragraphs. As it takes its first few steps, this immodest inquiry into a new modesty can certainly move within the horizons of the sub-rationalities which simple modernity developed and mutually insulated.

It is not an excess of rationality, but a shocking lack of rationality, the prevailing irrationality, which explains the ailment of industrial modernity. It can be cured, if at all, not by a retreat but only by a radicalization of rationality, which will absorb the repressed uncertainty. Even those who do not like this medicine of civilization, who find its taste unpleasant, simply because they do not like the medicine men of civilization, will perhaps be able to understand that this playful dealing with the earthly sources of certainty, this types-of-rationality experiment, is only retracing what has long been under way with vigour as a concrete experiment of civilization.

The invention of the political

This view must be made more specific and defended against at least three objections. First, anyone who abolishes the boundary between politics and nonpolitics deprives herself or himself of the basis of his argument. Where everything is somehow political, then somehow nothing is political any more. Isn't the necessity of political paralysis somehow being counterfeited into the virtue of sub-political mobility and emotionality, following the motto that if nothing works any more, then somehow everything works? Incidentally, 'The knowledge that everything is politics', as Klaus von Beyme writes, 'leads us astray if it is not supplemented with the insight that everything is also economics or culture'.[26]

Second, doesn't sub-politics end precisely where politics begins, namely where the 'real thing', the key question of power, is at stake, in such areas as military strength, foreign policy, economic growth and unemployment? Is the emphasis on sub-politics then just another manifestation of growing obedience?

Third, doesn't sub-politics reach as far and last precisely as long as it can be certain of the support of politics – law and money? Must one not then turn the argument around: doesn't the development of sub-politics presume a reactivation of the political centre and system? It is tempting to suspect that the formulation 'reinvention of politics' is pure wishful thinking. Even worse: isn't this invoking and working for the resurrection of a 'statist absolutism of reform' (Thomas Schmid) after its demise? I should like to block off and refute these objections by means of a conceptual and typological sharpening and differentiation of the political and politicization.

Politics of politics

The East–West antagonism was one gigantic cementing of the political. The antagonism fixed roles in every domain of society. On the small, everyday scale just as much as on the large geopolitical stage, normality and deviation, 'leadership', 'partnership' and neutrality were staked out and determined all the way down to the details of industrial production, municipal politics, family policy, technology policy, foreign aid policy and all the rest. It was the order of the Great Antagonism, and its eternal prolongation, which brought about and reproduced three things: tension, clear possibilities for orienting oneself and a world political order which could give itself the semblance of being non-political.

If it is permitted to compare the unrestrained character of the political to a creature from the animal kingdom, one can say a lion was sitting in the zoo and yawning. The keepers kept up and protected the cage and threw the lion a few bloody morsels to scare and amuse the zoo visitors looking on from all sides. 'Symbolic politics' was what many clever minds called this telegenic lion-feeding, this political circus. The training was general and omnipresent. Politics was becoming trivial. Everything was stage-management. Things that would have happened anyway and the way of presenting them followed the law of inverse proportionality: the smaller the scope of action and the differences between the parties, the more hot air.

With the collapse of the East–West antagonism, a paradoxical situation has arisen. Politics still takes place in the same old cages, but the lion is free. People pretend to be in the zoo – without the lion. They treat lions running at large like zoo lions, and they consider it narcissistic touchiness if the latter do not dutifully look for peaceful cages to lock themselves up. A bit of political wilderness has arisen in Europe, devoid of institutions, large and small, in all spheres of politics, even in those such as technology, industry and business which, not being politics, had hitherto been able to count on generally smooth implementation of their desires.

We distinguished above between official, labelled politics (of the political system) and sub-politics (in the sense of autonomous subsystemic politics). This return of the political beyond the East–West conflict and beyond the old certainties of the industrial epoch compels and justifies a further distinction, which runs transversely to those above, that is, the distinction between rule-directed and rule-altering politics. The former type can certainly be creative and nonconformist, but it operates within the rule system of industrial and welfare state society in the nation-state (or, in our terms, simple modernity). Rule-altering politics, on the other hand, aims at a 'politics of politics' in the sense of altering the rules of the game themselves. There are two things connected to this type of meta- or super-politics: first, the switching of the rule system and, second, the question of what system of rules one should switch to. Perhaps one should play gin rummy instead of bridge or vice versa.

Even inside simple politics, the bridge game, there are a number of individual variants of a more or less sophisticated type which one can play with various degrees of skill and mixed success. A completely different situation arises, however, if the rules of the game themselves are altered or switched. The height of confusion is attained when one plays both at once, bridge and the game of switching its rules. People play with swapped rule systems in order to change the rule systems themselves. Some continue to play bridge and are outraged as others attempt to invent and implement new displaced rules for the game during the bridge game. We face precisely this kind of hybrid of normality and absurdity everywhere today.

The game of classical industrial society, the antagonisms of labour and capital, of left and right, the conflicting interests of the groups and the political parties, continues. At the same time, many demand, and actually begin, to turn the rule system itself inside out, while it remains quite unclear, to put it figuratively, whether the future game will be bridge, ludo or football. Rule-directed and rule-altering politics overlap, mingle and interfere with one another. There are periods when one side dominates and then again periods when the other does so. While Europe is experiencing a regression back to rigid, bloody nation-state game variants of simple modernity, some forces in America are trying to set off for the new continent of inventing the political, trying out – and suffering from – the politics of politics.

The distinction between official politics and sub-politics, which is oriented to the systemic structure of society, must therefore be contrasted with the distinction between simple (rule-directed) and reflexive (rule-altering) politics. The latter measures itself by the depth, the quality of the political. The phrase 'politics of politics', or 'invention of the political', which aims at this, need not be meant normatively by any means. It only brings up for discussion what would have to happen if the subject of discussion everywhere (in the sense of opposing it) were to become reality – independent of whether these are dreams, nightmares or ideas on the way to realization. Thinking minimalistically, we are dealing today with the concrete operational idea of the invention of the political. Conceiving of it maximalistically, 'society' or groups in society are setting off on that mission. The distinction between official and reflexive politics can be applied to both politics and sub-politics as well as to the conditions for their politicization. Consequently a table results with six fields (Table 1).

The political, to the extent that it behaves peacefully or can be kept peaceful, takes place within the nation-state concept of democracy exclusively as a rule-directed wrestling match of parties over the feed troughs and levers of power with the goals of economic growth, full employment, social security, changing of governments in the sense of changing personnel or parties. That is democracy and that is how it takes place and manifests itself. Politics however, in the sense of a reconstruction of the governmental system, a transformation of government, a self-dissolution of government

Table 1

Place and type of the political	Quality or period of the political	
	simple (rule-directed)	reflexive (rule-altering)
Politics of the political system	symbolic politics, growth, full employment, technical and social progress	economic reactivation or metamorphosis of the state
Sub(system) politics	simple expert rationality, dominance of technocratic, bureaucratic action, private sphere	reform of rationality, political entrepreneurs, vocation as political action
Conditions of politicization	strike, parliamentary majority, governmental initiative, collective–individualistic solutions (e.g. car, insurance)	congestion, blockade and, as one variant, the struggle for consensus and reforms of the modernizations inside and outside the political system

both upward and downward by delegating decision-making authority to groups on the one hand and global agencies on the other – never! To put it a different way, politics in the nation-state structure and rule system is no departure into a new land of the political, the geopolitical or the global risk society. People quarrel over keeping and protecting the rules of the democratic and economic game in the nation-states. This model of politics is dubious for many reasons, not least because of a doubled inflation of demands. Governmental politics is supposed to be in charge of everything, and everyone is supposed to take part in it and to be aiming at maximizing his or her personal influence.

Even if no one can say from the depth of her or his heart that she or he believes that the transformation from a national economy of self-destruction to a global and democratic world civilization will really succeed, it will still be possible to achieve a consensus that the present obsolete institutions will be unable to achieve these goals under any circumstances. If one no longer wishes to close one's eyes to this, then one must leave the framework of *status quo* politics in one's objectives – economic growth, full employment, and social security – or at least open them up, expand them, rethink them and recompose them. That is precisely what the invention of the political aims to do. The same applies to Europe, to the world after the end of the Cold War, to the antagonisms between wealthy and starving regions of the earth which are now appearing openly and radically, to the problem of mobile economic and political refugees storming Fortress Europe and so on.

Inventing the political means creative and self-creative politics which does not cultivate and renew old hostilities, nor draw and intensify the means of its power from them; instead it designs and forges new content, forms and coalition. What is meant is a renaissance of the political which 'posits itself', to borrow an image from Fichte. That is to say, it develops its activity from activity, pulling itself up by its own bootstraps out of the swamp of routine. This does not mean the 'politics of convictions' (Max Weber) or a politics of lip service. On the contrary, the invention of politics requires a Machiavellian realism (see below), but does not exhaust itself therein. Instead, it practises and struggles for spaces, forms and forums of style and structure formation inside and outside the political system.

Metamorphosis of the state

One can say contradictory things about the modern state; on the one hand it is withering away, but on the other it is more urgent than ever, and both for good reason. Perhaps that is not so absurd as it appears at first. To reduce it to a formula: withering away plus inventing equals metamorphosis of the state. That is how one can sketch and fill out the image of a state that, like a snake, is shedding the skin of its classical tasks and developing a new global 'skin of tasks'. In a well-known interview, Hans Magnus Enzensberger says:

> The politicians are insulted that people are less and less interested in them . . . they would do better to ask what is the basis for that. I suspect that the parties have fallen victim to a self-deception . . . The core of today's politics is the ability of self-organization . . . That begins with the most ordinary things: school issues, tenants' problems or traffic regulations . . . Today the state is confronted by all sorts of groups and minorities of all kinds . . . not just the old organizations such as trade unions, the churches and the media. Even the athletes are highly organized. So are the homosexuals, the arms dealers, the motorists, the disabled, the parents, the tax evaders, the divorced, the

conservationists, the terrorists, and so on. They constitute ten thousand different power agencies in our society.[27]

In the old Europe, people always described

> the polity according to the model of the human body. The government was the supreme ruler, the head. This metaphor is definitively passé. No centre that predicts, controls and decides is available any more. The brain of society can no longer be localized; innovations and decisions on the future have not originated from the political class for some time now. On the contrary, only when an idea has become a banality does the coin drop for parties and governments ... The [German] Federal Government is relatively stable and relatively successful, despite and not because of the fact that it is ruled by those people grinning down at us from the campaign posters. Although the Minister of Posts does everything in his power to ruin the postal service, letters still arrive. Although the ruling Chancellor behaves like a bull in a china shop, trade with the East flourishes, and so on ... This paradox permits only one explanation: Germany can afford an incompetent government, because ultimately the people who bore us in the daily news really do not matter.[28]

The self-organization mentioned above does not, as Hermann Schwengel points out, 'mean the old liberal topos of the free social forces', for they are now turning against the political claim of the state. 'Self-organization means, more precisely, a reunification of these free forces in the deepest strata of society, in economic, community and political activity.' Self-organization means (reflexive) *sub-politicization of society*. 'The locus and subject of the definition of social well-being, of a specific political power technique, of the guarantee of public peace and of the provocative assertion of a political history of this and only this society [have] moved apart. They [are] just as accessible to economic and cultural institutions as to the political ones.'[29]

The authoritarian decision and action state gives way to the negotiation state, which arranges stages and conversations and directs the show. The ability of the modern state to negotiate is presumably even more important than its one-sided hierarchical ability to act, which is becoming more and more problematic. In late modernity at the tail end of the century, 'the [traditional] state is withering away as a "special creature", as the structure of a sovereignty and as hierarchical co-ordinator'.[30] Withering away need not be synonymous with failure, as in the widespread disgruntledness over political parties. On the contrary, success can kill too. The withering away of the state is often just the other side of the self-organization, the sub-politicization of society; it is a bit of redeemed utopia. Politics condensed down to symbolism characterizes the intermediate stage, in which the classical problems of the state in simple modernity have in part been solved and in part been forgotten in the thicket of active society, but where the governmental challenges of a reflexive modernity are not yet perceived at all.

Social scientists have difficulties with the concept of death. The collapse of the Eastern bloc, however, has demonstrated that there can be such a thing as a governmental stroke. Anyone who rules out the concept of an 'institutional death' forgets what we are dealing with everywhere in these days of radical social change: zombie-institutions which have been clinically dead for a long time but are unable to die. As examples one could take class parties without classes, armies without enemies or a governmental apparatus which in many cases claims to start and keep things going which are happening anyway.

If it is true that governmental tasks die and new ones must be defined and constituted, then the question arises of which tasks and how they are defined. Carl Böhret suggests an interesting criterion for this, the 'negotiating capability' of social interests. He considers this to be fulfilled where interests become capable of self-organization, where they are given voice and significance in the arenas of society and politics by organized agents. By contrast, the new government tasks that must be opened up are characterized in that they are not capable of negotiation but can and must be made so. An example would be the wounding of the vital and survival interests of the as yet unborn and the natural world around us, or the construction of a supranational and ideally global order. 'All problem fields that are in principle "negotiable" between groups of people and organizations can be "societalized". That means here that they can be worked out in the multilateral negotiating system, with the participation of the state. This increasingly also concerns the legal design where the governmental agent is primarily left with the central control of the context.' Put another way: the classical areas of symbolic politics can be moved out and delegated back to the organized sub-politics of society.

All aspects, however, which are 'not negotiable', because there is either the lack of a direct partner or because no interest can be represented effectively by such partners in a reasonable time, should in principle be handled as governmental and functional tasks. That always applies when the 'maxim of survival' is affected and there is a presumption of a 'generational responsibility' of protecting succeeding generations, but it also applies in the case of 'creeping catastrophes'.

For the foreseeable future, deregulation is only imaginable here at the price of disaster. In these areas, therefore, the state devotes itself to those problems which are without social competition for now, in ecology for instance. It is supposed to be allowed to claim a 'process monopoly' for this. The state must permit and even want the tasks assigned to it in each case not to belong permanently to it but rather to be worked off again and again ('societalized', that is) by the competition that occurs.[31]

It is not just a redefinition of governmental fields of responsibility which is at stake here but rather the radical issue of whether certain seemingly 'eternal' tasks and the institutions with jurisdiction over them have outlived their usefulness. Reflexive politics, then, does not mean just the invention, it means the clearing out of the political. Whether, for instance, the armed forces are part of the essence of the state (as almost all theories of the state from Hegel to Max Weber to Carl Schmitt would have us believe) is definitely dubious and must be made dubious in the age of ambivalence.

So this is not a plea for new governmental tasks within the old forms. Quite to the contrary, the core of the argument is that this new task simultaneously forces the state into a new form of managing tasks. The state must practise self-restraint and self-abnegation, give up some monopolies and conquer others temporarily and so forth.

Neither the 'laissez-faire' of a caretaker state nor the authoritarian overall planning of an interventionist state is appropriate for the operational needs of a highly differentiated modern society . . . The goal is the construction of realities in which the constructions of realities of other systems have some freedom of action. In the face of externalities that are no longer internally controllable, what is at stake are self-limitations of differentiated-out functional systems by a process of supervision, in which the perspective of mutual intervention – of politics in science perhaps, or of science in politics – is complemented by the perspective of the invention of mutually compatible identities.[32]

Beyond left and right?

Could it be that we still have the old landscape of political parties in Europe, but already signs and symptoms that it will be eroded down to its very deepest layers in the coming years? Is reflexive modernization then equivalent to a long-term earthquake which is radically altering the 'party geology'? Might all the unease that already takes our breath away today be just the calm before the storm? Or is this true and yet the exact opposite is brought about, that is, because people lose the support of the left–right political order, they restore the left–right order? Perhaps this actually has irreplaceable advantages. The spatial metaphor always applies everywhere and its application to the political is historically established and it tailors the (overtaxing) complexity in a bipolar manner which makes it susceptible to action, an asset whose value rises precisely with the disintegration of the world order.

Certainly, empirical political science confirms the relevance and significance of the left–right pattern in the perception of the populace. Things may be going the same way for those surveyed as for the social-scientist surveyors: they have no alternatives. In their helplessness, however, they help themselves to move on with the conceptual crutches of the past, even though they clearly sense the fragility of these antiquated crutches.

Is the transferral of the communist systems into capitalist systems a 'leftist' or a 'rightist' undertaking? Is the resistance to that process, that is to say, the protection of the 'achievements' of what remains of socialism, 'conservative' or 'progressive'? Are those who disturb the graveyard peace on the left by mercilessly exhibiting the perversions of socialism in all their concrete forms still promoting the cause of the 'class enemy', or are they already taking the role of a 'post-socialist left' and laying the basis of their claim on the future Europe?[33]

The political left–right metaphor, which was born with bourgeois society,[34] is probably unconquerable, unless it be 'dethroned' by alternatives. The co-ordinates of politics and conflict in the future will be cautiously and hypothetically located here and approached conceptually, as if with a dowsing rod, in three dichotomies: safe–unsafe, inside–outside and political–unpolitical. We are concerned here with three key questions: What is your attitude towards, first, uncertainty, second, towards strangers and, third, towards the possibility of shaping society?

Why these three key questions and oppositions and not others? We choose these because, in the perspective of the theory developed here, they have greater opportunities for implementation, or more clearly, opportunities for stylization and stage management than others. That is what is decisive, after all, and not the inherent validity and features of the aforementioned dimensions and categories. On the basis of the theory of reflexive modernization sketched out previously, it is plausible to assume, first, that even in the future it will still be possible to conduct counter-modernizations, second, that the continuation of self-destruction will deepen the battle lines between safe and unsafe, and, third, that the 'conflict of the two modernities' has yet to show its explosiveness politically and sub-politically.

There is little that should be surprising in the significance for the future of the inside–outside, us–them opposition. Considering nationalistic wars and looming refugee migrations, it hardly requires a theory of reflexive modernization to venture this prognosis. There might more likely be a need for that in explaining the how of those phenomena. Where institutions disintegrate, avalanches of possibilities descend upon those who must take action. In equal measure, an unsatisfiable need arises for simplicity and new rigidity. If alternative institutions that make possible and relieve action are not available, then the flight into the masquerade of the old certainties begins. These must be resurrected even while disappearing, as it were. This purpose is served by 'disguises' (in a quite literal sense) which combine two things: ascription (the strongest antidote to disembedding) and – paradoxically enough – constructibility. The hole cannot be filled in any other way.

That is to say, we are experiencing not the renaissance of the people, but the renaissance of the staging of the people (or the staging of the renaissance of the people). The latter gains the upper hand, in broadcasting stations and on title pages, because other types of change are blocked off, and nationalism, as bitter as this may sound to many, exudes the enticing aroma of self-determination. Here the different possibilities of counter-modernization – nationalism, violence, esoterica and so forth – can complement, mix, cancel, amplify and compete with each other.

Of what help is it to point out the staged nature of nationalism? Does it lose any of its danger thereby? No, but it does become more helpless, heterogeneous, and unstable; it acquires, so to speak, postmodern traits and loses the fatalistic and demonic quality that seduces people into dynamic nationalism. This neo-nationalism, which can probably be successfully staged in the long run, is a spectre which, like other spectres these days, needs broadcast space on television and the tacit sub-politics of the (still) democratic majority in the West, in order to be able to haunt effectively.[35]

Something which is at heart similar can also be said of the other two polarizations. The growth of controversies over manufactured threats causes the antagonisms safe-versus-unsafe to dig themselves in. Politicization obviously occurs issue-specifically. That means, however, that anyone who asserts safety on one side finds herself or himself in the ranks of the threatened on the other. Niklas Luhmann drew the conclusion from this that this opposition can not be handled institutionally, nor does it lead to clear front patterns.[36] The result, he claims, is a fluctuating conflict potential that can no more be limited than it can be sharpened into political disputes. It always remains underexposed here that the safety and insurance institutions themselves contain and maintain standards according to which they can be convicted of uninsured insecurity.[37]

And that is precisely what clears the way into sub-politicization and triggers the opposite impulses towards 'more of the same' and non-politics. The opposition between old and new modernity is a shock which encompasses and electrifies all fields of action in modern society. Uprisings encounter the resistance of the routines and those caught up in them. Reflexive, not simple, sub-politics must organize itself. Two patterns can be explored for this: the blockade and the coalition.

A general paralysis comes about along with sub-politicization; the modernizers as well as their critics run in place or get caught in the thicket of fomented points of view and interests. This petering out of the implementation process of industrialization, formerly so well oiled by consensus, slows the process and is the precursor of an anarchic self-limitation and self-control of previously unchecked industrialization as usual.[38]

The general confusion and opposition inside and outside the institutions necessitates and favours the formation of support networks crossing the boundaries of systems and institutions, which must be personally connected and preserved. In a certain way, then, the disintegration of institutions makes room for a refeudalization of social relationships. It is the opening for a neo-Machiavellianism in all areas of social action. Orderings must be created, forged and formed. Only networks, which must be connected together and preserved and have their own 'currency', allow the formation of power or opposing power.

Life-and-death politics

The antagonisms of the political world, such as liberalism, socialism, nationalism or conservatism, which rule in heads, parties, parliaments and in the institutions of political education, are the products of emerging industrialism. Those political theories talk about the problems of shaping nature and environmental destruction with all the insight of blind people talking about colours, and the same applies to the issues of feminism, to the critique of experts and technology and to alternative versions of science.

The concept of politics in simple modernity is based on a system of axes, one co-ordinate of which runs between the poles of left and right and the other between public and private. Becoming political here means leaving the private sphere in the direction of the public sphere, or conversely, that the demands of parties, party politics or the government proliferate into every niche of private life. If the citizen does not go to politics, then politics comes to the citizen.

Anthony Giddens calls this model 'emancipative politics' and delimits it against 'life politics'. 'Life politics concern political issues which flow from processes of self-actualization in post-traditional contexts, where globalizing tendencies intrude deeply into the reflexive project of the self, and conversely where processes of self-realization influence global strategies.'[39]

The exciting aspect of this view lies in the fact that here, in contrast to Christopher Lasch and his talk of 'Marxist culture', the political is achieved or makes its invasion in the passage through the private sphere, the back way around so to speak. All the things that are considered loss, danger, waste and decay in the left–right framework of bourgeois politics, things like concern with the self, the questions: who am I? what do I want? where am I headed?, in short all the original sins of individualism, lead to a different type of identity of the political: life-and-death politics.

Perhaps this new quality of the political will become comprehensible if one first pays attention to the hysterias that arise here. The pollution of air, water and foodstuffs certainly increases allergies in the medical, but also in the psychological sense of the word. Everyone is caught up in defensive battles of various types, anticipating the surrounding hostile substances in one's manner of living and eating. Those substances lie in ambush everywhere, invisibly. In other words, in ecological culture the most general and the most intimate things are directly and inescapably interconnected in the depths of private life. Private life becomes in essence the plaything of scientific results and theories, or of public controversies and conflicts. The questions of a distant world of chemical formulas burst forth with deadly seriousness in the inmost recesses of personal life conduct as questions of self, identity and existence and cannot be ignored. In global risk society, then, privacy as the smallest conceivable unity of the political contains world society, to use the image of the Russian dolls once again. The political nestles down in the middle of private life and torments us.

What constitutes the political, the politicizing aspect of life politics? First, inescapability, which, second, stands in contradiction to the principles of private sovereignty and, third, can no longer claim the character of natural constraints (in the original sense of the word). In contrast to the claims of modernity to order and decision-making, a new compulsory experience comes into being, which neither coincides with nor should be confused with the dependence on nature in earlier centuries or the class experience of the industrial epoch.

This is the experience of the 'nature fate' produced by civilization, in which the reflexive ego culture experiences and suffers the relentlessness of its technical constructivity and its global society. Now the microcosm of personal life conduct is interconnected with the macrocosm of terribly insoluble global problems. In order to take a breath without second thoughts, one ultimately has to – or ought to – turn the ordering of the world upside down.

This arouses an existential survival interest in scientific categories, sources of error, and perspectives, of which the earlier humanists could only dream. The philosophical issues of existentialism, for instance, become part of everyday life, almost burning issues. Søren Kierkegaard's concern with anxiety as the other side of freedom, for instance, or the issues of who defines and makes decisions on life and death and in what way, force themselves upon everyone in the distress of having to make a decision and become great issues which electrify everyone.

This new symbiosis of philosophy and everyday life shows up strikingly in the issues which people are forced to decide by advanced medicine and genetic engineering. Those developments are tantamount to a democratization of God. They force people into questions that earlier cultures and religions had projected on to God or the gods. The successes of reproductive medicine and genetic engineering will soon put parents and doctors in a position to select qualities of the coming generation negatively or, eventually, perhaps positively as well. It is already possible to recognize certain 'congenital diseases', as they are called, at an early stage and, in combination with abortion, to prevent the birth of a child with these probability characteristics. It is foreseeable that the choice of male or female offspring could also be 'regulated' in this way – unless there are explicit, difficult-to-monitor prohibitions which also apply mainly to a certain cultural group. And all of this is just the beginning of a long series of scientific revolutions.

The quality of the political which is emerging here is capable of changing society in an existential sense.[40] If the developments of human biology and genetics continue to be implemented solely as called for by the market, the constitution, freedom of research and the belief in medical progress, then the cumulative effect will be, in the truest sense of the word, a profound 'genetic' change of society, and not by parliamentary or governmental decision. Instead, this will occur through the unpolitical private sphere, the decision of millions of individuals, parents and mothers, with the advice of doctors and such bureaucratic test-tube creatures as 'genetic counsellors'. The utopias of eugenic progress from previous centuries will probably not be enforced from above with organized cruelty and brutality, as was National Socialist racial insanity (although that cannot be ruled out).

The 'executive branch' of the genetic cultural and social revolution in the future is the individual decision of the 'private individual'. The patient will become a revolutionary in his or her own cause. The genetic engineering revolution is extra-parliamentary. The formula 'the private is the political' thus acquires a secondary biotechnical meaning, which can quickly become its primary one. As was said, the history of humanity, its peril and its tragedy, is only just beginning, for technology, in its intensified application to the genetic realm, is becoming the birthplace of religious wars which, unlike their forebears in the late Middle Ages, can no longer be neutralized by the state. First intimations of the fundamentalist conflicts that face late biotechnical modernity can already be felt in the disputes over legalized abortion. In 'body politics', so emotionally charged with identity issues, religious wars between groups with conflicting lifestyles are waiting at every fork in the road.

Vocation as political action

One of the key questions will be the extent to which these antagonisms impact back on the guardians of rationality, the experts. After all, the question of power is raised in institutions when alternatives are worked out and expert groups rivalling over substantive issues collide.

Vocations and professions – understood as 'brand-name products' on the labour market, as commodity-like, licensed competence[41] – are the guardians of a certain form of normalized sub-politics. Personal-social identity is connected in these 'labour force patterns' with the right and the duty to arrange the substance of work. Vocational groups possess the productive intelligence and the power to arrange things in society. This can have varying meanings. Some contribute to the public welfare in a policy of small steps, others conduct health policy and still others 'improve the world' with genetic engineering. The professional form provides protection against the injustices of the labour market by protecting opportunities for strategic action even with respect to the plants, the purchasers of labour power.

There is a second factor connected to this: vocations and professions are (possible) foci of bourgeois oppositional politics. In addition to the struggles for social and legal security, the franchise and the right of assembly, this is a centre of obstinacy for self-assured individuality. The heterogeneity of the intelligentsia, the variability of its situations, intentions and views and the constant internal quarrelling, the contempt and lack of consideration its members practise in their dealings with one another – all of these make the intelligentsia anything in the world except a 'class' in any politically practicable sense of that term.

Third, professions are *de facto* agents in a global society of specialists, and this concretely existing supranationality predestines them to be agents of global solutions.

Fourth, the (reflexive) sub-politicization of the experts occurs to precisely the extent to which alternative rationalities and opportunities for action are produced and contrasted inside the professional and expert fields.

Technocracy ends with the alternatives which break open in the techno-economic process and polarize it. These alternatives become fundamental and detailed, professional and profitable, found careers, open markets and perhaps even global markets. They divide up the power bloc of the economy in this way and thereby make possible and enforce new conflicts and constellations between and inside the institutions, parties, interest groups and public spheres of all types, and as far as and as soon as all this occurs, the image of the indifferent self-referentiality of social systems shatters. The systems themselves become subject to arrangement. Like social classes, social systems also fade in the wake of reflexive modernization. Their continued existence becomes dependent upon decisions and legitimation, and therefore changeable. Opportunities for alternative action will therefore be the death of the individual-dependent systems.

An essential role is played here by the issue of how deeply alternative activity affects and even splits the ranks of expert rationality. Until now, this was unthinkable, or at least not a concrete threat. Three conditions have changed this: the transition from simple to reflexive scientization, the ecological issue and the penetration of feminist orientations into the various professions and fields of occupational activity.

Where the sciences and expert disciplines adopt and illuminate each other's foundations, consequences and errors, the same thing happens to expert rationality which simple scientization accomplished with lay rationality. Its shortcomings become discernible, questionable, capable of arrangement and rearrangement. The ecological issue penetrates into all occupational fields and makes itself felt in substantive controversies over methods, calculation procedures, norms, plans and routines. In any case, the existence of ecological splits in the occupational groups becomes an essential indicator and gauge of the stability of classical industrial society.

The same applies in a different way to feminist critiques of science and the professions, whenever they are not content with merely denouncing the professional exclusion of women but go on to criticize the professional monopoly on rationality and praxis and to redefine and compose specialist competence with inter-professional acumen and methodology. They do so, furthermore, not individually but organized and in a group.

This is how an ideal cracks up. Experts can solve differences of opinion, so the presumption goes, by means of their methodology and their scientific and technical norms. If only one conducts research long enough, then the opposing arguments will fall silent and unity and clarity will prevail. The exact opposite could occur. Research that inquires further and into more difficult questions, taking up all the objections and making them its own, this kind of reflexive research breaks up its own claims to clarity and monopoly; it simultaneously elevates both the dependence on justification and the uncertainty of all arguments.

It is an obvious objection that all of those things are speculations, which are being pushed aside by the hard maxims of free-market success. After all, many will say or hope, we are concerned with fleeting opinions, with agreements that can be revoked once and then granted again, with their banners largely fluttering in the wind of the economic climate. A juicy depression (no matter how regrettable its details might be), combined with mass unemployment eroding the substance and the self-confidence of the populace, drives away these spectres and resurrects the old guidelines of classical industrialization like the phoenix from the ashes.

This objection may apply under certain early conditions of ecological critique, but this is less and less true when business itself profits from the successes and hazards it has created. If sectors come into existence which build up their existence and their markets upon the recognition and elimination of hazards, then even the centres of economic power are split into orthodox believers and reformists, reformers, environmental Protestants, ecological converts. If it becomes an established view that ecological solutions, as well as ecological competency and intelligence in all fields of society, are conformist not only in terms of values but also with respect to the marketplace, in the long run perhaps even the world market, then trenches between losers and winners in the ecological competition for (economic) survival open up and become deeper. Ecology becomes a hit, a self-seller – at least in the form of ecological cosmetics or packaging. The resistance of the one half of the economy and society encounters a grand coalition of the alarmed public, the eco-profiteers and the eco-careerists in industry, the administration, science and politics. That means, however, that alternatives open up, co-operation becomes uncertain and coalitions must be forged, endured and fought out, which in turn cause further polarization. This precisely accelerates the circle of power disintegration in the institutions.

Along with the threat and the general perception of it, a highly legitimate interest in preventing and eliminating it arises. The ecological crisis produces and cultivates a cultural Red Cross consciousness. It transforms everyday, trivial, unimportant things into tests of courage in which heroism can be exhibited. Far from intensifying and confirming the general pointlessness of modernity, ecological threats create a substantive semantic horizon of avoidance, prevention and helping. This is a moral climate and milieu that intensifies with the size of the threat, in which the dramatic roles of heroes and villains achieve a new everyday meaning. Sisyphus legends spring up. Even negative fatalism – 'nothing works any more, it's all too late' – is ultimately only a variant of that. This is precisely the background against which the role of Cassandra can become a vocation or a career.

The ecological issue, the perception of the world in the co-ordinate system of ecological–industrial self-imperilment, turn morality, religion, fundamentalism, hopelessness, tragedy, suicide and death – always intermingled with the opposite, salvation or help – into a universal drama. In this concrete theatre, this continuing drama, this everyday horror comedy, business is free to take on the role of the villain and poisoner, or to slip into the role of the hero and helper and celebrate this publicly. Whether that solves anything is another matter. The cultural stages of the ecological issue modernize archaism. There are dragons and dragon-slayers here, odysseys, gods and demons, except that these are now played, split up, assigned and refused with shared roles in all spheres of action – in politics, law, the administration, and not least of all in business. In the ecological issue, a postmodern, jaded, saturated, meaningless, and fatalistic *pâté de foie gras* culture creates a Herculean task for itself, which acts as a stimulus everywhere and splits business into *Untergangster* (gangsters of doom) and Robin Hoods.

Drawing on Volker von Prittwitz, one can distinguish two systemical constellations in the ecological conflict.[42] The first constellation is the *blockade*, where polluter industries and affected groups face one another exclusively and spectacularly. This confrontational constellation begins to move only in a second constellation, in which (*a*) helper interests awaken and (*b*) the coalition of concealment between polluters and potential losers becomes brittle. This occurs to the extent that parts of business, but also of the professional intelligentsia (engineers, researchers, lawyers and judges), slip into the role of rescuer and helper, that is to say, they discover the ecological issue as a construction of power and markets, that is as expansion of power and markets. This, in turn, presupposes that industrial society becomes an industrial society with a bad conscience, that it understands and indicts itself as a risk society. Only in that way can helping and coping industries and careers develop themselves and their heroism, which both motivates and skims off profits. This presumes a turning away from mere criticism and the transition to the siege of the *status quo* by alternatives. The ecological issue must be worked down into other questions: technology, development, production arrangements, product policy, type of nutrition, lifestyles, legal norms, organizational and administrative forms, and so on.

Only a society which awakes from the pessimism of the confrontational constellation and conceives of the ecological issue as a providential gift for the universal self-reformation of a previously

fatalistic industrial modernity can exhaust the potential of the helping and heroic roles and gain the impetus from them, not to conduct
cosmetic ecology on a grand scale but to actually assure viability in
the future. Ecology cancels out objective apoliticism of the economic
sphere. The latter splits up in its sinfulness, it can be split all the way
into its management, into the personality and the identity of the
people on all levels of action. This splitting and susceptibility to
division into the sinful and those absolved of sin permits a 'political
trade of indulgences' and restores to politics the power instruments
of 'papal jurisdiction and misjurisdiction', the public exhibition and
self-castigation of the great industrial sinners, even the public tor-
ture implements of an 'ecological inquisition'. Most politicians shy
away from this in their kindness in keeping with public expectations. The professional swimmers-upstream in the ecological movement seem to lack the political charisma and realism to pull those
instruments out of the political tool chest by themselves.

NOTES

The text posits in much abbreviated form the argument of my book *Die
Erfindung des Politischen*, Frankfurt: Suhrkamp, 1993. For discussing and
rediscussing the themes of this essay I thank Elisabeth Beck-Gernsheim,
Wolfgang Bonss, Christoph Lau, Ronald Hitzler, Elmar Koenen, Maarten
Hajer and last but not least Michaela Pfadenhauer.

1 The notion of 'reflexive modernization' is used by A. Giddens in his
   books *The Consequences of Modernity*, Cambridge: Polity, 1990, and
   Modernity and Self-Identity, Cambridge: Polity, 1991, and by S. Lash
   in 'Reflexive modernization: the aesthetic dimension', *Theory, Culture
   and Society*, vol. 10, no. 1, 1993, pp. 1–24. I used it in my book *Risk
   Society: Towards a New Modernity*, London: Sage, 1992; in the context of ecological crises in my book *Gegengifte: Die organisierte
   Unverantwortlichkeit*, Frankfurt: Suhrkamp, 1988, English title *Ecological Politics in the Age of Risk*, Cambridge: Polity, 1994; in the context of
   sex roles, family and love in U. Beck and E. Beck-Gernsheim, *Das
   ganz normale Chaos der Liebe*, Frankfurt: Suhrkamp, 1990, English title
   The Normal Chaos of Love, Cambridge: Polity, 1994. See also W. Zapf
   (ed.), *Die Modernisierung moderner Gesellschaften*, Frankfurt: Campus,
   1991.
2 K. Marx and F. Engels, 'Communist Manifesto', *Werke*, vol. V, Berlin:
   Volksausgabe, 1972, p. 465. Cf. also M. Berman, *All that is Solid Melts
   into Air*, New York: Verso, 1982.
3 Cf. *Ecological Politics in the Age of Risk*, chapter IV.

4   This theme is developed in Part Two of my *Risk Society*.
5   U. Beck and E. Beck-Gernsheim (eds), *Riskante Freiheiten: zur Individualisierung von Lebensformen in der Moderne*, Frankfurt: Suhrkamp, 1994.
6   W. Bonss, 'Ungewissheit als soziologisches Problem', *Mittelweg*, vol. 36, no. 1, 1993, pp. 20f.
7   Z. Bauman, *Modernity and Ambivalence*, Cambridge: Polity, 1991.
8   Review by Z. Bauman, 'The solution as problem', *Times Higher Education Supplement*, 13 November 1992, p. 25.
9   Cf. François Ewald, *L'Etat Providence*, Paris: Grasset, 1986.
10 But then the pitch-black pessimism with which Bauman paints becomes antiquated, in the sense of empirically false.
11 W. Grant, W. Paterson and C. Whitston, *Government and the Chemical Industry*, Oxford: Clarendon, 1988; R. Bogun, M. Osterlund and G. Warsewa, 'Arbeit und Umwelt im Risikobewusstsein von Industriearbeitern', *Soziale Welt*, vol. 2, 1992, pp. 237–45; H. Heine, 'Das Verhältnis der Naturwissenschaftler und Ingenieure in der Grosschemie zur ökologischen Industriekritik', *Soziale Welt*, vol. 2, 1992, pp. 246–55; L. Pries, *Betrieblicher Wandel in der Risikogesellschaft*, Opladen: Westdeutscher Verlag, 1991; D. Nelkin (ed.), *Controversy: Politics of Technical Decisions*, London: Sage, 1992.
12 In this context W. Zapf wrote: 'Commenting critically, I would like to say that the position of Ulrich Beck is so fascinating because it holds firm both to the programme of modernization as well as to a fundamental critique of current society, including the majority of today's sociology. Beck wants a new modernity and a more insightful, more conscientious and more reflected, in short a reflexive theory. It is capable of winning over the adherents of the Critical Theory of the 1930s and 1960s, for whom Adorno's dictum applies: the totality is the untrue. It can assimilate the disillusioned Marxists, whose dreams of socialism have disintegrated, but who now are shown that free-market democracies must also fail because of their own contradictions. The theory is a modernized variant of the doctrine of late capitalism, where the ecological crisis now takes over the role previously played by the legitimation crisis of late capitalism. It is another theory of the third way beyond socialism and capitalism' ('Entwicklung und Zukunft moderner Gesellschaften', in H. Korte and B. Schäfers (eds), *Einführung in die Hauptbegriffe der Soziologie*, Opladen: Buddrich, 1992, pp. 204f.
13 'Individualization' has been discussed in Germany in social sciences, public and politics during the 1980s and 1990s. For documentation see Beck and Beck-Gernsheim, *Riskante Freiheiten*.
14 A. Heath and N. Britten, 'Women's jobs do make a difference', *Sociology*, vol. 18, no. 2, 1990, and the discussion that follows.
15 Giddens, *The Consequences of Modernity*, pp. 63ff; I. Wallerstein, *The Modern World System*, New York: Academic, 1974; T. Roszak, *Person/*

Planet: the Creative Disintegration of Industrial Society, London: Gollancz, 1979.

16 Giddens, *Modernity and Self-Identity*: see also S. Lash and J. Friedman (eds), *Modernity & Identity*, Oxford: Blackwell, 1992; S. Lash, *Sociology of Postmodernism*, London: Routledge, 1990.

17 B. Jessop, *State Theory*, Cambridge: Polity, 1990.

18 Cf. my *Risk Society*, Part Three.

19 At the same time, this very thing means a 'radicalization' of modernity. This does not mean an acceleration of acceleration but rather the vindication of the principles of modernity against their division by industrialism, their industrial form. To put it politically: self-limitation, self-criticism and self-reform of industrial modernity in the consistent application of modernity to itself.

20 G. Böhme, *Natürlich Natur: über Natur im Zeitalter ihrer technischen Reproduzierbarkeit*, Frankfurt: Suhrkamp, 1992.

21 On this see H. Willke, *Die Ironie des Staates*, Frankfurt: Suhrkamp, 1992.

22 On the following see, among others, M. Hoffmann-Riem and J. Schmidt-Assmann (eds), *Konfliktbewältigung durch Verhandlung*, Baden-Baden: Aspekte, 1990.

23 This is discussed in my book *Ecological Enlightenment*, New York: Humanity, 1993.

24 G. Schulze, *Erlebnisgesellschaft*, Frankfurt: Campus, 1992; S. Lash, 'Reflexive modernization'.

25 For the recontextualization of science see W. Bonss, R. Hohlfeld and R. Kollek, 'Risiko und Kontext', discussion paper, Hamburger Institut für Sozialforschung, May 1990. For the rethinking of subsystemic procedures see M. A. Hajer, *The Politics of Environmental Discourse: a Study of the Acid Rain Controversy in Great Britain and the Netherlands*, unpublished D.Phil. thesis, University of Oxford, 1993.

26 K. von Beyme, *Theorie der Politik im 20. Jahrhundert*, Frankfurt: Suhrkamp, 1991, p. 343.

27 H. M. Enzensberger, *Mittelmass und Wahn*, Frankfurt: Suhrkamp, 1991, pp. 230f.

28 Ibid., pp. 228f.

29 H. Schwengel, 'Die Zukunft des Politischen', *Ästhetik und Kommunikation*, vol. 65/6, 1987, p. 18.

30 C. Böhret, *Die Handlungsfähigkeit des Staates am Ende des 20. Jahrhundert*, unpublished manuscript, Speyer, 1992, pp. 9f.

31 Ibid.

32 Willke, *Die Ironie des Staates*, pp. 296, 303.

33 Since throwing 'leftist theory' out of the saddle, the question 'What is left?' (Steven Lukes) is beginning to split the remaining groups and splinter groups. We observe the novel phenomenon of a restorationist left. The old right-wing question is haunting many left-wing minds: was everything wrong just because a couple of Stalins and Honeckers made a mess of things? Even the individual in history is being redis-

covered, if the point is to play socialism off against its (mis)leaders and protect it in that way. Now the left is practising what it always criticized in the right, namely foreshortening history to the history of heroes, by claiming that individuals and not conditions brought about the collapse of communism. Against the triumphal shouting of victorious capitalism, so the question and demand goes, is it not incumbent upon people to stand up for the old principles, to distinguish ideal from concrete socialism, and to justify and proclaim the utopias of socialism now more than ever? Is it not particularly 'Western [German] opportunists' who are chasing after the Zeitgeist and opportunistically sacrificing the insights and outlooks of Western social critique?

34 S. Lukes, 'What's Left?', *Times Higher Education Supplement*, July 1992.
35 W. Heitmeyer, *Rechtsextremistische Orientierungen bei Jugendlichen*, Weilheim: Yurenta, 1991.
36 N. Luhmann, *Soziologie des Risikos*, Berlin: Springer, 1991.
37 Ibid.
38 The example of genetic engineering speaks against this, however: there are many evidences of resistance; see for example E. Beck-Gernsheim, 'Wider das Paradigma des Kriegsschauplatzes', *Ethik und Sozialwissenschaften*, vol. 3, 1992.
39 Giddens, *Modernity and Self-Identity*, p. 214.
40 For this see E. Beck-Gernsheim, *Technik, Markt und Moral*, Frankfurt: Suhrkamp, 1992 (English translation forthcoming from Humanity Press, New York).
41 Cf. U. Beck, M. Brater and H. J. Daheim, *Soziologie der Arbeit und der Berufe*, Reinbek: Rowohlt, 1980.
42 V. von Prittwitz, *Das Katastrophen-Paradox*, Opladen: Buddrich, 1990.

2 Living in a Post-Traditional Society

Anthony Giddens

In the social sciences today, as in the social world itself, we face a new agenda. We live, as everyone knows, at a time of endings. There is, first of all, the end not just of a century but of a millennium: something which has no content, and which is wholly arbitrary – a date on a calendar – has such a power of reification that it holds us in thrall. *Fin de siècle* has become widely identified with feelings of disorientation and malaise, to such a degree that one might wonder whether all the talk of endings, such as the end of modernity, or the end of history, simply reflects them. No doubt to some degree such is the case. Yet it is certainly not the whole story. We are in a period of evident transition – and the 'we' here refers not only to the West but to the world as a whole.

In this discussion I speak of an ending, in the guise of the emergence of a post-traditional society. This phrase might at first glance seem odd. Modernity, almost by definition, always stood in opposition to tradition; hasn't modern society long been 'post-traditional'? It has not, at least in the way in which I propose to speak of the 'post-traditional society' here. For most of its history, modernity has rebuilt tradition as it has dissolved it. Within Western societies, the persistence and recreation of tradition was central to the legitimation of power, to the sense in which the state was able to impose itself upon relatively passive 'subjects'. For tradition placed in stasis some core aspects of social life – not least the family and sexual identity – which were left largely untouched so far as 'radicalizing Enlightenment' was concerned.[1]

Most important, the continuing influence of tradition within modernity remained obscure so long as 'modern' meant 'Western'. Some one hundred years ago Nietzsche had already 'brought modernity to its senses', showing Enlightenment itself to be myth and thereby posing disquieting questions about knowledge and power. Nietzsche's was, however, the lone voice of the heretic. Modernity has been forced to 'come to its senses' today, not so much as a result of its internal dissenters as by its own generalization across the world. No longer the unexamined basis of Western hegemony over other cultures, the precepts and social forms of modernity stand open to scrutiny.

The orders of transformation

The new agenda for social science concerns two directly connected domains of transformation. Each corresponds to processes of change which, while they have their origins with the first development of modernity, have become particularly acute in the current era. On the one hand there is the extensional spread of modern institutions, universalized via globalizing processes. On the other, but immediately bound up with the first, are processes of intentional change, which can be referred to as the radicalizing of modernity.[2] These are processes of *evacuation*, the disinterring and problematizing of tradition.

Few people anywhere in the world can any longer be unaware of the fact that their local activities are influenced, and sometimes even determined, by remote events or agencies. The phenomenon is easily indexed, at least on a crude level. Thus, for example, capitalism has for centuries had strong tendencies to expand, for reasons documented by Marx and many others. Over the period since the Second World War, however, and particularly over the past forty years or so, the pattern of expansionism has begun to alter. It has become much more decentred as well as more all-enveloping. The overall movement is towards much greater interdependence. On the sheerly economic level, for example, world production has increased dramatically, with various fluctuations and downturns; and world trade, a better indicator of interconnectedness, has grown even more. 'Invisible trade', in services and finance, has increased most of all.[3]

Less evident is the reverse side of the coin. The day-to-day actions of an individual today are globally consequential. My decision to purchase a particular item of clothing, for example, or a specific type of foodstuff, has manifold global implications. It not only affects the livelihood of someone living on the other side of the world but may contribute to a process of ecological decay which itself has potential consequences for the whole of humanity. This extraordinary, and still accelerating, connectedness between everyday decisions and global outcomes, together with its reverse, the influence of global orders over individual life, forms the key subject-matter of the new agenda. The connections involved are often very close. Intermediate collectivities and groupings of all sorts, including the state, do not disappear as a result; but they do tend to become reorganized or reshaped.

To the Enlightenment thinkers, and many of their successors, it appeared that increasing information about the social and natural worlds would bring increasing control over them. For many, such control was the key to human happiness; the more, as collective humanity, we are in a position actively to make history, the more we can guide history towards our ideals. Even more pessimistic observers connected knowledge and control. Max Weber's 'steel-hard cage' – in which he thought humanity was condemned to live for the forseeable future – is a prison-house of technical knowledge; we are all, to alter the metaphor, to be small cogs in the gigantic machine of technical and bureaucratic reason. Yet neither image comes close to capturing the world of high modernity, which is much more open and contingent than any such image suggests – and is so precisely *because of*, not in spite of, the knowledge that we have accumulated about ourselves and about the material environment. It is a world where opportunity and danger are balanced in equal measure.

That methodical doubt – radical doubt – which paradoxically was always at the origin of the Enlightenment's claims to certainty, becomes thoroughly exposed to view. The more we try to colonize the future, the more it is likely to spring surprises upon us. This is why the notion of risk, so central to the endeavours of modernity, moves through two stages.[4] First of all it seems no more than part of an essential calculus, a means of sealing off boundaries as the future is invaded. In this form risk is a statistical part of the operations of insurance companies; the very precision of such risk calculations seems to signal success in bringing the future under control.

This is risk in a world where much remains as 'given', including external nature and those forms of social life coordinated by tradition. As nature becomes invaded, and even 'ended', by human socialization, and tradition is dissolved, new types of uncal-culability emerge. Consider, for example, global warming. Many experts consider that global warming is occurring and they may be right. The hypothesis is disputed by some, however, and it has even been suggested that the real trend, if there is one at all, is in the opposite direction, towards the cooling of the global climate. Prob-ably the most that can be said with some surety is that we cannot be certain that global warming is *not* occurring. Yet such a conditional conclusion will yield not a precise calculation of risks but rather an array of 'scenarios' – whose plausibility will be influenced, among other things, by how many people become convinced of the thesis of global warming and take action on that basis. In the social world, where institutional reflexivity has become a central constituent, the complexity of 'scenarios' is even more marked.

On the global level, therefore, modernity has become experimen-tal. We are all, willy-nilly, caught up in a grand experiment, which is at the one time our doing – as human agents – yet to an imponder-able degree outside of our control. It is not an experiment in the laboratory sense, because we do not govern the outcomes within fixed parameters – it is more like a dangerous adventure, in which each of us has to participate whether we like it or not.

The grand experiment of modernity, fraught with global hazards, is not at all what the progenitors of Enlightenment had in mind when they spoke of the importance of contesting tradition. Nor is it close to what Marx envisaged – indeed, among many other endings today we may speak of the end of Prometheanism. 'Human beings only set themselves such problems as they can resolve': for us Marx's principle has become no more than a principle of hope. The social world has become largely organized in a conscious way, and nature fashioned in a human image, but these circumstances, at least in some domains, have created greater uncertainties, of a very consequential kind, than ever existed before.

The global experiment of modernity intersects with, and influ-ences as it is influenced by, the penetration of modern institutions into the tissue of day-to-day life. Not just the local community, but intimate features of personal life and the self become intertwined with relations of indefinite time-space extension.[5] We are all caught up in *everyday experiments* whose outcomes, in a generic sense, are as open as those affecting humanity as a whole. Everyday experiments reflect the changing role of tradition and, as is also true of the global level, should be seen in the context of the *displacement and reappropriation of expertise*, under the impact of the intrusiveness of abstract systems. Technology, in the general meaning of 'technique', plays the leading role here, in the shape both of material technology and of specialized social expertise.

Everyday experiments concern some very fundamental issues to do with self and identity, but they also involve a multiplicity of changes and adaptations in daily life. Some such changes are lovingly documented in Nicholson Baker's novel *The Mezzanine* (1990). The book deals with no more than a few moments in the day of a person who actively reflects, in detail, upon the minutiae of his life's surroundings and his reactions to them. A paraphernalia of intrusion, adjustment and readjustment is revealed, linked to a dimly perceived backdrop of larger global agencies.

Take the example of the ice-cube tray:

> The ice cube tray deserves a historic note. At first these were aluminium barges inset with a grid of slats linked to a handle like a parking brake – a bad solution; you had to run the grid under warm water before the ice would let go of the metal. I remember seeing these used, but never used them myself. And then suddenly there were plastic and rubber 'trays', really moulds, of several designs – some producing very small cubes, others producing large squared-off cubes and bathtub-buttoned cubes. There were subtleties that one came to understand over time: for instance, the little notches designed into the inner walls that separated one cell from another allowed the water level to equalise itself: this meant that you could fill the tray by running the cells quickly under the tap, feeling as if you were playing the harmonica, or you could turn the faucet on very slightly, so that a thin silent stream of water fell in a line from the tap, and hold the tray at an angle, allowing the water to enter a single cell and well from there into adjoining cells one by one, gradually filling the entire tray. The intercellular notches were helpful after the tray was frozen, too; when you had twisted it to force the cubes, you could selectively pull out one cube at a time by hooking a fingernail under the frozen projection that had formed in a notch. If you couldn't catch the edge of a notch-stump because the cell had not been filled to above the notch level, you might have to mask all the cubes except one with your hands and turn the tray over, so that the single cube you needed fell out. Or you could twist all the cubes free and then, as if the tray were a frying pan and you were flipping a pancake, toss them. The cubes would hop as one above their individual homes about a quarter of an inch, and most would fall back into place; but some, the loosest, would loft higher and often land irregularly, leaving one graspable end sticking up – these you used for your drink.[6]

What is at issue here is not just, or even primarily, technology, but more profound processes of the reformation of daily life. Tradition here would appear to play no part whatever any more; but this view would be mistaken, as we shall see.

Insulting the meat

Among the !Kung San of the Kalahari desert, when a hunter returns from a successful hunt his kill is disparaged by the rest of the community, no matter how bountiful it may be. Meat brought in by hunters is always shared throughout the group, but rather than being greeted with glee, a successful hunt is treated with indifference or scorn. The hunter himself is also supposed to show modesty as regards his skills and to understate his achievements. One of the !Kung comments:

> Say that a man has been hunting, he must not come home and announce like a braggart, 'I have killed a big one in the bush!' He must first sit down in silence until I or someone else comes up to his fire and asks, 'What did you see today?' He replies quietly, 'Ah, I'm no good for hunting. I saw nothing at all . . . maybe just a tiny one'. Then I smile to myself because I know he has killed something big.

The twin themes of deprecation and modesty are continued when the party goes out to fetch and divide up the kill the next day. Getting back to the village, the members of the carrying group loudly comment upon the ineptness of the hunter and their disappointment with him:

> You mean you have dragged us all the way out here to make us cart home your pile of bones? Oh, if I had known it was this thin I wouldn't have come. People, to think I gave up a nice day in the shade for this. At home we may be hungry, but at least we have nice cool water to drink.[7]

The exchange is a ritual one, and follows established prescriptions; it is closely connected to other forms of ritual interchange in !Kung society. Insulting the meat seems at first sight the perfect candidate for explanation in terms of latent functions. It is a slice of tradition which fuels those interpretations of 'traditional cultures' which understand 'tradition' in terms of functional conceptions of solidarity. If such notions were valid, tradition could be seen essentially as unthinking ritual, necessary to the cohesion of simpler societies. Yet this idea will not work. There is certainly a 'functional' angle to insulting the meat: although it also leads to conflicts, it can be seen as a means of sustaining egalitarianism in !Kung (male) community. The ritualized disparagement is a counter to arrogance and therefore to the sort of stratification that might develop if the best hunters were honoured or rewarded.

Yet this 'functional' element does not in fact operate in a mechanical way (nor could it); the !Kung are well aware of what is going on. Thus, as a !Kung healer pointed out to the visiting anthropologist, when a man makes many kills, he is liable to think of himself as a chief, and see the rest of the group as his inferiors. This is unacceptable; 'so we always speak of his meat as worthless. In this way we cool his heart and make him gentle'.[8] Tradition is about ritual and has connections with social solidarity, but it is not the mechanical following of precepts accepted in an unquestioning way.

To grasp what it means to live in a post-traditional order we have to consider two questions: what tradition actually is and what are the generic characteristics of a 'traditional society'. Both notions have for the most part been used as unexamined concepts – in sociology because of the fact that they have been foils for the prime concern with modernity; and in anthropology because one of the main implications of the idea of tradition, repetition, has so often been merged with cohesiveness. Tradition, as it were, is the glue that holds premodern social orders together; but once one rejects functionalism it is no longer clear what makes the glue stick. There is no necessary connection between repetition and social cohesion at all, and the repetitive character of tradition is something which has to be explained, not just assumed.[9]

Repetition means time – some would say that it *is* time – and tradition is somehow involved with the control of time. Tradition, it might be said, is an orientation to the past, such that the past has a heavy influence or, more accurately put, is made to have a heavy influence, over the present. Yet clearly, in a certain sense at any rate, tradition is also about the future, since established practices are used as a way of organising future time. The future is shaped without the need to carve it out as a separate territory. Repetition, in a way that needs to be examined, reaches out to return the future to the past, while drawing on the past also to reconstruct the future.

Traditions, Edward Shils says, are always changing;[10] but there is *something* about the notion of tradition which presumes endurance; if it is traditional, a belief or practice has an integrity and continuity which resists the buffeting of change. Traditions have an organic character: they develop and mature, or weaken and 'die'. The integrity or *authenticity* of a tradition, therefore, is more important in defining it as tradition than how long it lasts. It is notable that only in societies with writing – which have actually become thereby less 'traditional' – do we usually have any *evidence* that elements of tradition have endured over very long periods. Anthropologists have virtually always seen oral cultures as highly traditional, but in the nature of the case have no way of confirming that the 'traditional practices' they observe have existed over even several generations; no one knows, for instance, for how long the !Kung practice of insulting the meat might have been in place.

I shall understand 'tradition' in the following way. Tradition, I shall say, is bound up with memory, specifically what Maurice Halbwachs terms 'collective memory'; involves ritual; is connected with what I shall call a *formulaic notion of truth*; has 'guardians'; and, unlike custom, has binding force which has a combined moral and emotional content.

Memory, like tradition – in some sense or another – is about organizing of the past in relation to the present. We might think, Halbwachs says, that such conservation simply results from the existence of unconscious psychic states. There are traces registered in the brain which make it possible for these states to be called to consciousness. From this point of view, 'the past falls into ruin', but 'only vanishes in appearance', because it continues to exist in the unconscious.[11]

Halbwachs rejects such an idea; the past is not preserved but continuously reconstructed on the basis of the present. Such reconstruction is partially individual, but more fundamentally it is *social* or collective. In fleshing out this argument, Halbwachs offers an interesting analysis of dreams. Dreams are in effect what meaning would be like without its organizing social frameworks – composed of disconnected fragments and bizarre sequences. Images remain as 'raw materials' that enter into eccentric combinations with one another.

Memory is thus an active, social process, which cannot merely be identified with recall.[12] We continually reproduce memories of past happenings or states, and these repetitions confer continuity upon experience. If in oral cultures older people are the repository (and also often the guardians) of traditions, it is not only because they absorbed them at an earlier point than others but because they have the leisure to identify the details of these traditions in interaction with others of their age and teach them to the young. Tradition,

therefore, we may say, is an *organizing medium of collective memory.*
There can no more be a private tradition than there could be a
private language. The 'integrity' of tradition derives not from the
simple fact of persistence over time but from the continuous 'work'
of interpretation that is carried out to identify the strands which
bind present to past.

Tradition usually involves ritual. Why? The ritual aspects of tradition might be thought to be simply part of its 'mindless', auto-
mation-like character. But if the ideas I have suggested so far are
correct, tradition is necessarily active and interpretative. Ritual, one
can propose, is integral to the social frameworks which confer integrity upon traditions; ritual is a practical means of ensuring preservation. Collective memory, as Halbwachs insists, is geared to social
practices. We can see how this is so if we consider not just the
contrast between memory and dreaming but the 'in between' activity of day-dreaming or reverie. Day-dreaming means that an
individual relaxes from the demands of day-to-day life, allowing
the mind to wander. By contrast continuity of practice – itself
actively organized – is what connects the thread of today's activities
with those of yesterday, and of yesteryear. Ritual firmly connects
the continual reconstruction of the past with practical enactment,
and can be seen to do so.

Ritual enmeshes tradition in practice, but it is important to see
that it also tends to be separated more or less clearly from the
pragmatic tasks of everyday activity. Insulting the meat is a ritualized procedure, and understood to be so by the participants. A
ritual insult is different from a real insult because it lacks denotive
meaning; it is a 'non-expressive' use of language. This 'isolating'
consequence of ritual is crucial because it helps give ritual beliefs,
practices and objects a temporal autonomy which more mundane
endeavours may lack.

Like all other aspects of tradition, ritual has to be interpreted;
but such interpretation is not normally in the hands of the lay
individual. Here we have to establish a connection between tradition's *guardians* and the truths such traditions contain or disclose.
Tradition involves 'formulaic truth', to which only certain persons
have full access. Formulaic truth depends not upon referential
properties of language but rather upon their opposite; ritual language is performative, and may sometimes contain words or practices that the speakers or listeners can barely understand. Ritual
idiom is a mechanism of truth because, not in spite, of its formulaic
nature. Ritual speech is speech which it makes no sense to disagree

with or contradict – and hence contains a powerful means of reducing the possibility of dissent. This is surely central to its compelling quality.

Formulaic truth is an attribution of causal efficacy to ritual; truth criteria are applied to events caused, not to the propositional content of statements.[13] Guardians, be they elders, healers, magicians or religious functionaries, have the importance they do in tradition because they are believed to be the agents, or the essential mediators, of its causal powers. They are dealers in mystery, but their arcane skills come more from their involvement with the causal power of tradition than from their mastery of any body of secret or esoteric knowledge. Among the !Kung the elders are the main guardians of the traditions of the group. Insulting the meat may be 'rationally understood' in terms of its consequences for the collectivity, but it derives its persuasive power from its connections to other rituals and beliefs which either the elders or the religious specialists control.

The guardians of tradition might seem equivalent to experts in modern societies – the purveyors of the abstract systems whose impact upon daily life Nicholson Baker chronicles. The difference between the two, however, is clear-cut. Guardians are not experts, and the arcane qualities to which they have access for the most part are not communicable to the outsider. As Pascal Boyer puts it, 'a traditional specialist is not someone who has an adequate picture of some reality in his or her mind, but someone whose utterances can be, in some contexts, directly determined by the reality in question'.[14]

Status in the traditional order, rather than 'competence', is the prime characteristic of the guardian. The knowledge and skills possessed by the expert might appear mysterious to the layperson; but anyone can in principle acquire that knowledge and those skills were they to set out to do so.

Finally, all traditions have a normative or moral content, which gives them a binding character.[15] Their moral nature is closely bound up with the interpretative processes by means of which past and present are aligned. Tradition represents not only what 'is' done in a society but what 'should be' done. It does not follow from this, of course, that the normative components of tradition are necessarily spelled out. Mostly they are not: they are interpreted within the activities or directives of the guardians. Tradition has the hold it does, it can be inferred, because its moral character offers a measure of ontological security to those who adhere to it. Its psychic underpinnings are affective. There are ordinarily deep emotional investments in tradition, although these are indirect rather than direct; they come from the mechanisms of anxiety-control that traditional modes of action and belief provide.

So much for an initial conceptualizing of tradition. The question of what a 'traditional society' is remains unresolved. I do not intend to deal with it at any length here, although I shall come back to it later. A traditional society, inevitably, is one where tradition as specified above has a dominant role; but this will hardly do in and of itself. Tradition, one can say, has most salience when it is not understood as such. Most smaller cultures, it seems, do not have a specific word for 'tradition' and it is not hard to see why: tradition is too pervasive to be distinguished from other forms of attitude or conduct. Such a situation tends to be particularly characteristic of oral cultures. A distinctive feature of oral culture, obviously, is that communications cannot be made without an identifiable speaker; this circumstance plainly lends itself to formulaic versions of truth. The advent of writing creates hermeneutics: 'interpretation', which is first of all largely scriptural, takes on a new meaning. Tradition comes to be known as something distinctive and as potentially plural. All premodern civilisations, however, remained thoroughly shot through with tradition of one kind or another.

If we ask the question, 'in what ways have modern societies become detraditionalized?', the most obvious tactic in providing an answer would be to look at specific forms of symbol and ritual and consider how far they still form 'traditions'. However, I shall defer answering such a question until later, and for the moment shall reorient the discussion in quite a different way. Tradition is repetition, and presumes a kind of truth antithetical to ordinary 'rational enquiry' – in these respects it shares something with the psychology of compulsion.

Repetition as neurosis: the issue of addiction

The question of compulsiveness lies at the origin of modern psychotherapy. Here is how one self-help book of practical therapy begins. 'This is a recording', it says, speaking of an individual's life-experiences – in our present activities we are constantly (in a largely unconscious way) recapitulating the past. The influence of past over present is above all an emotional one, a matter of 'feelings'.

Reasons can exist in two 'places' at the same time. You can be physically present with someone in the here and now, but your mind can be miles and years removed. One of our problems in relationships is that 'something' removes us from the present and we are not with whom we were with.

These recorded experiences and the feelings associated with them are available for replay today in as vivid a form as when they happened, and they provide much of the data that determine the nature of today's transactions. Events in the present can replicate an old experience and we not only remember how we felt, but we feel the same way. We not only remember the past, we relive it. We are there! Much of what we relive we don't remember.[16]

Compulsiveness in its broadest sense is an inability to escape from the past. The individual, who believes himself or herself to be autonomous, acts out a surreptitious fate. Concepts of fate have always been closely allied with tradition and it is not surprising to find that Freud was preoccupied with fate. 'The Oedipus Rex', he observes,

> is a tragedy of fate. Its tragic effect depends upon the conflict between the all-powerful will of the gods and the vain efforts of human beings threatened with disaster. Resignation to the divine will, and the perception of one's unimportance, are the lessons which the deeply moved spectator is supposed to learn from the play.

'The oracle has placed the same curse on us',[17] he continues, but in our case it is possible to escape. From Freud onwards, the dilemma of the modern condition is seen as overcoming the 'programming' built into our early lives.

Freud of course was much concerned with dreams, 'the royal road to the unconscious'. Freud's theory of dreams may or may not be valid in its own terms, but it is worthwhile considering its relation to the ideas of Halbwachs. For both Halbwachs and Freud dreams are memories with the social context of action removed. Let me now historicize this view. The period at which Freud wrote was one at which traditions in everyday life were beginning to creak and strain under the impact of modernity. Tradition provided the stabilizing frameworks which integrated memory traces into a coherent memory. As tradition dissolves, one can speculate, 'trace memory' is left more nakedly exposed, as well as more problematic in respect of the construction of identity and the meaning of social norms. From then onwards, the reconstruction which tradition provided of the past becomes a more distinctively individual responsibility – and even exigency.

As a good medical specialist, Freud set out to cure neuroses; what he actually discovered, however, was the emotional undertow of disintegrating traditional culture. The emotional life of modern civilization was essentially written out of Enlightenment philosophy, and was alien to those scientific and technological endeavours that were so central to the coruscating effects of modernity. Science, and more generally 'reason', were to replace the supposedly unthinking precepts of tradition and custom. And so, in a sense, it proved to be: cognitive outlooks were indeed very substantially and dramatically recast. The emotional cast of tradition, however, was left more or less untouched.[18]

Freud's thought, of course, is open to being understood in Enlightenment terms. From this point of view, Freud's importance was that he discovered a psychological 'track of development' comparable to that of the social institutions of modernity. The 'dogmatics' of the unconscious could be dissolved and replaced by veridical self-awareness; in Freud's celebrated, perhaps notorious, phrase, 'where id was ego shall be'. Some, more suspicious of the claims of Enlightenment, see Freud in a quite contrasting way. Freud shows us, they say, that modern civilization can never overcome those dark forces which lurk in the unconscious. Freud's own line of intellectual development in fact seems to veer from the first view towards the second over the progression of his career.

Yet perhaps neither of these perspectives is the most effective way of looking at things. Freud was dealing with a social, not only a psychological, order; he was concerned with a social universe of belief and action at the point at which, in matters directly affecting self-identity, *tradition was beginning to turn into compulsion*. Compulsion, rather than the unconscious as such, turned out to be the other side of the 'cognitive revolution' of modernity.

Freud's concrete investigations and therapeutic involvements – unlike most of his writings – concentrated upon the emotional problems of women, as mediated through the body. Yet the hidden compulsiveness of modernity was also manifest – although in a different way – in the public domain. What is Weber's discussion of the Protestant ethic if not an analysis of the obsessional nature of modernity? The emotional travails of women, of course, have no place in Weber's study – nor do the private or sexual lives of the purveyors of the entrepreneurial spirit. It is as if these things have no bearing upon the demeanour or motivation of the industrialist: a conceptual schism which reflected a real division in the lives of men and women.

Weber's work deals quite explicitly with the transition from tradition to modernity, although he does not put it in quite those terms. Religious beliefs and practices, like other traditional activities, tend to fuse morality and emotion. They have, as Weber makes clear, an adequate and visible motivational base. Just as we can quite easily understand the desire to accumulate wealth in the traditional world, where it is used to cultivate distinctive prerogatives, so we can also make sense of religious asceticism and its driven quality. The Hindu ascetic, for example, strives to overcome the toils of the world and enter a state of religious devotion.

The driven asceticism of the entrepreneur has no such obvious origins even though, just as obviously, it is inspired by passion and conviction. The outlook of the capitalist, Weber says, seems to the non-modern observer 'so incomprehensible and mysterious, so unworthy and contemptible. That anyone should be able to make it the sole purpose of his life-work, to sink down into the grave weighed down with a great material load of money and goods, seems to him explicable only as the product of a perverse instinct, the *auri sacra fames*'.[19] Weber himself shared this attitude of something akin to contempt in spite of his clarification of the intellectual puzzle posed by the capitalist spirit. Once the fulfilment of the calling of the entrepreneur 'cannot directly be related to the highest spiritual and cultural values', and is not the result of sheerly economic constraint, 'the individual generally abandons the attempt to justify it at all'. And so follows the famous quotation from Goethe: 'Specialists without spirit, sensualists without heart; this nullity imagines that it has attained a level of civilisation never before achieved.'[20]

What Weber calls 'economic traditionalism' is in his view characteristic of the vast bulk of economic activity in premodern civilizations. Economic traditionalism quite often recognizes material gain as a legitimate motive, but always grounds it in a wider morality, and includes, usually, a notion of excess. This was true both of Lutheranism and of all varieties of Puritanism. Luther, for example, understood work as a calling in a traditionalistic way, as part of an objective historical order of things governed by God.[21] The obsessional pursuit of divine grace has been part of many religions, but Lutheranism preserved some of that relatively relaxed attitude towards day-to-day life characteristic of non-monastic Catholicism. Puritanism is more driven. It was antagonistic towards most forms of traditionalism and more or less eliminated ritual within the religious sphere; it was also hostile to all types of sensuous culture.

It is tempting to link Weber's discussion of Puritan asceticism to psychological repression and many have in fact done so. Puritanism – and, following this, capitalism as an economic system – might seem to maximize self-denial. The pursuit of material gain on the part of the entrepreneur, after all, goes along with a frugal lifestyle and a horror of hedonism. In fact, some commentators have suggested that there have been two phases in the development of modern institutions over the past three centuries or so. The first was marked by the dominance of discipline and repression, the second by an upsurge of hedonism, perhaps associated with the rise of the consumer society.[22] Yet we might interpret the implications of Weber's work in quite a different fashion. The core of capitalist spirit was not so much its ethic of denial as its *motivational urgency*, shorn of the traditional frameworks which had connected striving with morality.

The capitalist, so to speak, was primed to repetition without – once the traditional religious ethic had been discarded – having much sense of why he, or others, had to run this endless treadmill. This was a positive motivation, however; success brought pleasure rather than pain. Hedonism differs from pleasure enjoyed in much the same way as the striving of the entrepreneur differs from economic traditionalism. In other words, almost by definition it too is obsessional: this is why it is much more closely related to the traits upon which Weber concentrated than may seem the case at first blush.

Modernity as compulsive: what does this mean and what are its implications? Although the connections need to be spelled out in greater detail, as with Freud we are speaking here of an *emotional drive to repetition*, which is either largely unconscious or poorly understood by the individual concerned. The past lives on, but rather than being actively reconstructed in the mode of tradition it tends to dominate action almost in a quasi-causal fashion. Compulsiveness, when socially generalized, is in effect *tradition without traditionalism*: repetition which stands in the way of autonomy rather than fostering it.

Freud spoke of obsession or compulsion; today we more commonly speak of addictions. The terminological difference is important, and helps bring out what is at issue. Compare the anorectic individual with Weber's entrepreneur. Each is driven by a this-worldly asceticism. Anorexia, however, is seen as a pathology, and (at present at least) is concentrated mainly in young women. It seems odd at first to regard anorexia as an addiction, because it appears more as a form of self-denial than as being 'hooked' on pleasure-giving substances. In this respect, however, it is no different from the capitalist spirit, and the point made about hedonism applies. In a world where one can be addicted to anything (drugs, alcohol, coffee, but also work, exercise, sport, cinema-going, sex or love) anorexia is one among other food-related addictions.

Addiction, it has been said, 'is anything we feel we have to lie about'.[23] It is, one could say, repetition which has lost its connection to the 'truth' of tradition; its origins are obscure to the individual concerned, although he or she may lie to others too. Thus alcoholics often hide their addiction even from those to whom they are closest, as part of denying it to themselves. Addiction, the author quoted above (a therapist) says, 'keeps us out of touch with ourselves (our feelings, morality, awareness – our living process)'; the individual's relations with others also tend to be obsessional rather than freely entered into. 'Ingestive addictions' (to food or chemicals) can be psychologically based, but addiction is primarily a social and psychological phenomenon rather than a physiological one. Thus in the field of alcoholism, a well known syndrome is that of the 'dry drunk', a person who exhibits most of the traits of the alcoholic, but without using the chemical. Many people, at least for some while, become more compulsive about their behaviour patterns after giving up alcohol than they were before.[24]

Why juxtapose addiction and tradition? There are two reasons. One is to focus on the compulsive traits of modernity as such, a matter to which I shall return later. The other, more important at this juncture, is because the topic of addiction provides an initial illumination of characteristics of a post-traditional order. In premodern societies, tradition and the routinization of day-to-day conduct are closely tied to one another. In the post-traditional society, by contrast, routinization becomes empty unless it is geared to processes of institutional reflexivity. There is no logic, or moral authenticity, to doing today what one did yesterday; yet these things are the very essence of tradition. The fact that today we can become addicted to anything – any aspect of lifestyle – indicates the very comprehensiveness of the dissolution of tradition (we should add, and this is not as paradoxical as it seems, 'in its traditional form'). The progress of addiction is a substantively significant feature of the postmodern social universe, but it is also a 'negative index' of the very process of the detraditionalizing of society.

Family and marriage counsellors sometimes use 'genograms' in helping individuals get along with – or split up from – one another. A genogram is very much like an anthropologist's map of a lineage in a traditional culture, save that it concentrates on the emotions. It traces out the emotional attachments of, say, the partners in a marriage backwards in time, reaching into the parents' and grandparents' generations. A genogram supposedly allows us to see how the emotional life of the present-day individuals recapitulates that of past generations – and provides the possibility of fruitfully escaping from this 'inheritance'.

One therapist, writing of experience with genograms, says 'I became aware, over and over again, of how tenaciously the past searches for its expression in the present'.[25] Most of the connections involved, again, are emotional and unconscious. Consider the case of Tom and Laura, described by Maggie Scarf.[26] Scarf began to construct a genogram for the couple by first of all asking what attracted the two to one another. Tom was a person who kept his emotions to himself, and he believed that this self-sufficiency was one of the things that Laura initially found attractive about him. Yet Laura's ideas about the relationship stressed 'sincerity', 'openness' and 'making oneself vulnerable'. 'It was as if each of them', Scarf says, 'had found, in the other, a missing aspect of something lacking in his or her own inner being.' Each had unconsciously recognized a complementary need in the other – the one for emotional communication, the other for independence of mind.

Repetition as disclosed by family analysis is often strikingly literal. Thus, for example, a woman whose upbringing has been affected by the fact that her father was an alcoholic marries a man who also turns out to be an alcoholic; perhaps she then divorces him, only to repeat a similar pattern. More commonly, the 'mode of being with the other' replicates what has been transmitted from the family context of childhood. As in the case of tradition, this is not a passive process but an active, albeit mainly unconscious, activity of recreation. Scarf observes:

> To some large or small degree, when we attain adult status, most of us have not put our childhood things behind us. In the very process of choosing our mates, and of being chosen – and then, in elaborating on our separate, past lives in the life we create together – we are deeply influenced by the patterns for being that we observed and learned about very early in life and that live on inside our heads. The fact that there may be *other options*, other systems for being in an intimate relationship, often doesn't occur to us, because we don't

realise that we *are* operating within a system, one which was internalised in our original families. What has been, and what we've known, seems to be the 'way of the world'; it is reality itself.

Repetition is a way of staying in 'the only world we know', a means of avoiding exposure to 'alien' values or ways of life. Laura's parents had each been married before, but she didn't find this out until she was in her early twenties. The discovery was a shocking one; she felt that they had deceived her previously. Although she was an outgoing person on the surface, she maintained an attitude of inner reserve. In her relationship with her husband, she seemed to want complete closeness and integrity, but actually they had an unconscious 'arrangement'. When she made a move towards closeness, he would react by asserting his autonomy. She depended upon him to preserve a necessary distance between them, while she expressed emotions in a public way which he could not do. He saw his own desire for emotional closeness to her as *her* need, for he seemed emotionally self-sufficient.

Going back through the relations between their parents and grandparents, parallel forms of symbiosis came to light – as well as many other similarities. Both had quite 'old' fathers, who were in their early forties when their children were born. Each had a parent who had regularly suffered from depression. These traits also went back a further generation. The relations between their parents 'reversed' their own, but otherwise paralleled it. Tom's mother was the depressed one in his family, while in Laura's case it was her father. Tom became an 'outsider', an 'observer', in his family, where neither conflict nor attachment between his parents was openly acknowledged; Laura was called upon to express emotions that were displaced on to her during family scenes.

I am not concerned here with how illuminating the therapist's analysis of the couple's relationship might be, or even whether genograms have any validity as representations of the past. So far as the post-traditional society is concerned, what is interesting is what I shall call the process of *excavation* involved. 'Excavation', as in an archaeological dig, is an investigation, and it is also an evacuation. Old bones are disinterred, and their connections with one another established, but they are also exhumed and the site is cleaned out. Excavation means digging deep, in an attempt to clean out the debris of the past.

The factors involved are severalfold: First, as mentioned, the past becomes emotional inertia when tradition becomes attenuated. Second, as in premodern societies, however, the past cannot simply be blanked out (although some psychological mechanisms have this effect) but must be reconstructed in the present. Third, the reflexive project of self, a basic characteristic of everyday life in a post-traditional world, depends upon a significant measure of emotional autonomy. Fourth, the prototypical post-traditional personal relation – the pure relationship – depends upon intimacy in a manner not generally characteristic of premodern contexts of social interaction.[27] The succession of the generations is stripped of the crucial significance it had in premodern orders, as one of the most central means for the transmission of traditional symbols and practices.

Choices and decisions

Let me follow the theme of therapy just a little further. Works of therapy almost always emphasize the issue of choice. Choice is obviously something to do with colonizing the future in relation to the past and is the positive side of coming to terms with inertial emotions left from past experiences. 'Who are you and what do you want?': the query sounds the ultimate in specious individualism. Yet there is something more interesting than this going on, which is essentially a way of looking at the social world.

The following is just a small sample of a very long list of 'choices' given by one author:

> Who you spend most of your time with
> What your favourite foods are
> Your posture
> How much or how little you smile
> How late you stay up at night
> Whether you smoke
> Whether you gossip
> Who you admire most
> How calm you are
> How you spend your holidays
> How often you feel sorry for yourself
> How much you worry
> How much patience you have
> How happy you are
> Who to talk to when you have a problem
> Whether you eat breakfast
> What you think about just before you go to sleep at night[28]

In post-traditional contexts, we have no choice but to choose how to be and how to act. From this perspective, even addictions are choices: they are modes of coping with the multiplicity of possibilities which almost every aspect of daily life, when looked at in the appropriate way, offers. The therapist advises:

> Look at what you can do, starting at any time you choose, by making conscious, *active* choices every time the opportunity comes up. It is what we do with these choices (and many other choices just like them) that will always determine not only how well each day works for us, but how successful we will be at anything we do.[29]

The logic is impeccable; for active choice surely produces, or is, autonomy. So why does the advice grate somewhat? One reason might be an objection from classical psychoanalysis. Choices are blocked, or programmed, by unconscious emotions, which cannot first be thought away by listing indefinite numbers of 'options'. Depending upon how fixed unconscious traits are presumed to be, one's genogram could be seen as setting clear limits to feasible options. To see day-to-day life as an amalgam of free choices thus flies in the face of psychological reality. Another reason might be the inevitability of routinization. Daily life would be impossible if we didn't establish routines, and even routines which are nothing more than habits cannot be wholly optional: they wouldn't be routines if we didn't, at least for longish periods of time, place them effectively 'beyond question'.

There is a third reason, however, which is to do with constraint and power. The choices that are constitutive of lifestyle options are very often bounded by factors out of the hands of the individual or individuals they affect. Everyday experiments, such as I described them earlier, are ways of handling options, and in this sense are certainly 'active'. Yet the nature of the options in question is clearly variable. Take the matter of the ice-cubes. The technological changes which impinge upon people's lives are the result of the intrusion of abstract systems, whose character they may influence but do not determine. The shifting design of ice-cube trays presumably responds in some way to consumer demand; but the design of the trays, and their construction, are controlled by large industrial corporations far removed from the control of the lay individual.

In coming to grips with the post-traditional order, then, we have to make a distinction between *choices* and *decisions*. Many of our day-to-day activities have in fact become open to choice or, rather, as I have expressed it previously, choice has become obligatory. This is a substantive thesis about everyday life today. Analytically, it is more accurate to say that all areas of social activity come to be governed by decisions – often, although not universally, enacted on the basis of claims to expert knowledge of one kind or another. *Who* takes those decisions, and *how*, is fundamentally a matter of power. A decision, of course, is always somebody's choice and in general all choices, even by the most impoverished or apparently power-less, refract back upon pre-existing power relations. The opening-out of social life to decision-making therefore should not be identified *ipso facto* with pluralism; it is also a medium of power and of stratification. Examples are legion, and span the whole gamut of social activity from minute features of day-to-day life through to global systems.

Nature and tradition as complementary

In respect of the progression of decision-making, we see a direct parallel between tradition and nature – one that is very important. In premodern societies, tradition provided a relatively fixed horizon of action. Tradition, as has been emphasized, involves active processes of reconstruction, particularly as filtered by its guardians. It is common to see tradition as intrinsically conservative, but we should say instead that it renders many things external to human activity. Formulaic truth, coupled to the stabilizing influence of ritual, takes an indefinite range of possibilities 'out of play'. Tradition as nature, nature as tradition: this equivalence is not as extreme as it may sound. What is 'natural' is what remains outside the scope of human intervention.

'Nature' in the modern era has become contrasted with the city; it is equivalent to 'countryside' and quite often has the connotation of a rural idyll:

> Oh there is a blessing in this gentle breeze
> A visitant that while it fans my cheek
> Doth seem half-conscious of the joy it brings
> From the green fields, and from yon azure sky.
> Whate'er its mission, the soft breeze can come
> To more grateful than me; escaped
> From the vast city, where I long had pined
> A discontented sojourner.[30]

There is some sense in such a usage. 'Nature' means that which lies undisturbed, that which is created independently of human activity. In one way the image is quite false, for the countryside is nature subordinated to human plans. Yet 'nature' in this meaning does preserve traits long associated with its separation from human contrivance. In many traditions, of course, nature was personalized; it was the domain of gods, spirits or demons. It would be misleading to see animism or other comparable outlooks as a merging of the human and natural worlds, however. Rather, the personalizing of nature expressed its very independence from human beings, a source of change and renewal set off from humanity, yet having a pervasive influence upon human lives. If nature was determined by decisions, these were not human ones.

One way to read human history, from the time of the rise of agriculture, and particularly the great civilizations, onwards is as the progressive destruction of the physical environment. Environmental ecology in the current period has arisen mainly as a response to perceived human destructiveness. Yet the very notion of 'the environment', as compared to 'nature', signals a more deep-lying transition. The environment, which seems to be no more than an independent parameter of human existence, actually is its opposite: nature as thoroughly transfigured by human intervention. We begin to speak about 'the environment' only once nature, like tradition, has become dissolved. Today, among all the other endings, we may speak in a real sense of the end of nature[31] – a way of referring to its thoroughgoing socialization.

The socialization of nature means much more than just the fact that the natural world is increasingly scarred by humanity. Human action, as mentioned, has long left an imprint upon the physical environment. The very invention of agriculture means clearing the natural ecosystem so as to create a habitat where humans can grow plants or raise animals as they want. Many now familiar landscapes of 'natural beauty', such as some of those in southern Greece, have actually been created by soil erosion following the placing of the land under cultivation in ancient times. Earlier on, the Sumerians, the originators of agrarian civilization, had destroyed the very land they had laboured to make fruitful.[32]

Until modern times, however, nature remained mainly an external system that dominated human activity rather than the reverse. Even in the most sophisticated of hydraulic civilizations floods or droughts were common; a bad harvest could produce devastation.

Risk here is of the old type. Natural disasters obviously still happen, but the socialization of nature in the present day means that a diversity of erstwhile natural systems are now products of human decision-making. Concern over global warming comes from the fact that the climate of the earth is no longer a naturally-given order. If global warming is indeed occurring, it is the result of the extra quantities of 'greenhouse gases' that have been added to the atmosphere over a period of no more than some two hundred years. Energy consumption has increased by a factor of some three hundred in the twentieth century alone; the fuel burned to provide the energy releases carbon dioxide into the atmosphere. A concomitant reduction in the world's natural 'sinks', which can absorb carbon dioxide, has exacerbated this effect. The overall consequence, even should the thesis of global warming prove mistaken, is the creation of new types of feedback effects and system influences.

The International Panel on Climate Change set up four possible emissions 'scenarios' and tried to assess the implications of each.[33] In the 'business as usual' scenario, where there is not much change from what seem to be the trends at the moment, the amount of carbon dioxide in the atmosphere will double in about twenty years into the new century. The introduction of very tight restrictions, one scenario, would stabilize the level; in each of the others, the level of increase would be geometric. All are just that – scenarios – which could reflexively influence what it is they are about. None of them, however, predicts a reversion. That is to say, henceforth and for the foreseeable future, with all its imponderabilities, we are dealing with a human rather than a natural order.

Some have said that the very idea of inanimate nature, so significant to the outlook and technology of the modern West, should be rejected today. Thus Rupert Sheldrake has suggested that 'once again it makes sense to think of nature as alive'; we might think of 'the entire cosmos' as 'more like a developing organism than an external machine'.[34] This process he specifically connects with the rebirth of tradition and ritual, as well as with an exploration of religion. 'A number of Westerners, myself included, have rejected the Christian religion and explored instead the religious traditions of the East, particularly Hinduism and Buddhism; others have attempted to revive aspects of pre-Christian paganism and the religion of the goddess.'[35] Whether or not such ideas and proclivities become widespread, such a process of selection is not a reawakening of tradition but something new. It is the adoption of tradition as itself a lifestyle decision; and no attempt to reanimate nature will reintroduce nature as it used to be.

The 'externality' of nature in premodern times did not only include the physical environment. It concerned also the body and, in close conjunction with tradition, whatever was counted as part of 'human nature'. All cultures have had systems of medicine and regimes of bodily training. But in the modern era the body and its physiological processes have been much more deeply invaded than before. Nowhere is this more evident than in the sphere of reproduction. The effects of detraditionalization and technology merge quite closely here, as in many other areas. The decision to have only a few children, for example, a demographic change of the first significance in modern societies in the nineteenth and early twentieth centuries, was part of the dissolution of traditional family systems, not a result of changes in technologies of contraception.

Technical changes, however, together with other innovations in reproductive technologies, have radically cut into 'external nature'. *In vitro* fertilization and embryo transplantation provide good examples. Not only can an individual or couple decide to have a child without having sexual intercourse, thus making a reality of virgin birth, but a variety of new possibilities, and dilemmas, open up as regards established kin categories and identities.

Tradition as contextual

Tradition is contextual in the sense that it is guaranteed by a combination of ritual and formulaic truth. Separated from these, tradition lapses into custom or habit. Tradition is unthinkable without guardians, because the guardians have privileged access to truth; truth cannot be demonstrated save in so far as it is manifest in the interpretations and practices of guardians. The priest or shaman may claim to be no more than the mouthpiece of the gods, but their actions *de facto* define what the traditions actually are. Secular traditions have their guardians just as much as those concerned with the sacred; political leaders speak the language of tradition when they claim the same sort of access to formulaic truth.

The connection between ritual and formulaic truth is also what gives traditions their qualities of exclusion. Tradition always discriminates between 'insider' and 'other', because participation in ritual and acceptance of formulaic truth is the condition for its existence. The 'other' is anyone and everyone who is outside. Traditions, one could say, almost demand to be set off from others, since being an insider is crucial to their character.

Tradition hence is a medium of identity. Whether personal or collective, identity presumes meaning; but it also presumes the constant process of recapitulation and reinterpretation noted earlier. Identity is the creation of constancy over time, that very bringing of the past into conjunction with an anticipated future. In all societies the maintenance of personal identity, and its connection to wider social identities, is a prime requisite of ontological security. This psychological concern is one of the main forces allowing traditions to create such strong emotional attachments on the part of the 'believer'. Threats to the integrity of traditions are very often, if by no means universally, experienced as threats to the integrity of the self.

Obviously in even the most traditional of societies not all things are traditional. Many skills and tasks, particularly those more removed from ritual or ceremonial occasions, are forms of 'secular expertise'. Such skills and tasks may often be informed by claims to generalizing knowledge, regarded as revisable in the light of new experience or changing conditions of operation. Malinowski showed as much many years ago. Yet the majority of skills are crafts; they are taught by apprenticeship and example, and the knowledge-claims they incorporate are protected as arcane and esoteric. The mystique demands initiation on the part of the fledgling participant. Hence the possessors of craft skills are often in effect guardians, even if those skills are kept relatively separate from the more overtly traditional apparitions of the society. Among the !Kung, for example, hunting is a skill developed by practice over many years, protected but not structured by initiation rites. A !Kung male can identify any local species by means of its footprints in the sand; he can deduce its sex, age, how rapidly it is travelling, whether or not it is healthy, and how long ago it passed through the area.[36]

Tradition claims a privileged view of time; but it tends to do so of space also. Privileged space is what sustains the differences of traditional beliefs and practices. Tradition is always in some sense rooted in contexts of origin or central places. Hunting and gathering societies may not have a fixed place of abode, but the area within which the group circulates is ordinarily accorded sacral qualities. At the other extreme, the 'great traditions' have created cultural diasporas spanning very large areas; premodern Christianity or Islam, for instance, stretched across massive geographical regions.

Yet such diasporas remained centred, either upon a single point of origin – Rome, Mecca – or upon a cluster of holy places.

The 'salvation religions' connected privileged place to quite impermeable cultural boundaries between insiders and outsiders. One is either a believer or a heathen. Other 'great traditions', most notably the 'exemplary religions' of the East, such as Buddhism or Hinduism, had more fuzzy zones of inclusion and exclusion. Yet the relation between tradition and identity always made the categories of friend and stranger (if not necessarily enemy) sharp and distinct. The stranger, it has been said (by Robert Michels), is the representative of the unknown. Although it might seem that the category of the stranger depends upon the territorial segmentation of premodern social systems, in fact it results more from the privileged and separatist character of traditionally conferred identities. The unknown is that culturally defined space which separates off the outside from the world of the 'familiar', structured by the traditions with which the collectivity identifies.

Tradition thus provided an anchorage for that 'basic trust' so central to continuity of identity; and it was also the guiding mechanism of other trust relations. Georg Simmel's definition of the stranger is somewhat different from that of Michels: the stranger is someone 'who comes today and stays tomorrow'.[37] The stranger, in other words, is not just someone who belongs to 'the unknown world out there' but a person who, by staying on, forces the locals to take a stand. One has to establish whether or not the stranger is a 'friend' if he or she does not go away again – which is not the same as accepting the stranger as one of the community, a process that may take many years, or even never happen. The stranger, as has been observed, is someone who:

> did not belong in the life-world 'initially', 'originally', 'from the start', 'since time immemorial', and so he questions the extemporality of the life-world, brings into relief the 'mere historicality' of existence. The memory of the event of his coming makes of his very presence an event in history, rather than a fact of nature . . . However protected the stay of the stranger is temporary – an infringement of the division which ought to be kept intact and preserved in the name of secure, orderly existence.[38]

The problem is: under what circumstances can the stranger be trusted? For tradition and the structural elements with which it is involved (such as kinship ties) sustain the networks of social relations along which trust flows. 'Familiarity' is the keynote of trust, which is often sustained by its own rituals. Ritual is important to trust because it supplies evidence of shared cultural community, and also because participation represents something of a public commitment which it is difficult later to go back on. In premodern societies, the extension of trust to newly encountered strangers normally takes the form of an extension of the 'familiar', either through ritual encounters or through the uncovering of kin connections.[39] A person may be trusted, at least provisionally, if some kind of kin relation, even very remote, is identified. Institutions like the Kula ring sustain trust between the different communities involved through ritual means, but the ritual is bolstered also by a more or less deliberate forging of kin bonds.

As Hans-Georg Gadamer has quite rightly stressed, tradition is closely bound up with authority. 'Authority' has a double sense: it is the authority which an individual or group has over others, the capacity to issue binding commands; however, it means also a reference-point of knowledge. Sometimes the two become merged, a matter of ideology or as a means of impersonalizing power; a directive will say 'issued by authority'. On the other hand, where an individual, for whatever reason, loses the aura which authority conveys, he or she is seen as charlatan. The two are therefore inevitably interdependent. A person who wields effective authority holds the aura of 'authority' in its more impersonal sense; correspondingly, of course, 'authority' must take the empirical forms of the giving of directives or judgements on the part of specific individuals.

Guardians and experts

In general we can make a distinction between rulers or officials (who give commands) and guardians (who supply interpretations), although the two categories are quite often merged in the same person. Max Weber was much concerned with the role of expertise in modern societies, but the contrasts he drew between tradition and expertise were primarily to do with the legitimacy of command systems. Those he discusses under the category of 'traditional authority' are mainly rulers rather than guardians, save in the context of his sociology of religion. Traditional authority is where 'masters are designated according to traditional rules and obeyed because of the traditional status'. Trust is generated not just by these traditional rules but by personal loyalty. The individual who has authority over others is, in Weber's words, a 'personal master' rather than a superior, one reason why traditional authority cannot be understood in terms of 'formal procedures'. Traditional rules are rarely clearly specified and always allow the master a wide area of freedom to do what he likes; he is free to do good turns for his subordinates, in return for gifts or dues. Household officials and favourites are often tied to the ruler in a patrimonial way, as slaves or dependants.

Authority in its more generic sense, in traditional cultures, is however the province of the guardians, and about this Weber says little. Those who hold authority – or effectively 'are' authority – in this way do or are so in virtue of their special access to the causal powers of formulaic truth. 'Wisdom' is the characteristic term which applies here. The wise person or sage is the repository of tradition, whose special qualities come from that long apprenticeship which creates skills and states of grace. Authority in its non-specific meaning is clearly a generative phenomenon. Whatever degree of trust may come from personal loyalty, the stability of traditional leadership depends in a much more integral way upon access to symbols which perpetuate the necessary 'aura'. Rulers may turn on their sages, Weber says, kings on their churchmen, because at any given point the masters possess greater secular power; but were the influence of traditions' guardians dispelled altogether, the power of a chief or prince would quickly come to naught.

Since he gives so much emphasis to domination, when he contrasts traditional with more modern forms of authority Weber focuses particularly upon 'rational-legal' authority. The dominance of the expert, in other words, is largely equated with the replacement of patrimonialism by bureaucracy. The prototypical expert is the bureaucratic official, performing the specialized duties of his office; the Puritan version of the calling played its due part in this transition. From this interpretation comes Weber's nightmare vision of a world imprisoned in the 'steel-hard cage' of bureaucratic domination.

Rational-legal authority rests upon 'a belief in the legality of enacted rules and the right of those elevated to authority under such rules to issue commands'.[40] Personal loyalty is downplayed as compared to due process of law or formal procedure. The keynote institution of rational-legal authority is the bureaucratic organization; discipline and control are characteristic of the conduct of the official and the organization as a whole.

The contrast Weber draws between traditional and rational-legal authority has been justly influential, as of course has his theory of bureaucracy. Yet his bureaucratic nightmare has not come to pass and it is not obvious that the 'official' is either the dominant figure of the age or the faceless autocrat whose diffuse power Weber feared. The compulsiveness that Weber unearthed in the Puritan ethic is not coupled to a 'disciplinary society' – whether in the manner of Weber or of Foucault – but to something else.

We need here to separate the expert from the official. Officials are experts, in a wide sense of that term, but expertise, in the context of the modern social order, is a more pervasive phenomenon than is officialdom. We should not equate experts and professionals. An expert is any individual who can successfully lay claim to either specific skills or types of knowledge which the layperson does not possess. 'Expert' and 'layperson' have to be understood as contextually relative terms. There are many layers of expertise and what counts in any given situation where expert and layperson confront one another is an imbalance in skills or information which – for a given field of action – makes one an 'authority' in relation to the other.

When we compare tradition with expertise we find major differences, just as in the case of comparing guardians with experts. We can sum these up, for the purposes of the present discussion, in the following way: First, expertise is disembedding; in contrast to tradition it is in a fundamental sense non-local and decentred. Second, expertise is tied not to formulaic truth but to a belief in the corrigibility of knowledge, a belief that depends upon a methodical scepticism. Third, the accumulation of expert knowledge involves intrinsic processes of specialization. Fourth, trust in abstract systems, or in experts, cannot readily be generated by means of esoteric wisdom. Fifth, expertise interacts with growing institutional reflexivity, such that there are regular processes of loss and re-appropriation of everyday skills and knowledge.

In its modern guise at least, expertise is in principle devoid of local attachments. In an ideal-typical way, it could be said that all forms of 'local knowledge' under the rule of expertise become local recombinations of knowledge derived from elsewhere. Obviously in practice things are more complicated than this, owing to the continuing importance of local habits, customs or traditions. The decentred nature of expertise derives from the traits to which Weber gives prominence, save that those do not concern only rational-legal procedures. That is to say, expertise is disembedding because it is based upon impersonal principles, which can be set out and developed without regard to context. To say this is not to downgrade the importance of art or flair; but these are qualities of the specific expert rather than the expert system as such.

The decentred character of expertise does not preclude the existence of 'authoritative centres', such as professional associations or licensing bodies; but their relation to knowledge-claims they seek to influence or regulate is quite different from that of centres of tradition in regard of formulaic truth. Although such might not always happen in practice, in principle their role is to protect the very impartiality of coded knowledge. In many ways expertise thus cuts across the formation of the bureaucratic hierarchies upon which Weber placed emphasis. It has become a commonplace to say as much about the role of professionals, whose global affiliations cannot be contained within the hierarchy of command within the organization. However, the phenomenon goes well beyond this example. In virtue of its mobile form, expertise is as disruptive of hierarchies of authority as it is a stabilizing influence. Formal bureaucratic rules, in fact, tend to deny that very openness to innovation which is the hallmark of expertise; they translate *skills* into *duties*.

Disembedding mechanisms depend on two conditions: the evacuation of the traditional or customary content of local contexts of action, and the reorganizing of social relations across broad time-space bands. The causal processes whereby disembedding occurs are many, but it is not difficult to see why the formation and evolution of expert systems is so central to them. Expert systems decontextualize as an intrinsic consequence of the impersonal and contingent character of their rules of knowledge-acquisition; as decentred systems, 'open' to whosoever has the time, resources and talent to grasp them, they can be located anywhere. Place is not in any sense a quality relevant to their validity; and places themselves, as we shall see, take on a different significance from traditional locales.[41]

Wisdom and expertise

There were various sorts of communication, but also dispute, between the diverse guardians of tradition in premodern contexts. Wrangles of interpretation were extremely common, and most traditional symbols and practices, even in small cultures, had strongly defined fissiparous tendencies. Difference in the interpretation of dogma, however, is not the same as disputes relating to expert knowledge (or, as should always be stressed here, claims to knowledge). The 'natural state' of tradition, as it were, is *deference*. Traditions exist in so far as they are separated from other traditions, the ways of life of separate or alien communities. The expert purveys universalizing knowledge. Experts are bound often to disagree, not only because they may have been trained in varying schools of thought but because disagreement or critique is the *motor* of their enterprise.

We sometimes speak, not without reason, of 'traditions of thought' in academic study, science and other areas relevant to the distribution of expertise. Gadamer has even made tradition, in his sense, the origin of all forms of linguistic understanding. The debate about 'presuppositions' and the importance of working within relatively fixed perspectives has spilled over into the philosophy of science. Yet the use of 'tradition' to describe such perspectives, while justifiable enough as shorthand, is clearly elliptical. The combination of scepticism and universalism that characterizes modern modes of enquiry ensures that traditions of thought are understood by sympathizer and critic alike to be relatively arbitrary. Experts trained in one particular approach may often be critical or dismissive of the views of those schooled in others; yet critique of even the most basic assumptions of a perspective is not only in bounds, but called for, expected and responded to.

The point is not just that, as Popper says, everything is open to doubt, fundamental though that is not just to intellectual enquiry but to everyday life in conditions of modernity. It is the *mixture of scepticism and universalism* which gives the disputes of experts their particular flavour. Experts disagree not just because they are defending different pre-established positions but in the very service of overcoming those differences. Pluralism here has a different form from the cultural diversity of premodern systems, and is clearly related to broad principles of democratization. Experts frequently disagree, but in the interests of a universalism that lends itself to public discourse. Such discourse is both the means of and produced by the conjunction of critique and universalism.

Discomforts for expert and layperson come from the very same source. Expert knowledge, and the general accumulation of expertise, are supposed to provide increasing certainty about how the world is, but the very condition of such certainty, not to put too fine a point on it, is doubt. For a long while, the tensions inherent in such a situation were masked by the distinctive status which science, understood in a specific way, enjoyed in modern societies – plus a more or less unquestioned dominance that the West held over the rest of the world. Furthermore, the very persistence of tradition, especially in contexts of everyday life, held back processes of evacuation that have today become far advanced. So long as traditions and customs were widely sustained, experts were people who could be turned to at certain necessary junctures; and, in the public eye, at least, science was in effect not very different from tradition – a monolithic source of 'authority' in the generic sense. The differences between guardians and experts were much less obvious than they have since become.

A non-traditional culture dispenses with final authorities, but the significance of this for day-to-day life was first of all muted by the factors described above. Even for those working in intellectual disciplines, 'science' was invested with the authority of a final court of appeal. What seems to be a purely intellectual matter today – the fact that, shorn of formulaic truth, all claims to knowledge are corrigible-(including any metastatements made about them) – has become an existential condition in modern societies. The consequences for the lay individual, as for the culture as a whole, are both liberating and disturbing. Liberating, since obeisance to a single source of authority is oppressive; anxiety-provoking, since the ground is pulled from beneath the individual's feet. Science, Popper says, is built upon shifting sand; it has no stable grounding at all. Yet today it is not only scientific enquiry but more or less the whole of everyday life to which this metaphor applies.

Living in a world of multiple authorities, a circumstance sometimes mistakenly referred to as postmodernity, is very consequential for all attempts to confine risk to the narrow conception referred to previously, whether in respect of an individual's life-course or of collective attempts to colonize the future. For since there are no super-experts to turn to, risk calculation has to include the risk of which experts are consulted, or whose authority is to be taken as binding. The debate over global warming is one among an indefinite range of examples that could be quoted. The very scepticism that is the driving force of expert knowledge might lead, in some contexts, or among some groups, to a disenchantment with all experts; this is one of the lines of tension between expertise and tradition (also habit and compulsion).

Science has lost a good deal of the aura of authority it once had. In some part, probably, this is a result of disillusionment with the benefits which, in association with technology, it has been claimed to bring to humanity. Two world wars, the invention of horrifically destructive weaponry, the global ecological crisis, and other developments in the present century, might cool the ardour of even the most optimistic advocates of progress through untrammelled scientific enquiry. Yet science can and indeed must be regarded as problematic in terms of its own premises. The principle 'nothing is sacred' is itself a universalizing one, from which the claimed authority of science cannot be exempt.

A balance between scepticism and commitment is difficult enough to forge within the philosophy of science, where it is endlessly debated; it is surely unsurprising, therefore, to find that such a balance is elusive when sought after in practical contexts of day-to-day life. Again this is as much true of the collective efforts of humanity to confront global problems as it is of the individual seeking to colonize a personal future. How can a layperson keep up with, or reconcile the diverse theories about, for example, the influence of diet upon long-term health? Some findings are at any time quite well established and it is sensible to act on them; for instance, giving up smoking almost certainly lessens the chance of contracting a specific range of serious illnesses. Yet it is only forty years ago that many doctors were recommending smoking as a means of enhancing mental and bodily relaxation. Many forms of scientific knowledge, particularly when they are bracketed to observable technologies, are relatively secure; the shifting sand is leavened with a measure of concrete. However, all must be in principle regarded as open to question and at every juncture a puzzling diversity of rival theoretical and practical claims are to be found in the 'moving' areas of knowledge.

In modern social conditions all experts are specialists. Specialization is intrinsic to a world of high reflexivity, where local knowledge is re-embedded information derived from abstract systems of one type or another. There is not a one-way movement towards specialization; all sorts of generalisms ride on the back of the division of labour in expertise. An example would be the general physician in the field of medicine; he or she is a non-specialist in medical terms, whose role is to know whether a patient needs a specialist and, if so, of what kind. Yet a 'general' physician is clearly a specialist when compared to lay members of the public.

It is of the first importance to recognize that all specialists revert to being members of the ordinary lay public when confronted with the vast array of abstract systems, and diverse arenas of expertise, that affect our lives today. This is far more than just an expansion of the division of labour in general. The guardians of tradition had their specialisms; the skills and position of the craft worker, for example, were usually quite separate from those of the priest. Specialist guardians, however, never became mere 'lay people'. Their possession of 'wisdom' gave them a distinct and general status in the community at large. In contrast to wisdom, 'competence' is specifically linked to specialization. A person's competence as an expert is coterminous with her or his specialism. Consequently, although some forms of expertise might command wide public esteem, a person's status within one abstract system is likely to be completely beside the point within another.

This situation decisively influences the nature of trust relations between experts and lay individuals, as well as trust in the abstract systems which the experts 'front'. Trust no longer depends upon a respect for the 'causal relation' believed to hold between a guardian and formulaic truth. The skills or knowledge possessed by experts are esoteric only in so far as they express their commitment to the mastery of a specialism; the individual who consults an expert could have sat in that person's place, had he or she concentrated upon the same learning process. Trust based purely on the assumption of technical competence is *revisable* for much the same reasons as knowledge purchased through methodical scepticism is revisable; it can in principle be withdrawn at a moment's notice. Hence it is not surprising that the purveyors of expertise often feel led to place a special premium on the services they have to offer, or to make particular efforts to reassure patrons at the point of contact with them. The degrees and diplomas hung on the wall of a psychotherapist's office are therefore more than merely informational; they carry an echo of the symbols with which figures of traditional authority surrounded themselves.

The problematic nature of trust in modern social conditions is especially significant when we consider abstract systems themselves, rather than only their 'representatives'. Trust in a multiplicity of abstract systems is a necessary part of everyday life today, whether or not this is consciously acknowledged by the individuals concerned. Traditional systems of trust were nearly always based on 'facework'; because of having special access to the esoteric qualities of tradition, the guardian was tradition made flesh. The disembedded characteristics of abstract systems mean constant interaction with 'absent others' – people one never sees or meets but whose actions directly affect features of one's own life. Given the divided and contested character of expertise, the creation of stable abstract systems is a fraught endeavour. Some types of abstract system have become so much a part of people's lives that, at any one time, they appear to have a rock-like solidity akin to established tradition; yet they are vulnerable to the collapse of generalized trust.

On the level of day-to-day life, forfeit of trust may take various forms, some of which are entirely marginal to the persistence of abstract systems themselves. It does not make much odds, for example, if a few people opt out more or less completely from surrounding abstract systems – by, say, establishing a small self-sufficient commune in a rural area. The fact that Jehovah's Witnesses reject much of the electronic technology of modernity has no particular impact on the wider society. Some dislocations or relapses in trust, however, are much broader in their implications. A progressive acceleration of mistrust in a bank, or a government, can lead to their collapse; the world economy as a whole is subject to vagaries of generalized trust, as of course are the relations between nation-states in the global political order.

Most important of all, trust in abstract systems is bound up with collective lifestyle patterns, themselves subject to change. Because of their local and centred character, traditional practices are embedded: they correspond to normative qualities that sustain daily routines. The notion of 'lifestyle' has no meaning when applied to traditional contexts of action. In modern societies, lifestyle choices are both constitutive of daily life and geared to abstract systems. There is a fundamental sense in which the whole institutional apparatus of modernity, once it has become broken away from tradition, depends upon potentially volatile mechanisms of trust. The compulsive character of modernity remains largely hidden from view so long as the Promethean impulse holds sway, especially when it is backed by the pre-eminent authority of science. When these factors are placed in question, however, as is happening today, the coincidence of lifestyle patterns and global processes of social reproduction come under strain. Alterations in lifestyle practices can then become deeply subversive of core abstract systems. For instance, a general move away from consumerism in modern economies would have massive implications for contemporary economic institutions.

Compulsiveness, I want to argue, is *frozen trust*, commitment which has no object but is self-perpetuating. Addiction, to recapitulate, is anything we have to lie about: it is the obverse of that integrity which tradition once supplied and which all forms of trust also presume. A world of abstract systems, and potentially open lifestyle choices, for reasons already explained, demands active engagement. Trust, that is to say, is invested in the light of the selection of alternatives. When such alternatives become filtered out by unexplicated commitments – compulsions – trust devolves into simple repetitive urgency. Frozen trust blocks re-engagement with the abstract systems that have come to dominate the content of day-to-day life.

Outside areas of compulsive repetition, the dialectic of loss and reappropriation offers clear contrasts with more traditional social orders. The esoteric quality of traditions is not something which is communicable from guardians to others; it is their very access to formulaic truth that sets them off from the rest of the population. Lay individuals come to share in this quality only infrequently – as in religious ceremonials, where they may temporarily have direct access to the realm of the sacred.

This situation is altered in a basic way when expertise comes widely to replace tradition. Expert knowledge is open to reappropriation by anyone with the necessary time and resources to become trained; and the prevalence of institutional reflexivity means that there is a continuous filter-back of expert theories, concepts and findings to the lay population. The reappropriation of expert knowledge, where compulsive behaviour-patterns do not apply, is the very condition of the 'authenticity' of everyday life. Habits and expectations tend to be reshaped in terms of the pervasive filter-back of information in a more or less automatic way. However, more deliberate and focused forms of re-engagement are common. As emphasized before, these can be individual or collective; they may cover idiosyncratic elements of a person's everyday life or be global in character.

Tradition in modernity

Modernity destroys tradition. However (and this is very important) a *collaboration between modernity and tradition* was crucial to the earlier phases of modern social development – the period during which risk was calculable in relation to external influences. This phase is ended with the emergence of high modernity or what Beck calls reflexive modernization. Henceforth, tradition assumes a different character. Even the most advanced of premodern civilizations remained resolutely traditional. Some brief comments upon the character of such civilizations will be worthwhile before taking up directly the issue of 'tradition in modernity'.

In premodern civilizations, the activities of the political centre never fully penetrated the day-to-day life of the local community.[42] Traditional civilizations were segmental and dualistic. The vast majority of the population lived in local, agrarian communities making up, as Marx said, 'a sack of potatoes'. Traditions participated in, and expressed, this dualism. The 'great traditions' were above all associated with the rationalization of religion, a process which depended upon the existence of scriptural texts. Rationalization here was not inimical to tradition; on the contrary, although the evidence cannot be forthcoming, we may suspect that it made possible the long-term existence of specific traditional forms well beyond anything found in purely oral cultures. For the first time a tradition could know itself to exist 'from time immemorial'. The great traditions were 'monumental' – in a material sense in so far as they produced great edifices, but also in a more non-physical way in the sense in which their classical texts were a testament to their power.

Because of the structural character of these civilizations, however, the great traditions were communicated only imperfectly to the local community, over which their hold was insecure. Local communities, in any case, remained oral societies. They bred a variety of traditions which either remained distant from or actively contested the filter-down of the more rationalized systems. Thus Weber showed in his studies of the 'world religions' that the rationalization of 'scriptoral tradition' became recontextualized within the community; magic, sorcery and other local practices broke up the unifying influence of the centralized symbolic order.

A very large part of the content of tradition, therefore, continued to be at the level of the local community. Such 'little traditions' were often influenced by the guardians of rationalized religions (priests, officials) but also responded to a variety of local conditions. Often there were linguistic differences as well as other cultural schisms between local communities and central elites.

As a result of the association that developed between capitalism and the nation-state, modern societies differ from all forms of pre-existing civilization. The nation-state and the capitalist enterprise were both power-containers, in which the development of new surveillance mechanisms ensured much greater social integration across time-space than had previously been possible.[43] In the early modern state, surveillance processes continued to draw upon traditional sources of legitimation, such as the divine right of the sovereign, and his or her household, to rule. Perhaps even more importantly, certainly to my analysis here, the power system of the early modern state continued to presume the segmentation of the local community. Only with the consolidation of the nation-state, and the generalization of democracy in the nineteenth and twentieth centuries, did the local community effectively begin to break up. Before this period, surveillance mechanisms were primarily 'from the top down'; they were means of increasing centralized control over a non-mobilized spectrum of 'subjects'. The time of the accelerating development of the nation-state was thus also one in which the general population became more closely drawn into systems of integration that cross-cut the local community level. Institutional reflexivity became the main enemy of tradition; the evacuation of local contexts of action went hand in hand with growing time-space distanciation (disembedding).

However, this was a complex process. Early modern institutions did not only depend upon pre-existing traditions but also *created new ones*. Formulaic truth, and associated rituals, were pressed into service in new arenas – the most important being the symbolic domain of the 'nation'. Eric Hobsbawm, among others, has drawn attention to the phenomenon. He notes that nineteenth- and twentieth-century ' "traditions" which appear or claim to be old are quite often recent in origin and sometimes invented'.[44] 'Invented traditions' are not necessarily constructed in a deliberate way, although this is sometimes the case. Thus for example many nineteenth-century buildings in Britain were put up or rebuilt in Gothic style. The contact claimed with the past in invented tradition, Hobsbawm says, is 'largely factitious' – in contrast to 'genuine traditions'. Invented traditions, Hobsbawm argues, proliferate in the context of early modern institutions. 'Ancient materials' are used for modern ends – most especially, to create legitimacy for emerging systems of power.

Hobsbawm's substantive thesis may be correct, but his concepts are more open to question. 'Invented tradition', which at first sight seems almost a contradiction in terms, and is intended to be provocative, turns out on scrutiny to be something of a tautology. For *all* traditions, one could say, are invented traditions. What gives tradition its 'genuineness', its authenticity, as I have remarked earlier, is not that it has been established for aeons; nor is it anything to do with how far it accurately encapsulates past events. In those most 'traditional' of all societies, oral cultures, after all, the 'real past', if those words have any meaning, is effectively unknown. Tradition is the very *medium* of the 'reality' of the past. In societies which have a recorded history, of course, 'continuity with a suitable past' can be established – and can be dissected by the historian with a critical eye. Yet how far such continuity is ever 'genuine' in Hobsbawm's sense is problematic and, to repeat, has nothing to do with a tradition's authenticity, which depends upon the connection of ritual practice and formulaic truth.

The interconnections between early modernity and tradition can be briefly described in the following way:

First, the fact that traditions, old and new, remained central in the early development of modernity indicates again the limitations of the 'disciplinary model' of modern society. Surveillance mechanisms did not by and large depend for their effectiveness upon the internalization of emotional control or *conscience*. The emerging emotional axis was rather one which linked compulsiveness and *shame* anxiety.

Second, the legitimating role of science, generally understood in a positivistic fashion, perpetuated ideas of truth which, in popular culture at any rate, retained strong ties with formulaic truth. The struggles between 'science and religion' concealed the contradictory character of its claims to unquestioned 'authority'. Hence many experts were effectively guardians and elicited appropriate forms of deference.

Third, the compulsive nature of modernity was not something that remained completely hidden or unresisted. One way of indexing this, as Christie Davies has shown, is by reference to common forms of humour and joking. Those places where Calvinism, the 'purest form' of the capitalist spirit, was strongest (e.g., Scotland, Switzerland, Holland) also became the butt of a certain style of joking. Jokes about the Scots, for example, in some part belong to a wider category of ethnic joking; but such jokes often focus full square on the Protestant ethic. A Scot sat at the bedside of an ailing friend. 'You seem more cheerful, John.' 'Aye, man, I thought I was going to die, but the doctor cae save my life. It's going to cost £100.' 'Eh, that's a terrible extravagance. Do ye think it's worth it?'

What are such jokes about if not compulsiveness, a rejection of the dogged stupidity characteristic of all compulsive behaviour? As Davies points out, the central characters in such jokes act out a caricature of the Protestant ethic – but clearly indicate that alternative attitudes are alive and well.[45]

Fourth, the compulsiveness of modernity was from its first origins gender-divided. The compulsiveness documented by Weber in *The Protestant Ethic* is that of a male public domain. In those institutional contexts where the capitalist spirit was dominant, women were effectively left with the emotional burdens which a 'striving instrumentalism' produced. Women began modes of emotional experimentation that were subsequently to have a great impact.[46] Yet traditional modes of gender difference, and gender domination, were at the same time actively reinforced by the development of newer traditions – including the emergence of an ethos of female 'domesticity'.

Fifth, tradition was called upon particularly in respect of the generation, or regeneration, of personal and collective identity. The sustaining of identity is thrown up as a fundamental problem by the maturation of the institutions of modernity, but – in tensionful and contradictory ways – this problem was 'resolved' by invoking the authority of tradition. The 'sense of community' of working-class neighbourhoods, for example, took the form, in some part, of a reconstruction of tradition; as did nationalism on the level of the state.

Globalization and the evacuation of tradition

The phase of 'reflexive modernization', marked as it is by the twin processes of globalization and the excavation of most traditional contexts of action, alters the balance between tradition and modernity. Globalization seems at first sight an 'out there' phenomenon, the development of social relations of a worldwide kind far removed from the concerns of everyday life. To the sociologist, therefore, it might appear as simply another 'field' of study, a specialism among other specialisms. The study of globalization would be the analysis of world systems, modes of interconnection which operate in the global stratosphere. So long as traditional modes of life, and especially the 'situated local community' persisted, such a view was not too far from the truth. Today, however, when the evacuation of local contexts has become so far advanced, it is quite inaccurate. Globalization is an 'in here' matter, which affects, or rather is dialectically related to, even the most intimate aspects of our lives. Indeed, what we now call intimacy, and its importance in personal relations, has been largely created by globalizing influences.

What ties globalization to processes of the excavations of traditional contexts of action? The connection is the disembedding consequences of abstract systems. The causal influences here are complex, and bound up with the multidimensional character of modernity.[47] I shall not analyse this directly here, but rather spell out the structural relations concerned. Tradition is about the organization of time and therefore also space: so too is globalization, save that the one runs counter to the other. Whereas tradition controls space through its control of time, with globalization it is the other way around. Globalization is essentially 'action at distance'; absence predominates over presence, not in the sedimentation of time, but because of the restructuring of space.

Processes of globalization today still to an extent follow certain early patterns established during the initial phase of modern social development. Capitalist enterprise, for example, is a disembedding mechanism *par excellence*, and is powering its way through previously resistant parts of the world just as thoroughly as it ever did. Paradoxically, state socialism, which saw itself as the prime revolutionary force in history, proved much more accommodating towards tradition than capitalism has been.

The first phase of globalization was plainly governed primarily by the expansion of the West, and institutions which originated in the West. No other civilization made anything like as pervasive an impact upon the world, or shaped it so much in its own image. Yet, unlike other forms of cultural or military conquest, disembedding via abstract systems is intrinsically decentred, since it cuts through the organic connection with place upon which tradition depended. Although still dominated by Western power, globalization today can no longer be spoken of only as a matter of one-way imperialism. Action at a distance was always a two-way process; now, increasingly, however, there is no obvious 'direction' to globalization at all, as its ramifications are more or less ever-present. The current phase of globalization, then, should not be confused with the preceding one, whose structures it acts increasingly to subvert.

Hence post-traditional society is the first *global society*. Until relatively recently, much of the world remained in a quasi-segmental state, in which many large enclaves of traditionalism persisted. In these areas, and also in some regions and contexts of the more industrially developed countries, the local community continued to be strong. Over the past few decades particularly influenced by the development of instantaneous global electronic communication, these circumstances have altered in a radical way. A world where no one is 'outside' is one where pre-existing traditions cannot avoid contact not only with others but also with many alternative ways of life. By the same token, it is one where the 'other' cannot any longer be treated as inert. The point is not only that the other 'answers back', but that mutual interrogation is possible.

The 'interrogations' which the West carried out of other cultures were for a long time one-sided – a series of investigations of a cryptic other which resembled nothing so much as the queries that men pursued into women. (Indeed there may very well have been quite close connections between these two sorts of interrogation.)[48] So far as non-Western cultures are concerned, the development of anthropology – a process which leads towards its effective dissolution today – gives a rough index of the phenomenon.

Anthropology has passed through three general phases. The first was one of taxonomy of the alien; early ethnography was a sort of collective voyage of the *Beagle*, circumnavigating the world in pursuit of the classification of exotic species. Taxonomic anthropology was often evolutionary. Evolutionism succeeded beautifully as means of categorizing the other as, if not inert, no more than a 'subject' of enquiry. Not that the enquiry was ever a casual or particularly comfortable one. The alien character of other traditions was a persistent source of compelling interest, puzzlement and generalized anxiety; any threat to Western dominance was, however, quashed by the neutralizing and distant effect of 'naturalized alienness'. One could say that the alienness of non-Western traditions was a real counterpart to the 'given' form of nature, an external environment of Western expansionism to be 'understood' and probably trampled over in much the same way.

A new phase was initiated when anthropology discovered what might be called the essential *intelligence* of other cultures or traditions. The other is discovered as just as knowledgeable as 'us', although living of course in different circumstances. Realization of such capability, and therefore of the implicit claims to equality of the other, were convergent with the invention of functionalism in anthropology. Functionalism recognizes the authenticity of other traditions, but relates that authenticity only to their inner cohesion, as situated cultural wholes. The integrity of traditions thus becomes acknowledged, but the 'dialogic' relation established is one that presumes the separateness of the alien. 'Intelligence' is entirely contextual; each culture is adapted to the milieu in which it is 'discovered'. The anthropological monograph can be deposited in the Western library where it stands alongside an indefinite array of

other studies. In social or material terms the juxtaposition of recording and real consequences remains cruel: the anthropologist, as
Lévi-Strauss sadly remarked, is the chronicler, and even in some
part the causal agent, of a disappearing world. The anthropological
monograph preserves, in much the same way as a protected relic
does, a testament to a way of life to which we can no longer directly
bear witness.

Compare the journeys of an itinerant anthropologist today. Nigel
Barley carried out anthropological research in Indonesia.[49] Barley's
work is different both in style and content from orthodox anthropology. It is chatty, witty and informal; it records his own feelings,
puzzles and mistakes in his encounters with the individuals whose
lives he went to study. He talks of the incidents, funny and dangerous, which happened during his time 'in the field' and of his 'subjects' as flesh-and-blood people rather than merely ciphers of a
larger collectivity. Interestingly, his books read more like novels
than academic texts – the presence of the author creates a biographical style as well as a strong narrative form. *He* is the *ingenu*, rather
than those whom he goes to 'investigate'; he is like a Lucky Jim of
the anthropological world. As an aside, but a very important one, it
might be noted that the recovery of a narrative style here turns
structuralism on its head. The 'absence of the author' in most pre-
existing anthropological studies is not a reflection of the fact that
texts speak for themselves; rather, the author is absent because such
studies are not full dialogic engagements with 'other cultures'.

A feature of Barley's writing is that the everyday world from
which he comes is pictured as just as baffling and problematic as the
one he enters in Indonesia. His attempts to buy cheap air tickets in
London meet with disaster; the only detailed map he can find of the
area he is going to visit dates from the 1940s and the place-names
are in Dutch; the advice he gets from anthropologists who have
worked in the area previously is contradictory. His ingenuousness,
and puzzled curiosity about the details of everyday life, actually
parallel very closely the outlook of the hero of *The Mezzanine*. The
alien culture is no more or less in need of interpretation than is his
culture of origin; at the same time, even the most exotic forms of
behaviour, when approached in a determined way, prove to have
elements of easy familiarity. Embarrassment and a certain diffuse
anxiety, occasionally laced with an awareness of danger, emerge as
the prime negative aspects of the anthropological encounter; on the
positive side, along with self-illumination, there is humour and the
pleasures of discovering a common humanity.

Wherever he goes, including the most apparently isolated of areas, he is never completely out of the tracks of tourists, and sometimes even stumbles across anthropologists. Local customs continue alongside images and information coming from both the national society and the wider world. Barley himself is introduced into the group he came to study as a 'famous Dutch tourist', come to 'honour the community and its old ways'.[50] One man whom the anthropologist met offered him hospitality in a charming traditional house in the village; he seemingly had resisted the intrusions of the modern world. Of course, it turned out that he had a degree in satellite communications from the Massachusetts Institute of Technology and actually lived most of the time in the city, where he had a modern house:

> His attachment to the traditional world was just as much an outsider's as mine was . . . He rubbed salt into my wounds by his relentless self-awareness: 'You see. I only learned to value the old way by going abroad. If I had sat in my village I would have thought of America as the Kingdom of Heaven. So I come back for the festivals'.[51]

Barley's anthropological trip was not just a one-way one; a group of his 'subjects' returned with him to London. Barley organized the visit by arranging with the Museum of Mankind that they would build a traditional rice-barn as an exhibit. Unlike the sophisticated individual just referred to, his companions had never previously been far away from their home village. They, presumably, wrote no books on their return, but we get at least some sense of their reactions to Barley's own mode of life and its wider cultural setting. They had their own puzzles, their own share of incidents and reactions; and, naturally, these only sometimes followed lines the 'anthropologist' expected. Yet their activities in London furthered Barley's grasp of their indigenous culture; for the process of building the rice-barn allowed him to document their methods of production in their entirety and to gather information that would have been very hard to come by in 'the field'.

'Return visits' are by no means unknown in anthropology. Franz Boas, for example, once shepherded some of the Kwakiutl around New York (they were apparently singularly indifferent to the grandeur of the city). Anthropologists have sometimes told candid inside stories of their field-work, although quite often these originated as private diaries, kept separate from their ethnographic reports. Thus Malinowski's field-work diaries of his experiences in the

Trobriands (and in England) remained unpublished until some while after his death. Today, however, anthropology is directly embroiled in the institutional reflexivity of modernity, and anthropology thus becomes indistinguishable from sociology. In British Columbia the present-day Kwakiutl are busy reconstructing their traditional culture using Boas's monographs as their guide, while Australian Aboriginals and other groups across the world are contesting land-rights on the basis of parallel anthropological studies.

In a post-traditional order, in Richard Rorty's memorable phrase, we see the formation – as a possibility rather than a fully-fledged actuality – of a cosmopolitan conversation of humankind. It is a social order where the continuing role of tradition, for reasons I shall go on to mention, is however edged with a potential for violence.

Detraditionalization

In the post-traditional order, even in the most modernized of societies today, traditions do not wholly disappear; indeed, in some respects, and in some contexts, they flourish. In what sense, however, or in what guises, do traditions persist in the late modern world? On a schematic level, the answer can be given as follows. Whether old or new, traditions in the modern world exist in one of two frameworks.

Traditions may be discursively articulated and defended – in other words, justified as having value in a universe of plural competing values. Traditions may be defended in their own terms, or against a more dialogical background; here reflexivity may be multilayered, as in those defences of religion which point to the difficulties of living in a world of radical doubt. A discursive defence of tradition does not necessarily compromise formulaic truth, for what is most consequential is a preparedness to enter into dialogue while suspending the threat of violence.

Otherwise, tradition becomes *fundamentalism*. There is nothing mysterious about the appearance of fundamentalism in the late modern world. 'Fundamentalism' only assumes the sense it does against a background of the prevalence of radical doubt; it is nothing more or less than 'tradition in its traditional sense', although today embattled rather than in the ascendant. Fundamentalism may be understood as an assertion of formulaic truth without regard to consequences.

In the concluding section I shall return to a discussion of the implications of these observations. For the moment, again in a rather schematic way, let me indicate some of the relations between tradition and quasi-traditional traits of the post-traditional society. I hope the reader will accept that such a relatively cursory account passes over a great deal which in another context would need to be unpacked – especially if a direct confrontation were to be made with some of the claims of postmodernism.

In the present day, the destruction of the local community, in the developed societies, has reached its apogee. Little traditions which either survived, or were actively created, during earlier phases of modern social development have increasingly succumbed to forces of cultural evacuation. The division between great and little traditions, which in some premodern civilizations survived for thousands of years, has today almost completely disappeared. Distinctions between 'high and low culture' of course still exist, and are associated with the persistence of a certain classicism in the former as compared to the latter; but this has only marginal connections with tradition as I have defined it.

The dissolution of the local community, such as it used to be, is not the same as the disappearance of local life or local practices. Place, however, becomes increasingly reshaped in terms of distant influences drawn upon in the local arena. Thus local customs that continue to exist tend to develop altered meanings. They become either *relics* or *habits*.

Habits may be purely personal forms of routinization. Many of the items listed on page 74, for example, are today likely to be matters of habit. They are individual routines of one kind or another, which have a certain degree of binding force simply by virtue of regular repetition. The psychological significance of such routines should not be underestimated. They are of basic importance for ontological security because they provide a structuring medium for the continuity of life across different contexts of action. In a post-traditional order habits are regularly infused with information drawn from abstract systems, with which also they often clash. A person might resolutely stick to a certain type of diet, for instance, even though a good deal of medical opinion condemns it. However, he or she may effectively be forced to shift if, as in the case of the ice-cube tray, manufacturing or design processes change.

Many personal habits effectively become collective as they are shaped by commodification, or as a result of generalizable influences of institutional reflexivity. Local customs are more genuinely collective habits when they are created by influences within an area or community; but those that are remnants of more traditional practices are likely to devolve into items in what some have called the *living museum*. Whether they are personal traits or more closely connected with social customs, habits have lost all tie with the formulaic truth of tradition. Their brittle character is indicated by the fuzzy boundary which separates them from compulsive behaviour; their compelling force can devolve into compulsive ritual, in specific instances into the obsessional neuroses which Freud was one of the first to describe and try to account for.

Artefacts once associated with both great and little traditions in the post-traditional order tend to become relics, although 'relic' should be extended to cover more than only physical objects. A relic, as I use the word here, covers any item in a living museum. Relics are not just objects or practices which happen to live on as a residue of traditions that have become weakened or lost; they are invested with meaning as exemplars of a transcended past. Consider the story of Wigan pier. George Orwell's *The Road to Wigan Pier*, first published in 1937, described Wigan as a dilapidated area which bore witness to the evils of industrialism. The road to Wigan pier was a personal journey but also described a downward trajectory of modern civilization. Orwell's account of the town was so scathing that it in fact aroused a great deal of local resentment.

Orwell was disappointed to find that Wigan pier no longer existed when he got to the town. The pier was not actually a walkway, still less was it anywhere near the sea; the term referred to an iron frame employed to empty coal into barges along a canal. It had been scrapped several years before Orwell arrived there. In the 1980s, however, the pier was rebuilt. The surrounding dock and warehouses were cleaned up and refitted, trees planted, and the area designated as a 'heritage centre'. The centre harks back not to the 1930s but to 1900; an exhibition, which recreates a mine and miners' cottages, occupies part of it. It invites the visitor to experience 'the way we were'. Ironically, Orwell has been drummed into service as part of the very 'heritage' he found so distasteful: visitors can take a drink in the Orwell pub.[52]

Relics are signifiers of a past which has no development, or at least whose causal connections to the present are not part of what gives them their identity. They are display items in a showcase, and Wigan pier is in this respect no different from 'true monuments', such as ruins preserved or refurbished palaces, castles and country homes. A material relic might seem to be something which literally 'stays in place' – which remains untouched by the vagaries of change around it. It would be more correct to say the opposite. A relic has no effective connection with the area in which it exists, but is produced as a visible icon for observation by whosoever happens to wish to visit. Like other museum pieces, it may be on the site where it originated, but whether it is or not has little relevance to its nature, which is as a signifier of difference. A relic is like a memory-trace shorn of its collective frameworks.

A living museum is any collage of such 'memory traces' presented for public display. In so far as they do not become habits, customs may fall into this category. The point about relics today is that only their association with a lapsed past gives them any significance. Relics were (and are) common in religious traditions, but there they had quite a different significance; they derived their importance not from simple connection with the past but from the fact that they participated in the domain of the sacred. As Durkheim pointed out, the sacred is indivisible; a small piece of Christ's cloak is as holy as any other seemingly more impressive religious object or practice.

The advent of modernity plainly does not spell the disappearance of collective ritual. Sometimes such ritual is proclaimed to go back for centuries, or even millennia; more commonly it is a relatively recent invention in the Hobsbawm mode. Max Gluckman makes a useful distinction between 'ritualism' and the 'ritualization of social relations' which has some purchase here.[53] 'Ritualism' exists where ritual activities are bound up with 'mystical notions', or what I would call formulaic truth. The 'ritualization of social relations' is where social interaction has a standardized form adopted as a way of defining the roles that people have on ceremonial occasions. Ritualism persists, or becomes revised, in some contexts, but in most instances has been displaced by ritualization (the two can come into conflict where, say, a person who never attends church wishes to have a church wedding). Ritualism and therefore tradition continue to exist and even flourish wherever formulaic truth forms a means of constructing interpretations of past time.

At about the same date as *The Road to Wigan Pier* was published, a crowd of some one hundred thousand people gathered just outside Pretoria, in South Africa, to celebrate the laying of the foundation stone for the Voortrekker Monument. Men and women turned out in the Voortrekker dress, fires were lit and *Die Stem*, the Afrikaner anthem, was sung. The Monument was built to celebrate

the anniversary of the Great Trek undertaken by the Boers a hundred years before and the victory of the covered wagons over the
massed forces of the Zulu army. The ritual, and the construction of
the memorial building, were not just continuations of pre-existing
traditions; they actually helped create a new version of Afrikaner
nationalism.

Such examples demonstrate that tradition is not just about cel-
ebrating an unchangeable past or defending the *status quo*. South
Africa at that point was still under the colonial control of the British;
the Afrikaners looked forward to the time at which they would
govern an independent country. In the words of one Afrikaner
political leader: 'The Great Trek gave our people its soul. It was the
cradle of our nationhood. It will always show us the beacons on our
path and serve as our lighthouse in our night.'[54]

Tradition, plainly, is bound up with power; it also protects
against contingency. Some have argued that the sacred is the core of
tradition, because it invests the past with a divine presence; from
this point of view political rituals have a religious quality. However,
one should rather see formulaic truth as the property which links
the sacred with tradition. Formulaic truth is what renders central
aspects of tradition 'untouchable' and confers integrity upon the
present in relation to the past. Monuments turn into relics once
formulaic truths are disputed or discarded, and the traditional
relapses into the merely customary or habitual.

Tradition, discourse, violence

Tradition is effectively a way of settling clashes between different
values and ways of life. Ruth Benedict expressed this in celebrated
fashion when she proposed that cultures make a selection from the
'arc of possible values' and outlooks on the world.[55] Once made,
however, and notwithstanding the changes that might occur, the
resultant traditions form a prism; other ways of life are distinct,
have an alien quality and their own centres. Tradition incorporates
power relations and tends to naturalize them. The world of 'traditional society' is one of traditional *societies*, in which cultural
pluralism takes the form of an extraordinary diversity of mores and
customs – each of which, however, exists in privileged space.

The post-traditional society is quite different. It is inherently
globalizing, but also reflects the intensifying of globalization. In the
post-traditional order cultural pluralism, whether this involves per-

sisting or created traditions, can no longer take the form of separated centres of embedded power.

Looked at analytically, there are only four ways, in any social context or society, in which clashes of values between individuals or collectivities can be resolved. These are through the *embedding of tradition*; *disengagement* from the hostile other; *discourse* or dialogue; and *coercion* or *violence*. All four are found in most environments of action, in all cultures, at least as immanent possibilities. However, quite different weightings of these factors are possible. In those societies in which tradition is a dominant influence, traditional beliefs and practices, as filtered through the activities of the guardians, take a great deal 'out of the play'. Embedded power is largely *concealed* and cultural accommodation takes the form above all of geographical segmentation. Disengagement here is not so much an active process as an outcome of the time-space organization of premodern systems, coupled to barriers which stand in the way of non-local communication.

With the emergence of modernity, however, and particularly with the intensifying of globalizing processes, these circumstances become more or less completely undermined. Traditions are called upon to 'explain' and justify themselves in a manner already alluded to. In general, *traditions only persist in so far as they are made available to discursive justification* and are prepared to enter into open dialogue not only with other traditions but with alternative modes of doing things. Disengagement is possible in some ways and in some contexts, but these tend to become more and more limited.

The Voortrekker monument subsequently became a symbol of the dominant ideology in South Africa in the postwar period. One could see the Apartheid doctrine fostered by that ideology as a deliberate 'refusal of dialogue' on the basis of enforced geographical and cultural segregation. As of 1993, central to the possibility of a democratic future for South Africa is the question of whether dialogic engagement is possible between Afrikaner nationalism and other cultural groups and power-interests in the country. In a period of ethnic revivalism, and resurgent nationalism in various areas of the world, the edge between dialogue and potential violence is plain to see.

Take as another instance the case of gender as tradition. Up to and well beyond the threshold of modernity, gender differences were deeply enshrined in tradition and resonant with congealed power. The very absence of women from the public domain suppressed any possibility that masculinity and femininity could be opened out to discursive scrutiny. Today, however, as a result of profound structural changes, combined with the struggles of feminist movements over many decades, divisions between men and women, up to and including the most intimate connections between gender, sexuality and self-identity, are publicly placed in question.

To place them in question means asking for their discursive justification. No longer can someone say in effect, 'I am a man, and this is how men are', 'I refuse to discuss things further' – statements that are normally carried in actions rather than stated in words. Behaviour and attitudes have to be justified when one is called upon to do so, which means that reasons have to be given; and where reasons have to be provided, differential power starts to dissolve, or alternatively power begins to become translated into authority. Post-traditional personal relations, the pure relationship, cannot survive if such discursive space is not created and sustained.

Yet, in very many cases it is not sustained. What happens? One possibility, obviously, is disengagement: today we live in the separating and divorcing society. A person can move on and look elsewhere. Even whole groups of people might do so. Where disengagement does not occur, and traditional relations are asserted, we enter the domain of potential or actual violence. Where talk stops, violence tends to begin. Male violence towards women today, both in the context of relationships and in the wider public arena, could be interpreted in this way.[56]

What applies in the area of personal relations and everyday life applies also to the global order and all levels in between. What I have just described could be seen as a male Clausewitzean theory of personal life: force or violence are resorted to once a 'diplomatic' exchange of views stops. Clausewitz's theorem still has its defenders, as well as its contexts of practical application, in the relations between states today. Cultural clashes in the global arena can breed violence; or they can generate dialogue. In general, 'dialogic democracy' – recognition of the authenticity of the other, whose views and ideas one is prepared to listen to and debate, as a mutual process – is the only alternative to violence in the many areas of the social order where disengagement is no longer a feasible option. There is a real and clear symmetry between the possibility of a 'democracy of the emotions' on the level of personal life and the potential for democracy on the level of the global order.

The post-traditional society is an ending; but it is also a beginning, a genuinely new social universe of action and experience. What type of social order is it, or might it become? It is, as I have said, a global society, not in the sense of a world society but as one of 'indefinite space'. It is one where social bonds have effectively to be *made*, rather than inherited from the past – on the personal and more collective levels this is a fraught and difficult enterprise, but one also that holds out the promise of great rewards. It is decentred in terms of *authorities*, but recentred in terms of opportunities and dilemmas, because focused upon new forms of interdependence. To regard *narcissism*, or even *individualism*, as at the core of the post-traditional order is a mistake – certainly in terms of the potentials for the future that it contains. In the domain of interpersonal life, opening out to the other is the condition of social solidarity; on the larger scale a proffering of the 'hand of friendship' within a global cosmopolitan order is ethically implicit in the new agenda sketched in right at the opening of this discussion.

Potentiality and actuality, needless to say, are two very different things. Radical doubt fuels anxiety, socially created uncertainties loom large; yawning gaps separate rich and poor on both local and more global levels. Yet we can discern clear prospects for a renewal of political engagement, albeit along different lines from those hitherto dominant. Breaking away from the aporias of postmodernism, we can see possibilities of 'dialogic democracy' stretching from a 'democracy of the emotions' in personal life to the outer limits of the global order. As collective humanity, we are not doomed to irreparable fragmentation, yet neither on the other hand are we confined to the iron cage of Max Weber's imagination. Beyond compulsiveness lies the chance of developing authentic forms of human life that owe little to the formulaic truths of tradition, but where the defence of tradition also has an important role.

NOTES

1   U. Beck and E. Beck-Gernsheim, *The Normal Chaos of Love*, Cambridge: Polity, 1995.
2   A. Giddens, *The Consequences of Modernity*, Cambridge: Polity, 1990.
3   P. Dicken, *Global Shift*, London: Chapman, 1992.
4   U. Beck, *Risk Society*, London: Sage, 1992.
5   A. Giddens, *The Transformation of Intimacy*, Cambridge: Polity, 1992.
6   N. Baker, *The Mezzanine*, Cambridge: Granta, 1990, p. 45.
7   R. B. Lee, *The Dobe !Kung*, New York: Holt, 1984, p. 49.
8   Ibid., p. 49.
9   P. Boyer, *Tradition as Truth and Communication*, Cambridge: Cambridge University Press, 1990.

10　E. Shils, *Tradition*, London: Faber, 1981.
11　M. Halbwachs, *The Social Frameworks of Memory*, Chicago: University of Chicago Press, 1992, p. 39.
12　Cf. A. Giddens, *The Constitution of Society*, Cambridge: Polity, 1984, pp. 45–51.
13　Boyer, *Tradition as Truth and Communication*, chapter 5.
14　Ibid., p. 112.
15　Shils says that there are 'factual traditions', without normative content. For me these fall into the category of customs. Shils, *Tradition*, pp. 23–5.
16　A. and T. Harris, *Staying OK*, London: Pan, 1985, p. 19.
17　S. Freud, *The Interpretation of Dreams*, London: Hogarth, 1951.
18　Giddens, *The Transformation of Intimacy*.
19　M. Weber, *The Protestant Ethic and the Spirit of Capitalism*, London: Allen & Unwin, 1976, p. 72.
20　Ibid., p. 182.
21　Ibid., pp. 84–6.
22　See, for instance, D. Bell, *The Cultural Contradictions of Capitalism*, London: Heinemann, 1979.
23　A. W. Schaeff, *Codependence: Misunderstood, Mistreated*, New York: Harper, 1986, p. 21.
24　Ibid., pp. 25–6.
25　M. Scarf, *Intimate Partners*, New York: Aullantine, 1987, p. 42.
26　Ibid. Quotations that follow are from this source.
27　A. Giddens, *Modernity and Self-Identity*, Cambridge: Polity, 1991.
28　S. Helmstetter: *Choices*, New York: Product Books, pp. 100–3. This is a selection from a list of one hundred day-to-day choices in the original.
29　Ibid., p. 104.
30　W. Wordsworth, *The Prelude*, Book One, lines 1–8.
31　B. McKibben, *The End of Nature*, New York: Random House, 1989.
32　C. Ponting, *A Green History of the World*, London: Penguin, 1991, chapter 5.
33　J. Broome, *Counting the Cost of Global Warming*, London: White Horse, 1992.
34　R. Sheldrake, *The Rebirth of Nature*, London: Rider, 1990, p. 153.
35　Ibid., p. 154.
36　Lee, *The Dobe !Kung*, pp. 47–8.
37　G. Simmel, 'The stranger', in Simmel: *On Individuality and Social Forms*, Chicago: University of Chicago Press, 1971, p. 143. On this question see also the important discussion in Z. Bauman: *Modernity and Ambivalence*, Cambridge: Polity, 1991, pp. 56–61.
38　Bauman, *Modernity and Ambivalence*, p. 60.
39　M. Weber, *Economy and Society*, Berkeley: University of California Press, 1978, vol. I, pp. 226–7.
40　Ibid., p. 215.
41　John Agnew, *Place and Politics*, London: Allen & Unwin, 1987.

42 Cf. A. Giddens, *The Nation-State and Violence*, Cambridge: Polity, 1985.
43 Ibid.
44 E. Hobsbawm, 'Introduction: inventing traditions', in E. Hobsbawm and T. Ranger, *The Invention of Tradition*, Cambridge: Cambridge University Press, 1983.
45 C. Davies, 'The Protestant Ethic and the comic spirit of capitalism', *British Journal of Sociology*, vol. 43, 1992.
46 Giddens, *The Transformation of Intimacy*.
47 For a discussion, see Giddens, *The Consequences of Modernity*.
48 See R. Hyam, *Empire and Sexuality*, Manchester: Manchester University Press, 1990.
49 N. Barley, *Not a Hazardous Sport*, London: Penguin, 1989.
50 Ibid., p. 138.
51 Ibid., p. 142.
52 R. Hewison, *The Heritage Industry*, London: Methuen, 1987.
53 M. Gluckman, *Custom and Conflict in Africa*, Oxford: Blackwell, 1970.
54 D. I. Kerzer, *Ritual, Politics and Power*, New Haven: Yale, 1988, p. 37.
55 R. Benedict, *Patterns of Culture*. London: Routledge, 1954.
56 Giddens, *The Transformation of Intimacy*.

3 Reflexivity and its Doubles: Structure, Aesthetics, Community

Scott Lash

What indeed might a critical theory look like in today's informationalized, yet more than ever capitalist, world order? If Marxism served pre-eminently as an *arme de critique* in a previous class-structured, nationally bounded manufacturing society, then what might instead replace Marxism in an era where axial principles of class, nation and industry have ostensibly yielded those of new identities, a global ordering and the production, circulation and consumption of communications? Commentators in a number of countries have for several years now posed just such a question and have proposed as today's critical successor to Marxism, on the one hand, the ethics of communicative rationality involved in the work of Jürgen Habermas, and, on the other, the analytics of discursive power instantiated in the writing of Michel Foucault.

I would like instead to argue in the pages that follow that crucial elements of such a turn-of-the-twenty-first-century critical theory can be found in the framework of 'reflexive modernity', which has been implicitly, when not explicitly, adumbrated in the first two sections of this book. But I should like to maintain that such a theory of reflexive modernity can take on this sort of critical power only when it is grasped radically against its own grain. That is, the theory of reflexive modernity can function best as critique only when understood fundamentally in terms of its own unarticulated other; when it is read counter to its own stated purposes and instead in the context of its unspoken assumptions. There are three ways in which I shall develop the theory of reflexive modernity in terms of its 'doubles', in terms of its own radical alterity. These correspond to the three parts of this chapter. First, reflexive modernization is a theory of the ever-increasing powers of social actors, or 'agency', in regard to structure. I will argue instead for a new set of structural conditions of reflexivity. I will argue that, though indeed there is a certain retrocession of *social* structures permitting greater scope to agency, there are new structural conditions of such 'free' and knowledgeable agency. I will argue that the receding social structures in this context are being largely displaced instead by *information and communication structures*.

Second, the theory as formulated by Beck and Giddens presupposes that reflexivity is essentially 'cognitive' in nature. This in the Enlightenment tradition of Kant through Durkheim and Habermas presumes critique by the universal (knowledgeable agency) of the particular (existing social conditions). I should like instead to draw attention not to the cognitive but to the *aesthetic* dimension of reflexivity. This is situated in the tradition – of Baudelaire through Walter Benjamin to Adorno – in which critique instead is *of* high modernity's unhappy totality, of high modernity's universals *through* the particular. Here the particular is understood as the aesthetic, and involves not just 'high art' but popular culture and the aesthetics of everyday life.

Third, the theory of reflexive modernization is a very 'strong programme' of individualization. The state of affairs which it describes is ever more one rendered by Beck's 'I am I', in which the 'I' is increasingly free from communal ties and is able to construct his or her own biographical narratives (Giddens). But the still further unfolding process of modernization has not just yielded the end-of-history convergence Fukuyama foresaw (especially in Eastern Europe) towards the 'I' of market democracy. Instead we have witnessed at the same time – and perhaps more than ever – a revenge of the repressed 'We' of ethnic cleansing, of eastern German neo-Nazi skinheads and the nationalist fragmentation of the former USSR. The third part of this chapter transforms the concept of aesthetic reflexivity into a more hermeneutic direction in an attempt to throw some light on the shifting ontological foundations of this recurrent phenomenon of *community* in late modernity.

Why 'reflexive' modernity?

Before I turn to a hermeneutic reconstruction of reflexive modernity theory, let us examine some of its virtues as a critical theory.

Here I want to look first at how it is in important respects a creative departure from the seemingly endless debates between modernists and postmodernists. I want further to show how, in contrast to the high abstraction of both modernist and postmodernist versions of critical theory, it has an immediate applicability to social analysis, that it constitutes a turn towards a *zeitdiagnostische Soziologie*. In this context I want also to gain some analytic purchase on the crucial features of the theory.

Modernist social theory has been criticized for presupposing a utopian 'metanarrative' of social change. To this, postmodern analysts such as Foucault have counterposed what seems to be a dystopic evolutionism. The idea of reflexive modernity seems to open up a third space, a fully different and more open-ended scenario. The idea might be best understood in a context suggested by Horkheimer and Adorno's *Dialectic of Enlightenment*, in which reason or modernization, initially emancipatory from the premodern static order of the *ancien régime* – in opening up possibilities for free expression, budding democracy and the free markets of liberal capitalism – then turned upon itself. Enlightenment or modernization in the era of *organized* capitalism instead becomes its own haunting double – as the public sphere opened up by market exchange turned into its other of hierarchically structured monopoly capitalist firm; as democratic individualism in political life turned into the clockwork impersonality of legal-rational bureaucracy; as the creative drive of the aesthetic modernist avant-gardes became the prison-estates of tower blocks and housing projects of the 1960s; as the anti-clerical emancipatory potential of classical physics turned into the nature-destroying science of the late twentieth century.

Reflexive modernization theory, however, holds open another possibility for this turn of modernization in which 'system' advances seemingly inexorably to destroy the 'life-world'. It points instead to the possibility of a positive new twist to the Enlightenment's dialectic. What happens, analysts like Beck and Giddens ask, when modernity begins to reflect on itself? What happens when modernization, understanding its own excesses and vicious spiral of destructive subjugation (of inner, outer and social nature) begins to take itself as object of reflection? This new self-reflexivity of modernity, on this view, would be a lot more than the belated victory of 'free will' over the forces of 'fate' or 'determinism'. It would instead be a development immanent to the modernization process itself. It would be a condition of, at a certain historical point, the development of functional prerequisites for further modernization. In the late twentieth century, if modernization as economic growth is to be possible, the work-force must acquire substantial information-processing abilities and thus must be highly educated. The framework of problem-solving, questioning and the like involved in this education process is also a condition of acquisition of the sort of knowledge that can be turned as rational critique upon the 'system' itself. If modernization presupposes increased individualization, then these individuals – less controlled by tradition and convention – will be increasingly free also to be in heterodox opposition to the dystopic consequences of modernization.

And indeed this is the sort of distinction that reflexive modernization makes in regard to 'simple' modernization. If simple modernization gives us the vertically and horizontally integrated, functionally departmentalized meso-economic firm, then the new reflexivity on the rules and resources of the latter yields flexible disintegration into networked districts of small, relatively autonomous knowledge-intensive firms. If simple modernization's totalizing inversion of the social rights of the Enlightenment project is the impersonality of the bureaucratic welfare state, then its reflexive counterpart understands that welfare services are a client-centred coproduction and advocates a decentralized citizen-empowering alternative set of welfare arrangements. If the politics of simple modernity serve up, on the one hand, the abstract 'blueprint Marxism' of the Eastern European past, and, on the other, the Western combination of capitalist state bureaucracy and abstract procedural parliamentarism, then reflexive modernity proffers a politics of radical, plural democracy, rooted in localism and the post-material interests of the new social movements. In brief, if simple modernization means subjugation, then reflexive modernization involves the empowerment of subjects. If simple modernization gives us Foucault's scenario of atomization, normalization and individuation, then the reflexive counterpart opens up a genuine individua*liz*ation, opens up positive possibilities of autonomous subjectivity in regard to our natural, social and psychic environments. Though, as Giddens warns, even reflexive modernity is a 'juggernaut', as the consequences of reflexivity can unanticipatedly result in new insecurities, in new forms of subjugation.

At issue here is no longer the straightforward and dichotomous juxtaposition of tradition and modernity, dear to the hearts of the giants – Weber, Durkheim, Simmel and Tönnies – of classical sociological theory. At issue instead is a three-stage conception of social change – from tradition to (simple) modernity to reflexive modernity. On this view simply modern societies are not fully modern. In this context reflexive modernity comes *after* simple modernity. Put another way, traditional society here corresponds to *Gemeinschaft*; simple modernity to *Gesellschaft*; and its successor to a *Gesellschaft* that has become fully reflexive. The motor of social change in this process is individualization. In this context *Gesellschaft* or simple modernity is modern in the sense that individualization has largely broken down the old traditional structures – extended family, church, village community – of the *Gemeinschaft*. Yet it is not fully modern because the individualization process has only gone part way and a new set of *gesellschaftlich* structures – trade unions, welfare state, government bureaucracy, formalized Taylorist shopfloor rules, class itself as a structure – has taken the place of traditional structures. Full modernization takes place only when further individualization also sets agency free from even these (simply) modern social structures.

It is necessary to call attention to the very different nature here of traditional and simply modern social structures. Though both presuppose a not fully developed individualization, the sort of structures they presuppose is vastly different. That is, whereas traditional societies presuppose *communal* structures (and I want to understand 'structure' in Giddens's sense of 'rules and resources'), simply modern societies presuppose *collective* structures. These collective structures assume that communal ties are already broken down, and the 'We' has become a set of abstract, atomized individuals. Thus social class, as Tönnies emphasized, was not *gemeinschaftlich* but *gesellschaftlich*. It was a collectivity which already presupposed facelessness, already presupposed the impersonality of social relations. If communities presume shared *meanings*, then collectivities presume merely shared *interests*. Marx himself understood class (for itself) emphatically not as a matter of shared meanings. Indeed the formation of classes in capitalism entailed that workers were set free from the earlier peasant *Gemeinschaften* as individuated bearers of labour power, who would only come together as a collectivity when the common conditions of workers were understood as shared interests. The understanding of the working class as *Gemeinschaft* is in many respects a peculiarly British phenomenon, due to the uneven modernization of British society, and to the fact that Britain – in terms of social class – has made the transition directly from tradition to reflexive modernity, skipping over, so to speak, the stage of simple modernity. In comparison, *la classe sociale* in France, as Touraine observes, has been understood not in terms of community but in respect to class struggle as *la raison*.[1] In Germany canonically the working class was also not conceived as community but as exemplified in Social Democratic politics, a *gesellschaftlich* collectivity which was at the same time the basis of and excluded from civil society. Cultural critics such as Nietzsche were thus able to wish a plague on the houses of both utilitarian capital and equally utilitarian organized labour.

It is not just the class structures of simple modernity that are abstract and impersonal: equally abstract and impersonal are, for example, phenomena of nation and nationalism, which Benedict Anderson has argued are rooted in an atomized polity and abstract homogenous space and narrative time.[2] Indeed the whole notion of 'society' in modernity is abstract, characterized not by the concrete and particular relationships of the *Gemeinschaft* but by abstract relationships such as impersonality, achievement and universalism – which Talcott Parsons saw as constituting the institutional norms of his *Social System*. Durkheim and his fellow 'positivists' were attacked by the classical humanist tradition in France for essentially the same sort of abstract vision of the social. Indeed Georg Simmel's 'sociological expressionism' was at points an explicit attempt to counterpose the 'life-force' of the inner self against the general and impersonal abstract norms of the social.[3]

The point in this context is that this initial, 'simple' stage of modernity is not just *halfway* modern, but halfway *modern*, and that even its collectivity is grounded in atomization and individuation. It is that further individualization in the second, reflexive phase of modernity has set free individuals also from these collective and abstract structures such as class, nation, the nuclear family and unconditional belief in the validity of science. Thus reflexive modernity is attained only with the crisis of the nuclear family and the concomitant self-organization of life narratives; with the decline of influence on agents of class structures – in voting behaviour, consumption patterns, trade union membership; with the displacement of rule-bound production through flexibility at work; with the new ecological distrust and critique of institutionalized science.

This said, what indeed, it might be wondered, is 'reflexivity'? To this question two answers must be given. First there is *structural* reflexivity in which agency, set free from the constraints of social structure, then reflects on the 'rules' and 'resources' of such structure; reflects on agency's social conditions of existence. Second there is *self*-reflexivity in which agency reflects on itself. In self-reflexivity previous heteronomous monitoring of agents is displaced by self-monitoring. Beck's *Risk Society* and Giddens's *Consequences of Modernity* mainly address *structural* reflexivity. Beck here foregrounded reflexivity on the institutions of science in the framework of ecological critique, while Giddens's focus is more general reflexivity regarding the rules and resources of society. Beck and Beck's *Das ganz normale Chaos der Liebe* and Giddens's *Modernity and Self-Identity* and *The Transformation of Intimacy* are largely about *self*-reflexivity, in the shift to autonomous monitoring of life narratives and of love relationships.[4]

Each sort of reflexivity in turn can take place either, on the one hand, via the mediation of 'expert-systems'; or, on the other, against the grain of such expert-systems. Here is where the remarkable convergence of Anthony Giddens's and Ulrich Beck's theories ends. For Giddens reflexivity in modernity is via a 'double hermeneutic', in which (while the first medium of interpretation is the social agent) the second medium of interpretation is expert-systems. Thus for him, as at the turn of the nineteenth century for Durkheim, sociology itself is a key expert-system in structural reflexivity. That is, in late modernity a growing proportion of the population has access in more or less diluted form to sociological concepts as a hermeneutic medium of reflection – and potentially as an impetus for social change – on the rules and resources of social structure. For Giddens *self*-reflexivity, or the self-organization of life narratives, takes place in contradistinction, via such expert-systems as psychology and psychoanalysis. For Giddens reflexivity in modernity involves a shift in trust relations, so that trust is no longer a matter of face-to-face involvement but is instead a matter of trust in expert-systems. For Beck, in strong contrast, reflexivity in modernity entails a growing freedom from and critique of expert-systems. Structural reflexivity thus involves a freedom from the expert-systems of dominant science. Self-reflexivity involves a freedom from and critique of various psychotherapies. Reflexivity is based not in trust but in distrust in expert-systems.[5]

The problem of 'insecurity' figures importantly in both authors' conceptual frameworks. This is striking because, as I've argued elsewhere, Giddens's concern – like that of classical sociologists like Durkheim – is with the problem of order, while Beck's – like the tradition running from Marx through Habermas – is with change.[6] For both, reflexivity aims to achieve the minimization of insecurity. In Beck's *Risk Society* which thematizes social change, reflexivity – made possible by individualization – is to bring about social change through the minimization of environmental hazards. This is just one of the forms of meaningful social change that reflexive agency can achieve in the risk society. Thematized in Giddens's case is 'ontological insecurity'. Although Beck has achieved fame for the concept of the risk society, insecurity is far more basic to Giddens's *problematique*. For Giddens the problem of order is formulated on the basis of such ontological insecurity. The problem is precisely how we can cope with not so much environmental but psychic and social hazards, and maintain reasonable levels of order and stability in our personalities and in society. His answer is through the mediation of expert-systems.[7]

Giddens draws importantly on ethnomethodology for his idea of hermeneutically mediated reflexivity. Only whereas ethnomethodology asks the question how we *routinely* achieve *meaning*, Giddens in effect asks how do we *consciously* achieve *ontological security*? Whereas ethnomethodology would seem to want to dispute expert-systems (and in particular Durkheimian and other versions of positivist sociology) and instead look behind them at 'habits' and routine activities, Giddens wants to argue that such insecurity is only, or at least best, coped with via the use of expert-systems. The notion of 'ontological insecurity' is drawn from the work of R. D. Laing on existential psychology.[8] The term's tenor is Heideggerian and would seem to call for a 'hermeneutics of retrieval', whereby one would through hermeneutic interpretation gain access to the ontological foundations of our social and psychic worlds. This would seem to be the apparent way to gain a basis in some sort of ontological security. This would entail hermeneutic interpretation, the laying open (*Auslegung*) and hermeneutic dismantling of the subject–object thinking of expert-systems in order to be able to show their foundations in forms of being, in ways of life.[9] Giddens like Laing eschews this sort of hermeneutic interpretation and instead finds his double hermeneutic and solution for ontological insecurity in expert-systems themselves.

The point at issue for the moment however is that whereas Beck sees expert-systems similarly as obstacles to the achievement of security, Giddens sees them as instruments which help us just to achieve such security. And however one might want to dispute the normative implications of Giddens's theory, its purchase on late modernity's empirical reality is considerable. Though Giddens's largely positively valued expert-systems seem to be very much the same thing as Foucault's (wholly negatively valued) 'discourses', they are in fact a much broader concept.

Whereas Foucauldian discourses are frameworks regulating the systematic occurrence of serious speech acts, expert-systems are much wider in scope. They refer at the same time to the practices of say professionals and other experts; they have a strong institutional aspect; they can also refer to the expertise objectified in machines such as aeroplanes and computers, or in other objective systems such as monetary mechanisms.[10]

And this broad purchase, yet immediate empirical applicability, is precisely the virtue of both Beck's and Giddens's theories of reflexive modernity. What they represent is the development of what is known in Germany as a *zeitdiagnostische Soziologie*. After two decades of dominance of the German social-theoretical landscape by the interminable struggle between Habermas's communicative action and Niklas Luhmann's autopoetic systems theory, the impact of Beck's *Risikogesellschaft* was quintessentially that of social theory finally coming back down to earth. This was true in terms of the accessibility of both the ideas and the presentation – *Risk Society* and *Das ganz normale Chaos der Liebe* are two of the best selling social science books in continental European history – and are read widely by the educated lay public. It was also true in that Beck addressed how social change in its broad outlines was also change of everyday lives. The publication of *Consequences of Modernity*, followed by *Modernity and Self-Identity* and *The Transformation of Intimacy*, represented also a *zeitdiagnostisch* turn in Anthony Giddens's intellectual history. Previously one read Giddens to learn about Giddens and his social theory – his notions of time-space distanciation, of structuration theory. Now a whole new audience was introduced to Giddens's far more accessible new work. Now people who wanted to read about trust, risk, relationships, the crisis of modernity, the role of expert-systems have begun to consult his work. There has been a new interest in Giddens among the Labour Party; and the wider British 'left', who previously saw his work as very ivory-tower stuff, now consult it alongside *eminences grises* such as Stuart Hall as among the most penetrating analyses of social change. With the decline of academic Marxism at the end of the 1970s, sociology too lost its place at centre stage of what was current in the world of theory. After more than a decade in which literary critics, art and architecture writers and philosophers have dominated the 'theory scene' – and one thought one heard the death knell of sociology in favour of the much more fashionable 'cultural studies' – it is gratifying that sociology can address the same major problems of the contemporary era with such political purchase and analytic power.

Enough by way of introduction and kind things said. Let us get to the 'beef' of the matter at hand. Let us return to the theory of reflexive modernity. Let us at the same time turn to the creative destruction of this theory of agency, the cognitive and individualism and its concomitant reconstruction as a theory also of structure, the aesthetic and community.

Agency or structure?

The reflexive modernization thesis has for its core assumption the *Freisetzung* or progressive freeing of agency from structure. This is perhaps most powerfully instantiated in social change in economic life, and in particular in the development of a new framework of what might be called 'reflexive accumulation', for economic growth. This takes place via the freeing of agency from structure. Or rather structure effectively forces agency to be free in the sense that structural, capital accumulation is possible only on the condition that agency can free itself from rule-bound 'fordist' structures. This process has been commonly understood in terms of 'flexible specialization' in which increasingly specialized consumption entails more flexible ways of producing. Specialized consumption in this context encourages firms to produce smaller batches of a given product, on the one hand, and to widen the array of products on offer, on the other. For this to be possible firms and workers in firms must *innovate* that much more quickly. And such ever more rapid innovation is a question of a lot more than just 'flexibility'. Quicker innovation entails that a lot more work must proportionally go into the designing of new products. It entails that a far greater proportion of the production process than heretofore must be accounted for by a knowledge-intensive 'design process' and a smaller proportion by the material 'labour process'. Knowledge-intensivity necessarily involves *reflexivity*. It entails self-reflexivity in that heteronomous monitoring of workers by rules is displaced by self-monitoring. It involves (and entails) 'structural reflexivity' in that the rules and resources (the latter including the means of production) of the shopfloor, no longer controlling workers, become the object of reflection for agency. That is, agents can reformulate and use such rules and resources in a variety of combinations in order chronically to innovate.

So far so good. The *Freisetzung* thesis of reflexive modernity theory (where agency is set free from structure) has thus considerable explanatory potential regarding the flexibilization of production. But let us pause for a moment. Let us step back and ask the question which Beck and Giddens do not, with sufficient urgency pose: Why, we might ask, do we find reflexivity in some places and not in others? Why in some economic sectors and not in others? There is to be sure a massive increase in the number of reflexive producers in the (operating systems and applications) software sector, in computer and semiconductor production, in the business services, in machine building in, for example, Germany. But what about the postfordist creation of the millions of 'junk jobs' of downgraded manufacturing jobs in, for example, the apparel sector of the last decade and a half; what of the creation of the massive 'MacDonalds proletariat' in the services; the systematic creation of large armies of unemployed, especially among young males? What about all of these new labour market positions which have been 'downgraded' to a position below that of the classical (fordist) working class? Are there in fact alongside the aforementioned 'reflexivity winners' whole battalions of 'reflexivity *losers*' in today's increasingly class-polarized, though decreasingly class-conscious, information societies? Further, outside of the sphere of immediate production, just how 'reflexive' is it possible for a single mother in an urban ghetto to be? Ulrich Beck and Anthony Giddens write with insight on the self-construction of life narratives. But just how much freedom from the 'necessity' of 'structure' and structural poverty does this ghetto mother have to self-construct her own 'life narratives'?[11]

To account for such systematic inequalities in our globalized informational capitalism, as well as the systematic inequalities between core and peripheral nations, we must, I believe, address the *structural conditions of reflexivity*. But what can these structural conditions be if reflexivity, as delineated above, has developed only through the retreat, the retrocession of social structures? If reflexivity by definition involves the *Freisetzung* of agency from structure, then how indeed can inequality in late modernity have a structural explanation? The answer to this would seem to be that reflexivity and inequality of 'reflexivity chances' must then have for condition of existence an interarticulated set of *non*-social structures. If so then what in fact are these non-social structures? What indeed underpins reflexivity is then neither the social (economic, political and ideological) structures of Marxism, nor the (normatively regulated and institutional) social structures of Parsonsian functionalism, but instead an articulated web of global and local networks of *information and communication structures.* One might best understand this new context in contrast to industrial capitalism, in which 'life chances' and class inequality depend on an agent's place in and access to the mode of production. In reflexive modernity, life chances – the outcome of who are to be the reflexivity winners and who the reflexivity losers – depend instead on place in the 'mode of information'.[12] Life chances in reflexive modernity are a question of access not to productive capital or production structures but instead of access to and place in the new information and communication structures.

Reflexive production: upgrading the working class

The idea of 'information structures' has been introduced in the work of the Japanese industrial sociologist Kazuo Koike in the context of a comparison of Japanese and American firms. Koike analysed internal labour markets in large firms in the two countries, and found that the incentive patterns for promotion in Japan were tightly linked to the acquisition of knowledge or information, while in the USA promotion was mainly independent of knowledge acquisition. The concept was subsequently further developed by the institutional economist Masahiko Aoki also to encompass information *flows*. Here in the Japanese firm information flows are optimized through the trust relations which exist between the firm and its workers, subcontractors, and between firms and financiers. This stands in contrast to the blocking of information flows in low-trust, market-governed firms in the USA and UK.[13] Information structures thus consist of, first, networked channels in which information flows and, second, spaces in which the acquisition of information-processing capacities takes place.

Reflexive production, in this context, is possible only in the presence of optimal levels of information flow and knowledge (or information-processing) acquisition. And certain modes of institutional governance of information structures are favourable to reflexive production, while others are not. Japanese 'corporatist' governance of information structures is, for example, more conducive to reflexive production than market governance in the USA and UK. Crucial here is the extent to which information structures overlap with production systems in a given sector or a given country. Crucial is the question of who in a production system is included in, and who is excluded from, the information structures. Thus Aoki has drawn on Ronald Dore's juxtaposition of Japanese 'relational contracting' with Anglo-American market-governed 'arms-length contracting'. In Japanese subcontracting, the frequent permanent and temporary exchange of personnel between subcontractor and parent firm, the joint programmes of product development and the shared identity between workers in subcontractor and parent firm optimize information flow. In the USA and UK not only is information flow impeded by the absence of these material and symbolic exchanges, by the absence of these trust relationships, but the subcontractors are excluded from the information structure of the parent firms' production system altogether.[14] In Japanese as in German production systems, financial contracting typically takes place to a greater extent via banks than in the Anglo-American world. Institutional economists have complained for some time about the inability of banks in the USA and UK to act rationally and put an end to their bad habits of short-term loans at quite high interest rates. But perhaps free market rational-choice assumptions are not the solution but rather the problem. It is instead perhaps the proclivity of the Anglo-Saxon institutions for neo-classical, cost-benefit thinking of the calculating rational actor that has predisposed them to the failure of such short-termism. This rational choice, neo-classicism, stands polar opposite to the relational contracting of the Japanese and German banks, the fact that their relationship with industry is more one of 'status' than 'contract', the fact that corporatistic (as distinct from neo-classical) trust relations enable also a flow of symbols between financial and industrial contractors. It is the shared meanings, the shared 'world' of the two, which explains the tendency of banks in Japan and Germany to lend long and at lower interest rates. And in return they are included in the information structures of the industrial firm. Financial contracting through equities is, to be sure, increasingly common in Japan and Germany. But in Japan again shareholding is much longer-term and dividends are much lower than on the Anglo-American model. Although the outcome is reaped in capital gains, the motive for Japanese shareholders to engage in such 'risk-sharing' with industrial firms is again the trust context of their relationship.[15] The result is inclusion in the information structures of the firm's production system. The short-termist Anglo-Saxon financial contractors often do not even show an interest in being included in these information structures.

Finally, employment contracting in Japan in comparison with the Anglo-Saxon world is also relational rather than arms-length, the straightforward cash nexus being complemented by symbolic exchange of shared identity. This need not be at all 'primitive'; indeed many of us as university teachers or, say, graduate students have relationships with our departments that are strongly networked in terms of symbolic exchange and shared identity. In this context Japanese workers will say they work 'in the firm' while their British or American colleagues work 'for the firm'. What this involves is a certain measure of risk-sharing among Japanese workers – who, for example, will work at quite low levels of pay for the first years of their careers. But it also involves inclusion of the Japanese worker in the firm's information structure. There is a certain informational *quid pro quo* involved in this. The worker contributes to information flow through giving voice to tacit knowledge in, for example, quality circles. In return he or she has access to much more information in regard to how the production process is run. Here information flow is inextricably intertwined with knowledge acquisition. Moreover, Japanese workers as consumers effectively participate in risk-sharing with industry. Their propensity to maintain high levels of savings at low interest rates are effectively loans to industry.[16]

In Germany too, corporatist governance of production systems makes possible inclusive information structures and highly reflexive production. This traditionalist institutional governance allows for very modern production, while seemingly modern market governance in the Anglo-Saxon world effectively inhibits the modernization of production systems. In Germany there are, so to speak, three pillars of such corporatist governance: the technical college system, the collective bargaining structure and the apprenticeship.

The technical colleges (*technische Fachhochschulen*) are the basis for the successful highly networked industrial districts in for example Baden-Württemberg and Nordrhein-Westphalia. The technical colleges are colleges of higher education, not elite technical or engineering universities. Their closest counterparts might be the English polytechnics as they were first set up, or state or city engineering schools in the USA. The knowledge taught in the technical colleges is, however, much more concrete, trade-based and hands-on than the comparatively abstract, theoretical learning in their Anglo-American counterparts. The typical departmental structure for such a college will not be, say, a physics and a physical chemistry department but instead departments of shipbuilding, machine-tool engineering, ceramics and the like. Technical colleges are the linchpin for information structures in German industrial districts. They work through the establishment by college teachers of consultancy offices and technology-transfer services for the firms, and through the circulation of personnel through colleges and firms.[17]

The technical colleges are not particularly effective in districts dominated by larger firms, which finance in-house much of their own R&D and training. They are also not effective where firms are small and not very innovative. There is sufficient incentive for college lecturers to send their students and spend some of their own working years only in firms which are innovators. Through the circulation of personnel over the course of their careers through the technical colleges and firms there takes place considerable information flow and acquisition of information-processing capacities. It is not at all untypical for an already apprenticed young man, after several years working in a firm, to go on to a technical college for two years to acquire credentials to become a technician, after which he will either go back to work for the same firm or join another medium-sized firm in the same industrial district. After several more years' work, this man might return to the technical college for further courses and the acquisition of credentials as an engineer. After this, this man may work as an engineer for another firm in the district. Perhaps at the age of forty he will take on a lecturing job in one of the nearby colleges, where he will send his students on projects for up to one year working in the district's firms. Simultaneously he might be spending two days a week running a technology transfer office, providing consultancy services to local firms.[18]

In the circulation of personnel between firms and colleges, there is not just information flow and knowledge acquisition but the further facilitation of each by the comparative egalitarianism of the German industrial occupational structure. There is significantly more work-life mobility from skilled worker to technician to engineer than in other countries. Moreover, the status differences between engineer, technician and skilled worker are much less pronounced than elsewhere. This is conducive to an occupational universe concentrated around the 'middle mass'. Here engineers are seen not so much as higher-ups in hierarchy but as professionals, fellow professionals with just a different specialized *Beruf* (trade, craft or profession), who can work side by side with skilled workers.[19] Both the mobility and the status equality facilitates the free exchange of ideas and hence information flow as well as knowledge acquisition.

The second pillar is the corporatist representational structures of the works councils and co-determination, and the sectoral neo-corporatist collective bargaining structures. These have been described at length elsewhere.[20] The point is that each of these furthers trust relations. These are not the more particularized, personalized trust relations of the Japanese firm. They are more abstract and institutionalized trust relations, and lead to the forgoing of opportunism, between trade unions and management. All of this facilitates information flow, especially via the works councils, but also positive training policies, which itself is the third pillar of the *deutsche Modell*.

Wolfgang Streeck has argued that it is irrational for any one capitalist to invest heavily in training workers, though it is eminently rational for capitalists as a class to invest in such training.[21] This is because any single capitalist who invested in training would in all likelihood lose his or her trained workers through external labour markets to another capitalist. The first employer would not then recoup the costs invested in training, while the second would be a 'free rider' at the expense of the first. Streeck's insight here is not entirely accurate. It is rational for any one capitalist to invest in training when – as is often the case in Japan – he or she knows that trained workers are likely to stay their whole careers in his or her firm. But the principle of what Streeck argues holds: the Japanese case is not one of neo-classical, market governance of training but of institutional governance through 'enterprise corporatism'. And that market-regulated training is the worst possible solution for the information structures of reflexive production.

There seem to be two solutions to Streeck's proposed regulation of training by capitalists as a class. On the one hand, there is the state-regulated education of workers until the age of about eighteen common in France and Japan. On the other, there is the corporatistically regulated apprenticeships in Germany and Austria, and these form our third 'pillar'. They are regulated on a local level – through chambers of commerce, trade unions, employees' associations and state representatives from the departments of education. Where capitalists organize such training collectively through the state, education tends to be school-based; learning is theoretical, of abstract numerical and verbal competencies. Where they organize training collectively through the 'local corporatism' of the German-speaking world, education is based in the workplace; learning is more practical and hands-on.[22] In the Anglo-Saxon world we have unfortunately neither the one nor the other. Apprenticeship structures in both the UK and the USA are mainly a thing of the past. As for state-organized secondary schools, young people either leave early (UK) or learn very little at all while there (USA).

In contrast to Aristotle's *zoon politikon* and Enlightenment Rational Man, the German apprenticeship seems to take on Marxian *homo faber* assumptions. That is, to be without a skill is somehow to be beyond the pale in terms of what it is that makes human beings human. If there are 720,000 school-leavers in a given year and only 715,000 apprenticeship places, it is a national scandal. The twenty-two-year-old salesman of video recorders, Sega consoles, walkmen and CD players in an electronics goods shop on the high street or shopping mall will have done an apprenticeship and know the detailed electronics of what he is selling you. The young woman of the same age in a bakery will have similar detailed knowledge of all the kinds of bread she is baking and selling to customers. The apprenticeship is still based on a *Meistermodell*, reminiscent of medieval guilds, in which workers progress from apprenticeships to journeyman to master. Skilled mechanics in large machine tool firms who are work team leaders at the age of thirty-five will often be at the same time master craftsmen. Loyalty and community here (which in Japan is connected with the enterprise) in Germany is in the context of the *Beruf*, of the trade or professional community. This is instantiated in lower wage levels of German apprentices who in the UK and elsewhere commonly earn some 75 per cent of adult wages.[23] The *quid pro quo* for such monetary sacrifice is the acquisition of knowledge for the apprentices. In Japan as well, (in strong contrast with the UK, Italy and France) wages of school-leavers entering firms are on the order of 50 per cent of those of adult workers.

At issue here is a process not of reflexive modernization but of 'reflexive *traditionalization*'. This is traditionalization in Robert Bellah's sense of an ethics of commitment and obligation, not to the self (which we do see in Anglo-American production systems) but to a *community*, this community being the firm in the Japanese case and the *Beruf* in the German.[24] This is reflected in the forgoing of adult wages by very young workers. This reflexive traditionalization is not a matter of individualization but one of reflexive *communities* with practices motivated by and oriented to a set of 'substantive goods'. Such substantive goods are, in Alistair MacIntyre's sense, 'internal goods' – that is, not goods external to practices, such as monetary reward, power or prestige, but goods internal to practices – workmanship or the good of the firm. These substantive goods also, in Charles Taylor's sense, set themselves off in contradistinction to 'procedural goods'.[25] In contrast to the procedural shopfloor ethics of demarcation disputes and a primary focus on the 'discursive will-formation' of shopfloor democracy, a substantive shopfloor ethics will be rooted in the *Sittlichkeit* (the ethical life of particular, shared and customary practices) of the trade or company community and will devote primary focus to craftsmanship and making a high quality product.

This traditionalization and community is *reflexive* in that it mediates abstract power relations, either where trade unions and democracy are well instituted, as in Germany, or where such power structures are hierarchical and paternalistic, as in Japan. Although it is often said (and true in some respects) that globalization is forcing Germany and Japan to move in the direction of Anglo-American market regulation, these traditional structures are reflexive in another way. And that is that it is the small, old-fashioned firms in Japan and Germany which actually do come the closest to market regulation of work relations, while the largest, most modern, most high-tech firms in both countries come closest to the traditionalist and communitarian models. This traditionalization is reflexive finally in the sense that large numbers of firms, in the Anglo-Saxon world and elsewhere, previously with individuated forms of economic regulation, now choose to attempt to institute precisely such non-market structures.

Reflexivity winners and reflexivity losers: (new) new middle class and underclass

Premodern, and communal–traditional forms of regulation, as we have just seen, can be conducive to information flow and acquisition which are the structural conditions of reflexive production. The training and access to information flows which this presupposes involves an upgrading of the new 'reflexive' working class in regard to the classical, fordist proletariat. These sorts of information structures are a condition of existence of the contemporary working class *tout court*, in that where they are absent products are not internationally competitive, and working-class jobs disappear. Hence the proportion of manufacturing workers in the total labour force today is on the order of 50–75 per cent higher in Germany than in the Anglo-American world.

If communal regulation is optimal for the scope and power of information and communication structures in production systems, then individualized (and market) regulation is optimal for them in *consumption* systems. Flows of not just information and communications but also money articulate primarily with not production but consumption systems in the market-driven Anglo-American social economies. Here financial contractors of firms tend to contract more in the interests of their own consumption needs than the interests of the firm, with resulting short-termism in stock ownership. Hence the phenomenon of leveraged buyouts. Hence the vastly higher proportion in the Anglo-American world of loans to direct consumption (bank credit cards, hire purchase, overdrafts, shop credit-card usage) and of mortgages to homebuyers than in Japan, Germany and elsewhere. Consumption is also massively more *individualized* in the market-driven Anglo-Saxon countries. All sorts of areas in which consumer decisions are made by 'structure' in Germany and Japan are left to individual decision in the USA and UK. And this more reflexive consumption is carried out with the help of expert-systems. A middle-class (or even working-class) individual in the UK or USA is apt to buy and sell four houses in her lifetime, undergoing thereby four sets of financial transactions with surveyors, architects, lawyers, estate agents and building societies. Her German or Japanese counterpart will mostly rent her whole life long or, if she buys a house, do so only once, hence undergoing none of these economic transactions with expert-systems. The Anglo-American individual is that much more likely to be divorced, or divorced more than once, entailing more lawyers, more house purchases, etc.; to have a personal tax accountant, to use a personal finance officer, to hire at points in her life physical training specialists and physio- and psychotherapists. In market-driven economies this frequently economic-transacting individual is that much more likely to be a 'she' than in corporatist countries. Her mode of consumption will open up ever more activities and occupational places in the advanced consumer services. This is matched by the filling of these occupational places with vast (and recently vastly greater) numbers of female personnel, as is indicated in the 1990 United States Census. A given Anglo-American will typically be involved in inordinately more economic transactions with these consumption-experts in her life than will her German or Japanese counterpart. Hence these occupational places, and the middle class in general, are so very much larger in the USA and UK than in Germany and Japan. The proportion of the workforce active in the advanced services (which are expert-systems) is approximately twice as high in the Anglo-Saxon countries as in corporatist ones. A great deal more than half of those employed in these advanced service jobs in the Anglo-American world are active in the consumer services, while the preponderance in the corporatist countries are in the producer services.[26]

The reflexive working class in the wake of the demise of organized capitalism is paradigmatically linked to the information and communication (I&C) structures in three ways: as newly individuated consumers; as users of informationalized means of production (in, for example, computer numerically controlled tools) and as producers of consumer and producer goods (for example, televisions, fax machines, fibre-optic cable) which function as means of production and consumption inside the I&C structures. The expanded middle class in reflexive modernity *work inside* the I&C structures. They do so very largely as the *'experts' inside the expert-systems*, which themselves are 'nodes' of accumulated information and accumulated information-processing capacities stockpiled, as it were, at various locations inside the I&C structures. There is a crucial distinction between the new middle class in reflexive, as distinct from simple, modernity. Simple modernity's new middle classes grew in size as adjuncts to the accumulation of manufacturing capital. Their characteristic economic activity was as expert engineers, as marketing specialists in the sphere of circulation, in sales, finance and other services as part and parcel of – and in service of – the wider circuits of accumulation of manufacturing capital. In simple modernity there was considerable growth in these services, where the bulk of the new middle class, or 'service class', worked. This growth resulted from the increased 'roundaboutness' in the production of manufacturing goods.[27]

In reflexive modernity the tables are turned. The working class and the production of manufacturing goods become instead a crucial moment in, though subordinated to, the roundabout production of *informational* goods. With the production of informational goods becoming the new axial principle of capital accumulation, the (new) new middle class is created. This new class embraces occupational places which have developed from the new principle of accumulation. But now the middle class is no longer a 'service class', that is, a class in the service of the reproduction needs of manufacturing capital. In its expanded form, it becomes more a 'served' than a service class, as its mainly information-processing labour is no longer subsumed under the needs of manufacturing accumulation. In reflexive modernity the accumulation of capital is at the same time (increasingly) the accumulation of information.[28] Thus the means of production as constant fixed capital (hardware) and constant circulating capital (software) are informationalized. At the same time variable capital as labour power and the commodities produced (both consumer and producer goods) take on an increasingly high and predominant proportion of informational content. The point is that the accumulation of information (and of capital) in the I&C structures becomes the driving force of reflexive modernity, just as the accumulation of manufacturing capital and its associated social structures had been in an earlier modernity. And reflexive modernity's upgraded (and reduced) working class as well as its expanded middle class find their basis in this informational displacement of the 'motor of history'.

If the transformed middle class works in the information and communication structures, and the reflexive working class for and with these structures, then there is a third paradigmatic class in reflexive modernity who are fundamentally *excluded* from access to the I&C structures. If the post-industrial middle class (mainly) and the upgraded working class (marginally) are the 'reflexivity-winners' of today's informationalized capitalist order, then this third class who are downgraded from the classical proletariat of simple modernity are the 'reflexivity losers', the bottom and largely excluded third of our turn-of-the-twenty-first-century 'two-thirds societies'. A large portion of this new lower class are very much in the position of what it makes sense to call an 'underclass'. William J. Wilson's underclass thesis has been a powerful and positive ethical–political intervention, calling the attention (of politicians, policy-makers and social scientists) for the first time in a long time to the plight of the urban ghettos as well as the increased class polarization of post-industrial societies. Wilson's thesis is in the first instance not about race but about social *class*. It is quite straightforwardly that in the shift from manufacturing to informational production a new class is created which is structurally downwardly mobile from the working class. In terms of relations to the I&C structures we will see that this underclass includes the 'ghetto poor' but also incorporates much of the information society's 'excluded third'.[29]

The subsiding of social structures in reflexive modernity is especially felt by the underclass. In the ghetto there is a general emptying-out of social structures, of the institutions of socio-economic and cultural regulation. Thus, the large fordist factories in the USA and elsewhere have either shut down or moved to regions and suburban and ex-urban locations which are geographically out of reach of the black population. Along with labour markets, consumer commodity markets move out as shopping malls and centres find locations that blacks have to travel distances to shop in and are rarely hired to work in. Other structural institutions of regulation also move out of what is becoming the 'impacted ghetto' – the large industrial trade unions, welfare state agencies victim to cuts in public spending, the church, the respectable black middle and working classes – and very effectively, the family.[30] The result is not individualization but anomie, and a deficit of regulation. The result is the gang-bonding of young males and racial violence. This of course applies not only to the urban minority ghettos but to the white ghettos of Britain's council estates in Liverpool, Glasgow and Newcastle where working-class fathers breed underclass sons. Where fathers who worked in the mines, on the docks, in the steel mills, in large chemical and machine-building plants have sons who leave school at sixteen without an apprenticeship and invariably find little in the way of steady employment until the age of twenty-five. Of sons who when employed at all are unable to find the industrial labouring jobs they were brought up to do, but wind up behind a counter at Dixons, as a cleaner at the local airport or a porter at the local college.

The same is, above all perhaps, true in Eastern Europe, in eastern Germany or Poland, where the factory jobs that fathers could depend on have disappeared for the sons. Where other instances of socio-economic regulation, like (state-run) trade unions or the police, have subsided or been fully delegitimated. Where the population of the most able young people has emptied out to seek work in western Germany. Here socio-economic 'governance' previously by the state, through state-regulated corporations and networks, was to be displaced by market regulation. But markets are institutions as well, with specific social, legal and moral preconditions. And to a disturbing degree the previously existing modes of institutional governance has not been replaced by market governance at all but instead by a deficit of governance, a deficit of socio-economic regulation. As in black America a generation of youth which has been brought up 'learning to labour', a generation of Eastern European working-class kids has grown up only to find this time that there are no working-class jobs.[31] 'Learning to labour', as Paul Willis described it, is also and perhaps mainly the acquisition of a specific sort of *male* habitus. Without an outlet in working-class jobs, the alternative is gang-bonding, the (football) terraces and racial or racist violence. That is, the heteronomous monitoring of simple modernity has not been replaced by reflexive modernity's self-monitoring. Instead, in the absence of the displacement of social

structures by the I&C structures, the outcome is neither heteronomous nor self-monitoring but very little monitoring at all.

The subsiding of the social structures and the increased freedom
for agency is experienced by all social classes in reflexive modernity. It is only in the case of the underclass that these social
structures are not displaced by the information and communication
structures. The labour process, for example, of this new lower class
is substantially less informational and substantially more material
in content than that of the middle class and working class. The
means of production of for example a new lower-class 'MacDonalds
proletarian', a garment sector worker, a house servant, a shopping
mall employee are substantially less informational in content than,
say, the CNC (computer numerically controlled) tools of the reflexive working class. So, typically, is the content of the product which
is manufactured. All jobs, as Ganssmann notes, contain information-processing and material-processing components. One indicator of the proportion of each is the length of job-task cycle.[32] This
can range from the unusually long-cycle job tasks of, say, the cor-
poration lawyer who works for six months on a given merger or
acquisition, or the university professor who works for three years
on a major research project, to the three to four hours necessary for
a skilled mechanic to repair a machine. The more design-intensive
work is, the more innovation-intensive, and the more long-cycle, job
tasks are. But these cycles are significantly shorter in the new lower-
class jobs, from the subcontracted cleaners of the state schools to the
check-out workers at the supermarkets.

Exclusion from information and communication structures takes
place for the new lower class not just on the job. Their residences are
also affected. The maps of communications geographers graphi-
cally expose the locations of fax machines, large satellite receivers
and senders, fibre-optic cable, international computer networks and
the like. In these, one is struck by the heightened informational and
communicational density in the downtown districts of central cities,
with their concentrations of head offices, of finance and of business
services; the intermediate levels of density in the suburbs, the locations of factories and many advanced consumer services; and the
sparseness of the ghetto and underclass areas. What one sees is a
patchwork of such 'live zones' or 'tame zones' in the urban central
business districts and the 'dead zones' or 'wild zones' of the ghettos.[33] And as civil society, as the public sphere itself, becomes increasingly superimposed on the I&C structures, exclusion from

them becomes exclusion from *citizenship*, effectively both political and cultural exclusion from civil society. That is, if in simple modernity citizenship's obligations were mainly to the nation-state, in reflexive modernity they are instead to the self, to responsible self-monitoring. Citizenship's rights in simple modernity, featuring equality before the law, political rights and the social rights of the welfare state, have been transformed into reflexive modernity's rights of access to the information and communication structures. Reflexive modernity's new lower class, which is increasingly in many respects effectively an underclass, is deprived of both obligations and rights, of what now is no longer social but predominantly cultural citizenship.

There are three modes of formation, of the 'making' of this new lower class, which is indeed a 'class not in but of civil society'. First, there is downward mobility from the working class as instantiated in the black American ghetto and the British council estates. Second, there are the vast number of migrants setting up businesses and working in the informal sector of the economy, in the apparel industry, and for example the Asians running the small shops of the West's big cities. Third, there is the systemic exclusion of women from the I&C structures. In countries like Germany this exclusion of women (and minorities) is exacerbated by the corporatist institutions of the apprenticeship, the welfare state and the education system, in which women perform welfare services, not in firms operating through the market, not by working in jobs in the welfare state, but (as excluded from labour markets) in the home. Hence the very low labour-force participation rate of women in Germany and Austria.[34] Even in the absence of enhanced corporatist exclusion, women in neo-liberal labour markets are shunted away from the information-intensive end of the labour force and disproportionately into new lower-class positions. Moreover, outside of work-life, the line separating the 'live zones' from the 'dead zones', which sets off middle-class neighbourhoods from the ghettos also runs right through the centre of the private sphere of the household. Here men typically have access to equipment highest in the informational content, such as the camcorder, the remote-control switch of the television and operation of the time-shift on the video recorder, while women – with less access to the 'brown goods' – tend to concentrate their usage in the 'white goods' of refrigerator, cooker and vacuum cleaner, washer and dryer in which there is a higher ratio of mechanical components to electronic components. This holds even for the young boys, and not girls, who have privileged access to the Sega and Nintendo consoles, the home computers and electric guitars.

Although the new lower class or underclass is quite clearly a class category, defined by access to not the mode of production but the mode of information, the personnel filling these class positions are typically determined by more particularistic, 'ascribed' character-istics – by race, country of origin and gender, and, in some countries like Britain where class has always had a caste-like dimension, by large numbers of young white (ex-)working-class males. Here too the new lower class comes to resemble the underclass not only as delineated with social-scientific precision in Wilson's work but also its metaphoric rendering in the *Unterwelt* of Wagnerian opera and Fritz Lang's film *Metropolis*. Like Lang's (lumpen-)proletarians the underclass is recognizable by ascribed, often physical features. Lang's underclass was also decipherable as not a service but a servant class. And the increased activity of the new lower class in literally servant jobs in the homes and (as waitresses, taxi-drivers, etc.) in the public leisure lives of the higher echelons of the central business district's middle class, as well as the continuing servant activity of large numbers of women in the homes of their husbands and children, seems to qualify them for this. Finally Lang's *Unterwelt* was metaphoric for the then German working class, who suffered caste-like exclusion from civil society, although civil society itself was built on the back of their labour. Much the same could be said for the new lower class today.

Most significant might be the particular ways that the ghettos, that women are *not* excluded from the I&C structures. This is first through comparatively open access to the education system. Thus women, it is well known, are entering the professional schools and universities on an unprecedented scale. And blacks in the USA for example have increased enormously their relative and absolute education level, only to find that the requisite jobs have disap-peared. The other is that through television, including satellite and cable, radio, video recorders and the like, the new lower class may not be on the information-*manipulating* end, but they most surely are on the communications, and especially symbol and image-com-munication, *receiving* end of the I&C structures. This disparity – between acquisition of symbol-processing capacities and access to symbol flow in the I&C structures, between access to the sending of symbols and their reception – has been and will increasingly be a potent mix for the heterodox political and cultural critique by blacks, by women, by other ethnic minorities – from the 'wild zones' themselves.

Reflexivity: cognitive or aesthetic?

But not only does knowledge flow through these information and communication structures, not only do conceptual symbols function as structural conditions of reflexivity in modernity, but so does an entire other economy of signs in space. This other semiotic economy is one of not conceptual but mimetic symbols. It is an economy that opens up possibilities for not cognitive but aesthetic reflexivity in late modernity. The conceptual symbols, the flows of information through the information and communication structures cut, to be sure, two ways. They represent, on the one hand, a new forum for capitalist domination. Here no longer is power primarily lodged in capital as the material means of production. In place of this is found the power/knowledge complex – now largely linked to supra-national firms – of the mode of information.[35] On the other hand, as outlined at length above, these flows and accumulations of conceptual symbols constitute conditions of reflexivity. The same is true of the 'mimetic' symbols, of the images, sounds and narratives making up the other side of our sign economics. On the one hand as the commoditized, intellectual property of the culture industries they belong to the characteristically post-industrial *assemblage* of power.[36] On the other they open up virtual and real spaces for the popularization of aesthetic critique of that same power/knowledge complex.

This second, not cognitive but aesthetic, moment of reflexivity is fundamentally mimetic in nature, and as such is very much in the tradition not of Enlightenment high modernity but of modernism in the arts. It has, partly in the context of ethnicity and the issue of 'neo-tribalism', become transferred into a basis for a new, at the same time situated and contingent, ethics. This aesthetic dimension of reflexivity finally is the grounding principle of 'expressive individualism' in everyday life of contemporary consumer capitalism.[37]

The conceptual and the mimetic

Reflexivity, by *definition*, would seem to be cognitive in nature. 'Aesthetic reflexivity' would, on the face of it, seem to be a contradiction in terms. So the question which must be asked is how can aesthetics, how can an aesthetic 'moment' or aesthetic 'source' of the self, be 'reflexive'? Let us try initially to approach this question by focusing on the *object* on which art, or our aesthetic sensibilities, might be reflexive. Here there can be reflexivity, on the one hand, on the natural social and psychic worlds of everyday life; and on the other there can be reflexivity on 'system', on the modes of commodification, bureaucraticization and other operations by which the 'system' colonizes any and all of these life-worlds. Aesthetic reflexivity on everyday life takes place via a mode of not conceptual but *mimetic* mediation. Thus such thinkers as Nietzsche and Adorno stand the Platonist hierarchy of the conceptual and the mimetic on its head. Nietzsche in his early essay 'Über Lüge und Wahrheit' contends that mimesis provides greater access to the truth than conceptual thought. He proclaims that theoretical concepts are little better than desiccated versions of mimetic metaphors, and that in their abstract and sterile fixedness they lack the suppleness necessary for truth. He maintains that the concept in particular cannot have access to processes of 'becoming' – his example is the unfolding blooming of a flower – in natural and cultural processes.[38]

Adorno also has recourse to the notions of the mimetic in his idea of aesthetic critique. In the Enlightenment tradition of critical theory – from Kant to Marx to Habermas – critique is of the particular by the universal (be this universal a categorical imperative, the proletariat or communicative rationality). Against this, for Adorno, as for Nietzsche, critique instead is of the universal by the particular; or critique of 'the subject' from the point of view of 'the object'. The notion of aesthetic reflexivity which I am advocating here is closer to Adorno's rather than Nietzsche's on several counts. First, I should like to take seriously the process of *mediation* which Adorno, and not Nietzsche, proffers.[39] For Adorno if Platonic and Cartesian conceptual reflection involves a great deal of abstract mediation, then aesthetic reflection involves not ultimate but 'proximal' mediation. In Nietzsche's aesthetic there is a blunt immediacy of the mimetic, which is neither of a different quality than nor in a different 'world' to everyday life. It seems to me that, in the absence of mediation, it is problematic to speak of reflexivity at all.

Second, reflexivity as developed in this book – in a complex dialectic of structure and agency – is implicitly Hegelian, and Adorno, though thoroughly heterodox, is surely an Hegelian. Hegel himself, we will recall, had a strongly inflected notion of aesthetic reflexivity. In his *Aesthetic Writings* and in *The Encyclopaedia*, he conceives art as in the realm of absolute reason, as the most 'finite' sphere in this realm, less mediated than religion and philosophy.[40] Adorno's Hegel is of course that of only a 'negative dialectic', of a persistent critique not *through* the universal, or through totality, but *of* the universal and *of* totality. Here comparison with Herbert Marcuse is instructive. Marcuse also privileged the aesthetic–sensual dimension – but could only imagine the triumph of cognitive reason's unhappy totality, where Eros was nullified in a totalizing repressive desublimation and any hope of aesthetic resistance sublated in what became 'one-dimensional man'. Adorno, though still profoundly the pessimist, in contradistinction to Marcusian one-dimensionality, saw space for determinate negation precisely in the aesthetic dimension. Yet, unlike neo-Nietzschean deconstructors of the subject by the 'object', Adorno, though understanding the aesthetic to be in the position of the particular, still preserves 'moments' of the subject in the object.[41]

This understanding of Adorno, pervasive in the German-speaking world from the outset of the 1980s, shows how vastly wide of the mark has been his reception by the mainstream of Anglo-American cultural studies and sociological theory.[42] In this Adorno has been identified with 'production aesthetics', with high modernism and with the transcendental subject of an abstract aesthetic rationality. But as we have just seen, Adorno's aesthetic utopia was one of a radical particular set against the universal, of the non-identical (aesthetic) object – which in its intrinsic difference and heterogeneity – can never be subsumed by the abstract subject of identity-thinking. Thus when Adorno understands art as the working through the possibilities of the aesthetic material, he is speaking of a very hands-on, 'tectonic' notion of material. When he praises Schoenberg's twelve-tone music it is not as 'conceptual music' arranged in structural sequence, but of the very texture, the very grain of the tonality. His unhappiness with pastiche in painting is not due to an abstract purism of, for example, structural *combinatoires* of facet-planes in cubism. It is because of an explicitly material notion of the qualities and possibilities of the paint. This is particularly thematized in one of his last talks – to the Hochschule für Gestaltung at Ulm, in some respects the West German postwar heirs – including Alexander Kluge – of the design tradition of the Bauhaus.[43] Historians of architecture have noted a tradition in modernism which is material and 'tectonic', with forebears in bridge-building and engineering and whose foremost exponent is Mies van der Rohe. This they have contrasted with a more conceptualist tradition with roots in abstract art, and prototypically instantiated in Corbusier. In the framework of this juxtaposition Adorno's mimetic materialism is clearly on the side of Mies and the engineers.

This mimetic materialism has been foregrounded recently in a book on Adorno by Fredric Jameson. Jameson, also importantly influenced by Hegel, extends this Adornonian 'aesthetic materialism' to suggest a negative dialectics of *popular* culture. This provides for him an effective 'postmodernism of resistance' in contradistinction to the postmodernism of domination enunciated in Jameson's earlier work.[44] Jameson is in this sense suggesting that the cultural logic of late capitalism, though seemingly one-dimensional, though ostensibly identitarian, creates – in an immanent dialectical movement – its own non-identical critique. This too is aesthetic reflexivity, but at issue are not reflexive subjects but the already reflexive *objects* produced by the culture industries and circulating in the global information and communication structures. These objects are already at least trebly reflexive – as symbol-intensive intellectual property, as commoditized and as advertised. They are at the same time mimetic in a more radical vein than that propounded by either Nietzsche or Adorno. That is, philosophers will often counterpose the mimetic (as aesthetic) to the conceptual (as theory). But, in the space of the aesthetic, we can make a distinction more typical of linguists between 'semiosis' and 'mimesis'. In semiosis, meaning is produced rather on a Saussurean model through the differences, valences and identities between elements in a *langue*. Mimesis, in contrast, signifies 'iconically', through resemblance.[45]

It is crucial in this context that the objects of the culture industries are differently reflexive than cultural objects were in the earlier era of liberal capitalism. That is, they are reflexive, they are mimetic in a far less mediated way. If nineteenth-century realist narrative as cultural object is reflexive through highly mediated semiosis, then ideal-typically organized capitalist cinema – in its diachronic, tonal visuality – is a cultural object which is reflexive through less mediated iconic representation.[46] For modes of signification to be less highly mediated (by the subject) is, at the same time, for them to be more highly *motivated* by the phenomenon which is represented. The most proximally mediated, and most highly motivated form of signification, is of course 'signal'. And the culture industries, especially television, signify increasingly like signal – in sports programmes, in the news, in 'live' crime and divorce shows, in talk shows, in immediate audience revelation programmes like 'Donahue' and 'Oprah Winfrey'. In fact the greater part of the information which flows in the information and communication structures signifies as signal.

What are the implications of this for aesthetic reflexivity? For aesthetic critique? Let us here perhaps have another look through Adorno's eyes. We must understand Adorno in spite of his mainstream cultural studies reception. This misreading has dismissed Adorno because of his rejection of popular culture's vulgarity. This misses the point, it is interminably repeated, that popular culture can in fact serve not domination, but 'resistance'. Adorno's scepticism, however, towards the culture industries was not because their products were too much like low culture, but indeed because they were too much like *high* culture. That is, he rejected them not because they exemplified the proximal mediation of 'mimesis' but because they exemplified the *ultimate* mediation of 'the concept'. To come under the sign of the commodity is to partake of the abstraction – as Marx too was well aware in his notion of exchange-value – of the concept, of identitarian reification. Thus in effect Adornonian mimesis advocates 'low culture' against high culture. Critique could come via popular culture but only when it was deconstructed (quite literally in Derrida's sense) from under the sign of the commodity.

In a similar vein, Walter Benjamin's notion of 'allegory' promulgated a version of mimesis – as 'die Sprache der Dingen', as, literally, the sounds of the city – but this is far less mediated than even Adornonian mimesis.[47] In contrast to Adorno's Hegelian assumptions, Benjamin did not even speak the language of mediation. His allegorical mimesis shares properties with signal in being, like surrealist representation, very highly motivated. But neither Adorno nor Benjamin, of course, saw even the most proximal modes of mimesis as mere copying. Both saw an unbridgeable gap between 'speech' and 'phenomenon'. The very proximal mimesis of the culture industries was captured by Adorno under the notion of 'hieroglyphic writing'.[48] Like hieroglyphics, popular culture seems to signify: not abstractly through semiosis but most immediately, through resemblance. Yet for us in the modern West, hieroglyphics also take on indecipherable levels of abstraction. So may the culture industries, which can take the immediacy of popular cultural experience and metamorphose it into the unhappy utilitarian abstraction of the commodity.

Aesthetique, ethique, ethnique

This theory of reflexive modernity or any theory of reflexivity is reflexive in so far as it concerns the mediation of everyday experience – whether this mediation is conceptual or mimetic. A theory of reflexivity only becomes a *critical* theory when it turns its reflection away from the experience of everyday life and instead on to 'system'. Aesthetic reflexivity – either of cultural forms or of experiencing individuals – is not conceptual but mimetic. It is reflexive in so far as it operates mimetically on everyday experience; it becomes *critical* only when its point of mimetic reference becomes 'system', of commodities, bureaucracy, or reification of life forms. The same is true for cognitive reflexivity, in which mediation is conceptual. Of theorists of cognitive reflexivity, Habermas's for example is primarily a *critical* theory, in that the transcendental, intersubjective and discursive truths of communicative rationality are explicitly aimed at critique of system in order to win space for the life-world. In this sense, cognitive reflexivity in both Beck and Giddens is *not* primarily critical, not primarily aimed at the logic of commodity and bureaucracy, but instead – like such earlier theories of simple modernization as Durkheim's – aimed at the transformation of tradition.

In one very important way the theory of reflexive modernity, with its rather one-sided emphasis on the cognitive, or 'conceptual', dimension seems to compound the unhappy identity integral to the process of simple modernization. I am speaking of the notion of 'risk' which both Beck and Giddens set up against a core problem, even a core ontology, of insecurity. Now risks can be understood as dangers, but, in so far as today's society presumes increased individualization, risks are mainly things that individuals take. If I want to innovate at work, I must take not just responsibility but risks. New products are always also a matter of risk-taking. The shrewd gambler must be a risk-taker. If I am to be a good poker player, I must take responsibility – that is, know how much I can afford to lose – but also risks. As a poker player when I take risks, I must act 'probabilistically'. I will know that a great deal of the outcome of a hand is inexplicable, and a matter of contingency (*fortuna*),[49] but a great deal of the rest is cognizable through probabilistic calculation based on the cards already showing, the memory of any discards, the cards turned over by other players and the betting patterns of the other players.

In this sense social life today probably does have more to do with risk than with insecurity, more to do with how the 'transcendental subject' of high modernity has been brought down a few pegs and can only at best be a probabilistic calculating subject. Thus 'expert science', though often imbricated in a formal discourse of certainty, must act probabilistically *vis-à-vis* the natural environment. Even when the experts are the object of critique, through the reflexivity of the lay public, what is disputed is partly the expert's discourse of certainty.[50] This however does not mean that the answers of a critical *public* – themselves often dependent on the advice of other experts – are any less probabilistic. The risk society is thus not so much about the distribution of 'bads' or dangers as about a mode of conduct centred on risk. This is seen not just in relationship to environment, or work, or poker playing. It is instantiated in the self-construction of life narratives described by Beck and Giddens, in which a probabilistic calculative mode of regulation imparts narrativity to the life-course. Through such risk-taking probabilistic calculation, we often find ourselves in situations of 'shame', that is, being exposed in our contradictory, fragmented autobiographies. In the same fashion we calculate, 'hedonistically', our leisure time.[51] We carry out our sex lives in such probabilistic calculation, in risk-taking encounters with the ontological insecurity of AIDS. Even quantitative sociology has become part of the risk society, as the metaphysics of Karl Pearson's probabilistic correlation coefficient replaced the security of explanation of a previous positivism. In the newer, perhaps more modest positivism, contingency (insecurity) is rendered as 'unexplained variance'.[52]

Is the risk society a last attempt on the part of the modernist subject now only probabilistically to control the out-of-hand and increasingly rampant insecurity and 'excess' of a triumphant postmodernity? Do the expert-systems of reflexive modernization colonize ever more regions of the life-world? It is possible perhaps to maintain a precarious agnosticism on this question and at the same time agree with Zygmunt Bauman that answer might be to avoid altogether the metaphysics of risk and instead to live with contingency, even to affirm ambivalence.[53] What Bauman is suggesting is, it seems to me, a radically different sort of poker. Here the player is less the probabilistic risk-taker, but instead the sometimes foolhardy addict of the all-night games, the player who pushes kings-over-threes to the hilt, the punter who bets more than he or she can afford to lose. This poker player, like Georg Simmel's 'adventurer', is not out for risk-taking but in search instead of a zone of contingency in a social space increasingly cross-hatched by ever more, and ever more pervasive, expert-systems.[54]

Bauman, unlike Beck and Giddens, could not see 'another modernity' as a new and reflexive era succeeding an old and 'simple' one. Instead his other modernity, one closer to aesthetic modernism, would run *parallel* to its Cartesian and utilitarian counterpart. Bauman's culture of alterity is on the one hand the mimetic critique of high, Enlightenment modernity. It is at the same time the dark side of the Enlightenment. As 'id', it stands counterposed to 'ego'; as insecurity it encounters the calculating subject; as *fortuna* it underpins the *cogito*. Bauman, however, gives to this other modernity an ethnic twist. In the place of the aesthetic, in the place of insecurity as disruptive mimesis, in the place of *fortuna* or ambivalence, for him, stands the Jew. Thus the Jew, like Simmel's 'stranger', is the visitor who 'comes today and stays tomorrow'. Aesthetic modernism, Susan Sontag somewhere wrote of Proust – who belonged to both – would be unthinkable in the absence of those two 'confraternities', of homosexuals and Jews. On this view, the homosexual and the Jew are neither same nor clearly other; they instead are disruptive of classifications; they embody ambivalence.

Bauman's project is ultimately an ethical one. It is a project that he may articulate best, but shares with thinkers such as Lyotard, Rorty, Derrida, Levinas and Adorno. The idea is to construct an aestheticized ethics and understand it in terms of ethnicity. In this the Holocaust is understood as the final triumph of 'the concept', the victory of identitarian and Cartesian modernity. The implication is that no totalizing critical movement such as Marxism, no transcendental ethics like the Kantian imperative, is possible after the Holocaust. All that is possible is determinate negation or aesthetic critique, where even ethics can only be an *ethique aesthetique*, or an ethics of non-identity.[55] Habermas in *The Philosophical Discourse of Modernity* characterizes this sort of thinking, in contrast to 'symbol', as *allegory*. He observes that if 'symbol' is somehow Protestant in its allowing for totality, 'allegory' is perhaps Jewish in its imperative (thus Derridean *écriture* always defers the meaning of the signifier) that the name of God must not be spoken.[56]

For these philosophers of allegory, the pivotal text of course is Kant's *Critique of Judgement*. For Kant, 'judgement in general is the faculty of thinking the particular as subsumed under the universal'.[57] In his *Critique of Pure Reason* and *Critique of Practical Reason*, this general rule posed no problem. But in consideration of the work of art and (not mechanical, but) organic nature there seemed to be some complications. In life forms and art, it seemed to Kant, Aristo-telian teleology rather than mechanical causality was at work. In the development of a work of art or an organism, the universal is no longer a principle (whether as in Socratic nominalism or Platonic realism) external to the object under consideration, but the universal is operative, as it were, 'autopoetically', internal to the organism (work of art) itself.[58] In aesthetic judgement the universal is no longer located in a transcendental (real or ideal) subject. Instead Kant likened such judgement to English Common Law, in which a previous particular case becomes the framework within which a subsequent particular is assessed. If this is so, then, one wonders, why speak of judgement at all? Perhaps what is called for, as Bauman suggests, is an end to the ethics of judgement.[59] On this view an *ethique aesthetique* is the triumph of the aesthetic over judgement itself. It is the revenge of the object on the subject, the retribution of difference on identity.

The 'I' or the 'We'

A number of these philosophers of allegory liken this inversion of subject and object, of universal and particular involved in aesthetic reflexivity, to another set of phenomena in the context of more directly social practices. In this, the abstract morality of Kant's cat-egorical imperative is challenged by the ethical life of Hegelian *Sittlichkeit*. Often this is contextualized in contemporary politics with abstract Eastern European 'blueprint Marxism' standing in for Kantian morality, and the complex particularity of a given specific culture as exemplifying *Sittlichkeit*. This is the move that for exam-ple Lyotard makes in *Le Différend*, Maffesoli in *Ethique aesthetique* and implicitly Terry Eagleton in *Ideology of the Aesthetic*. One possi-ble consequence of this, the danger of such particularism, is an emergent 'neo-tribalism' and ethnocentrism of ethical–aesthetic communities. This is a danger which Bauman staves off through prescribing – drawing on Levinas – an ethics of interpretation for the other, and to which for example Rorty counterposes not a universalism of 'emancipation' but a 'cosmopolitan' pragmatics of translation between speech communities.[60]

One is initially gratified, but then soon uneasy in the face of such arguments. How, one might ask, can Bauman or Rorty speak so quickly of translation to the other before a convincingly substantial sense of shared meanings among 'the same' is established? Are perhaps these 'neo-tribes', much like Benedict Anderson's 'imagined communities', not tribes or communities at all but merely associations of atomized individuals? Why, further, does Bauman, like Adorno, have to construe the Third Reich purely in terms of 'technology', of bureaucratic modernity, and ignore the proximal communal meanings of the premodern yet still existent *ethnie*?[61] Why do almost all of these 'allegorists', these 'deconstructors', insist on understanding Hegelian *Sittlichkeit* as 'difference', as complexity or the non-identical, instead of as community and shared cultural practices?

What I am pointing to is a substantial deficit in any sort of convincing notion of 'community', of the 'we' in these analyses. And to understand today's barbaric if fragmented new nationalisms, as well as the collective representations of the new social movements, not to mention other kinds of contemporary ethics of practice, some fundamental thinking about the 'we' is surely needed. What I am further arguing is that a neglect of shared meanings, a systematic impossibility of the 'we', is systematically integral to allegorical thinking. I am claiming that analysts in the tradition of allegory from Nietzsche to Benjamin and Adorno, to Derrida, Rorty and Bauman, presume a radical individualism – surely not a utilitarian but an aesthetic individualism: not an individualism of a controlling ego but the individualism of a heterogenous, contingent desire – which itself is hardly conducive to community.

What I am contending is that any understanding of the 'we' under the star of aesthetic reflexivity, under the star of such a mimetic critique of the concept, is impossible. To have access to community, it may be necessary to break with such abstract aesthetic subjectivity. It may be necessary to reject the 'method' suggested by deconstruction in favour of the 'truth' advocated by hermeneutics. Cognitive reflexivity posed the calculating subject versus contingency, and the conceptual versus the mimetic. Aesthetic reflexivity's renewal of this hierarchy, with the embrace of contingency and mimesis, remain arguably located in the same metaphysical universe. To have any access to the 'we', to community, we must not deconstruct but hermeneutically interpret and thus evade the categories of agency and structure, subject and object, control versus contingency and the conceptual versus the mimetic. This sort of interpretation will give access to ontological foundations, in *Sitten*, in habits, in background practices of cognitive and aesthetic individualism. It will at the same time give us some understanding of the shared meanings of community.

Aesthetic reflexivity – as allegory, or deconstruction – is unceasingly anti-foundationalist. Thus Baudrillard's sign-value deconstructs the 'essentialism' of Marxian exchange-value. Thus the Lacanian symbolic reveals the foundationalism in orthodox Freudian ego psychology; Deleuze deconstructs Lacan's prison-house of language and Oedipus for his own libidinal economics of desire; Derrida, De Lauretis and Iragaray in turn can find a phallocentric metaphysics of presence in Deleuze, which they counter with an alternative female economy of desire;[62] while feminists of the 1990s take the foundations away from even De Lauretis's 'essentialist' naturalism. In each case there is the initial anti-foundationalist challenge of aesthetic subjectivity to rationalist individualism, and then further attacks by even more 'anything goes' versions of aesthetic subjectivity on the incumbent form of the latter. In each case it is forms of control which are deconstructed from the standpoint of contingency or ambivalence. The previous modes of ambivalence are shown really to have been modes of control, and they in turn are deconstructed, and so on.

Where and when, if ever, will this incessant process of deconstruction end? Does it lead to one after another often increasingly *kitsch* theory replacing the last one, on the model of rapidly changing styles in our 'throw-away societies'? What all of these ideas do is to deconstruct the universal from the point of view of the particular. And though, as Tönnies observed, the individualized *Gesellschaft* is to universalism what the *Gemeinschaft* is to particularism, none of today's ubiquitous and incessant deconstruction leads to any grasp of the 'we', but just to ever less foundational, ever more Faustian forms of the aesthetic 'I'. Thus Lyotard's title of an early book, *Dérive à partir de Marx et Freud*, is emblematic of our own 'casting ourselves adrift', through the chronic deconstruction of whatever foundations, whichever essentialisms still remain. The point, however, is that Marx and Freud, along with Christ, 'the eternally deconstructed', were themselves original and paradigmatic deconstructors. They were along with Nietzsche the founding figures among the 'masters of suspicion'. The practitioner of what Ricoeur calls a 'hermeneutics of suspicion'[63] is in principle suspicious of some sort of good universal from the standpoint of a deceitful, hidden, *sournois* particular. Thus the unseemly, sweaty labour process of the satanic mills and Lang's *Metropolis* is the truth of the noblest Christian and Enlightenment ideals. And the debased particularly of the id is the truth of the noblest sublimations of the ego.

In its persistent challenge to ever new universals, in its chronic aesthetic reflexivity, present-day deconstruction does not under-mine, or 'cast adrift from' Marx and Freud, but only repeats, in ever more rapid cycles, what the masters (of suspicion) inaugurated. In counterposition to this, one wonders if it may be not that Marx and Freud had not gone far enough, but that they already had gone too far. It may well be that the notion of the Enlightenment ego – from classical physics and economics – that was their prime target had already gone too far. What is needed perhaps for any sort of group of community, of the 'we', of national and other collective identity is not any sort of hermeneutics of suspicion at all. What may well instead be needed is perhaps a 'hermeneutics of *retrieval*'. Such a hermeneutics of retrieval, unlike the masters (and today's journey-men) of suspicion, will not unendingly sweep away foundations but will attempt to lay open the ontological foundations of commu-nal being-in-the-world. A hermeneutics of retrieval will not sus-piciously put the lie to first substantive and then procedural goods, but will seek to point to a grounded set of substantive goods as the basis of any sort of communal ethics. A hermeneutics of retrieval will not, in Faustian suspicion, chronically be on the lookout for 'transcendental signifieds', it will not chronically defer and deny meaning. It will, instead of marvelling in the free play of the signifier, modestly 'look beneath' that signifier to gain access to the shared meanings which are conditions of existence, indeed *are* the very existence, of the 'we'.

From subjectivity to community

One particularly fruitful attempt at understanding community and collectivity today is found in the cultural studies literature. This literature has been invaluable in understanding social change, as Stuart Hall and others have provided necessary tools for analysis of the declining significance of social class, the increased significance of cultural, in comparison with social, factors, and the increased importance of leisure in comparison with the sphere of production. All of this has massive implications for changes in forms of com-munity and collective identity. Cultural studies has increasingly been concerned with the media, and has argued that what is impor-tant here is not cultural production but instead cultural consump-tion. Analysts such as Fiske have contended that even the most mass-produced of Hollywood films, even the most apparently politically and aesthetically retrograde soap operas, even the sort of popular muzak produced for example by Stock, Aitken and Waterman, can have politically progressive effects. These writers argue that even such cultural objects do not necessarily serve dominant ideologies, but can be used in cultural consumption by audiences for collective struggles against domination.[64] The point I want to make here is not so much about the relative merits of, say, Fiske's political judgement or even about the relative merits of producer-driven versus consumer-driven accounts of popular culture. The point instead concerns the possibility of cultural community, and the very terms 'producer', cultural 'text' or cultural 'object' and 'consumer' are telling in this context. That is, cultural communities, the cultural 'we', are collectivities of shared background practices, shared meanings, shared routine activities involved in the achievement of meaning. The cultural studies model would seem to rule this out. The cultural studies model instead resembles that of neo-classical economics, with 'producers' and 'consumers' abstracted from shared and embedded practices and instead operating as rational-choice-making individuals with 'preference schedules', with cultural 'products' to choose from on the marketplace. Unfortunately the sort of model that Fiske and his colleagues work with is pervasive not only among professors but in everyday life, and would seem to be a reason why cultural communities are indeed very thin on the ground today.

A more sophisticated approach within this framework is found in Dick Hebdige's writings on subcultures. Hebdige's understanding here moves away from producerist and consumerist perspectives to a stronger focus on cultural processes and embedded cultural practices. He speaks of 'authenticity' in the context of sub-cultural community precisely as instantiated in those subculture members whose way of life is the most distanced from consumerist mentalities. This focus on subculture is also a focus pre-eminently on *reflexive* community.[65] That is, if we are 'thrown' into the collective meanings and practices of the being-in-the-world of simple community, we reflexively 'throw ourselves' into the communal world of youth subculture, as we decide to become involved in them, or even with others come to have a hand in creating them. A problem with the idea of subcultures as conceived in cultural studies is the idea of 'resistance through rituals'. In this 'rituals' are conceived as the symbolic construction of subcultural identity. These are typically constructed through the 'bricolage' of a disconnected set of signifiers from previous styles.[66] For example Teddy

Boy subculture involves drawing on Edwardian, black American and a variety of other signifiers. The problem is that this whole focus on freely playing *combinatoires* of signifiers tends to ignore the whole basis of subcultures, or any community, which are shared meanings or shared signifieds.

The sort of cultural communities at issue here are evoked by Heidegger's discussions of 'world' in Division One of *Being and Time*. Here 'the world', conceived initially by Heidegger along the lines of a model of a metaphorical workshop (as a world, as a community), can exist only on the basis of the accessibility of meaning. When the workshop is functioning, Heidegger notes, focus is never on the sign or signifier; instead signs are seen immediately as meanings. It is only when there is breakdown that focus is on the sign.[67] When a community like a football team is functioning, the meaning of signs like a shout, a nod of the head, is transparent. Footballers read each other's signifiers already as meanings. It is only when there is breakdown that the goalkeeper must confer with his central defenders about gestures and sounds and take the signifier as problematized. In other words the movement to subject–object modes of thought takes place only with the breakdown of shared practices and shared meanings of the 'we', and to start from the subject–object assumptions of subcultures as a bricolage of signifiers and then try to understand 'the we', as does much of the cultural studies literature, is itself indeed problematic.

Perhaps the most influential and deeply considered attempt to grasp community beginning from considerations of the subject is in the work of Jürgen Habermas. Habermas's commitment to understanding community is profound. His theory is of 'communicative' action and his background in hermeneutics must be taken seriously. His commitment is not to Enlightenment abstraction or to contemporary expert-systems. He wants instead to preserve and widen the sphere of the 'life-world', conceived in a way consistent with Schutz's and Heidegger's idea of 'world'. The difference is that, instead of starting from the collective meanings of *Kultur* and proceeding to a defence of *Zivilisation*, Habermas takes his starting point from the individualism of *Zivilisation* and wants to arrive at the *Sittlichkeit*, the community, of *Kultur*. That is, Habermas wants to use the Enlightenment to protect the life-world from the excesses of the negative (and unintended) consequences of the Enlightenment. What Habermas specifically wants is a life-world of embedded social practices, that is, a *Sittlichkeit* (concrete ethical life) in Hegel's sense that is grounded in the intersubjectivity of communi-

cative action. Is this possible? Can such transcendental intersubjectivity be a basis for community? Surely in this context
communicative intersubjectivity can be a basis for 'the social' or for
'society'.[68] The social, or society, as defined by classical sociologists
such as Durkheim has been understood as consisting of abstract
rules and norms regulating action in institutions. Durkheim himself
was attacked by classical humanists in the first decade of the twentieth century in France for just this sort of scientistic and 'clockwork'
idea of society. Habermas's transcendental intersubjectivity – transcendental in that the subjects are disembedded from worlds of
shared practices – is surely a good basis for the social in this sense.
But so is Talcott Parsons's equally transcendental intersubjectivity
of ego and alter, through which his sociology of action can yield the
normatively governed institutional structures of functionalism. But
community – *Gemeinschaft, Sittlichkeit* – is a far cry from these abstract rules. Instead it is based on *Sitten*, which are customs and by
definition not rules; it is based in habits, not in judgements, but 'prejudgements'. When Gadamer polemically pits truth against method
in *Wahrheit und Methode,* he is not just referring to the advocacy of
ideographic versus methodological rulebound approaches in the
human sciences. He is also referring to the truths revealed by community, by *Sittlichkeit* in everyday life.

For Habermas communicative rationality is a means by which
intersubjectivity can roll back the claims of 'system' and expand the
space of the life-world. This takes place through communicative
interaction, in which speech-acts or utterances are potentially 'discursively redeemable validity claims'. Habermas recognizes that
communicative rationality takes place on the basis of the sort of pre-
understandings and background assumptions which are the domain of hermeneutics. But the great part of his attention is devoted
not to these but to the examination of discursively redeemable
validity claims. How can this cope with community? Now community in any substantial sense must be 'worlded'. It must be rooted in
shared meanings and background practices. These practices have
purpose, have their own specific 'telos'. These practices involve
other human beings. They also involve things, which are not 'objects' but *'Zeuge',* in Heidegger's sense – that is, tools, 'gear', including language and informational tools,[69] which we dwell among and
invest significantly with affect. Everyday activities in the 'we' are
involved in the routine achievement of meaning; they are involved
in the production of substantive goods, which themselves are also
meanings. Though activities are guided by such substantive goods

whose criteria are set internal to a given practice, this guiding is not by rules but by the example of such present and traditional practices.

Now consider the discursively redeemable validity claims of communicative rationality. In this the communications involved are understood as speech acts. Why should Habermas want to use speech-act theory? Surely speech-act-based sociolinguistics and conversation analysis have been criticized precisely because they look at utterances (a 'text', a 'corpus') in abstraction from everyday embedded social practices. Speech-act theory, observes Hubert Dreyfus, presumes the regulation of different sorts of utterances by 'rules', which goes against the anti-nomothetic, *sittlich* basis of community.[70] Further, Habermas looks at such speech acts between subjects as 'validity claims'.[71] Hence the assumption right away is that meaning is not shared but seemingly chronically contested. Utterances are assumed to be in the first instance about attempts to establish or overturn positions of power. Speech acts become power plays. But in fact, in most communities of practice, communication does not in the first instance or usually involve power plays, but involves developing successfully a common collective practice. When a goalkeeper signals to his right fullback, at issue is the successful development often of an attacking pattern through the middle of the field and out to the wings, rather than in the first instance power relations between keeper and defender. When a colleague from another university – in the international sociological community – whom I esteem and who esteems me, rings me and asks me to get the article in the post to the journal she edits, at issue immediately is the production of a common product, rather than the power relations between her and me. Indeed if there were not sufficient shared meanings – and a bracketing out of speech acts as validity claims between us – it is unlikely that she and I would share enough common ground to be involved together in the project. Habermas's theory, it has been claimed, involves too weak a notion of power. I would like to argue rather the opposite – that it has too *strong* a notion of power; that it claims to see power in places where power just isn't, and in doing so cannot account for the shared meanings necessary for community. Why, one might ask, is communicative rationality a 'universal pragmatics'? Pragmatics in linguistics looks at power and what words do. Why does Habermas not instead proffer a *semantics*, focusing on the *meaning* of expressions?[72]

Finally for Habermas these validity claims are 'discursively re-deemable'. This means that where a validity claim is contested, the interlocutors must move into the realm of 'discourse' – in which arguments are systematically brought forward in support of the communications. The realms of discourse which Habermas is referring to are theoretical discourse, ethical or practical discourse, and aesthetic-expressive discourse. In this context comparison with Giddens is instructive. That is, the individualistic assumptions of Giddens's reflexive modernity, and its potential deficiencies in understanding community or the 'we', are in important ways also those found in communicative rationality. Both theorists, for example, assume an abstract or 'transcendental' subject–subject relation as starting point. For Habermas this is intersubjectivity; for Giddens it is the *intra*-subjectivity of the self-monitoring social agent. For Giddens modern reflexivity passes through the 'loop' of, or is mediated by, 'expert-systems'. For Habermas the equivalent of expert-systems are the 'discourses' which attest to the validity of the subject's utterances. Though not all expert-systems are such legitimating and speech-act redeeming discourses, all of Habermas's discourses would also be expert-systems.

Let us return to the notion of community implicit in Heidegger's 'workshop' model in *Being and Time*. Here being-in-the-world involves not 'subjects' but situated human beings absorbed in routine (or pre-reflexive) practices or activities with not objects but *Zeuge* (tools, 'gear', equipment) and involved in shared meanings and practices with not 'subjects' but other finite human beings. It is only with the breakdown of routine activity that human beings become subjects and the *Zeuge* become objects, as repair becomes necessary.[73] It is only with the breakdown of shared meanings that human beings become 'subjects' for one another. This is where the expert-systems, this is where the legitimating discourses, come in; that is, to repair the breakdown so that practices and shared meaningful activities can resume once again. But when the expert-systems and discourses *chronically* intervene, when they intervene 'preventively' and pervasively, then the practices, shared meanings and community become increasingly marginalized, made progressively less possible. The problem does not seem to be, as many have argued, that Habermas's discourse ethics is too abstract to have much purchase on reality. The problem may instead be that it has *too much* purchase on reality. It is more likely that social reality itself has become too abstract, too pervasively interpenetrated by expert-systems and legitimating discourses. It is more likely that neither the incessant discourse of the concept and cognitive reflexivity nor the interminable deconstruction of mimesis and aesthetic reflexivity might be the best mode of access to truth. What could be an alternative? Perhaps only in involved engagement, in having concern for things and people in a shared world. Perhaps not the incessant noise of the signifier of either discourse or deconstruction, but instead the already shared meanings of everyday social practices, make thinking and truth (and community) possible.

Charles Taylor in *Sources of the Self* seems to have begun from far more promising assumptions in developing a truly reflexive hermeneutics and notion of community. We have already observed that the 'discourse ethics' of cognitive reflexivity disputes the notion of substantive goods and instead proffers a highly proceduralist notion of the good. Taylor doesn't deny the validity of this but instead parries by showing how such procedural ethics are themselves a substantive good and 'source' of the modern self. We have also noted that the deconstruction ethics of aesthetic reflexivity wants to do away with both substantive and proceduralist notions of the good. Again Taylor doesn't counter this, so much as show how such deconstructive anti-foundationalism is itself a foundation, indeed is itself a substantive good and source of the modern self. So far so good. But there is more. Taylor is a Hegel scholar and a communitarian. In his *Hegel* he insisted that we must understand community and ethics in terms not of Kant's abstract morality but of Hegel's *Sittlichkeit*, which he contextualized in the writings of the Romantic philosophers among Hegel's contemporaries. In this context it would seem that Taylor wants us to understand 'sources', not in terms of a reflexive subject; and that reflexivity lies not in the subject, nor the self, but instead in the *sources* of the self. It is that reflexivity must be present in the background practices, in the 'ever-already there' of the world into which the self is thrown.[74]

Taylor seems then to offer us a notion of reflexive community in which the shared background assumptions are already reflexive. Here I think he is surely on the right track. But at the same time this line of approach raises a number of sticky, perhaps insurmountable, issues. First, Taylor seems to be telling us that we only *think* we are living in the presence of an impoverishing deficit of *Sittlichkeit*. He seems to be saying instead that we already have community, if only we knew where to look for it. This he does mostly by assertion. One may ask here if this isn't mostly a case of wishful thinking at best. At worst, if we already have community, then we are let off from needing reflexively to create it. Further, what if we agree with Taylor that both the cognitive-utilitarian and aesthetic-expressive dimensions of modern reason are sources of the self? Are these grounds for rejoicing? Or are these 'sources' themselves so emptied-out, so abstract, that they instead are perhaps emblematic of 'system' having already finally colonized the life-world? Taylor, like many other thinkers, finds two traditions present in the aesthetic source of the self – on the one hand 'symbol' and on the other 'allegory'. Here the tradition of 'symbol' would embrace Goethe, Schiller, Schleiermacher and for example T. S. Eliot. 'Allegorists' would include Baudelaire and the *poètes maudits*, but also Benjamin, Derrida and Foucault. 'Symbol' arises from the Romantic tradition and is understood in terms of nature, totality, organicism, community and meaning. Allegory is in contrast cynical, urban, artificial, radically individualist and highlights the materiality rather than the transparency of the signifier. Taylor, then, for me inexplicably and surely unconvincingly, puts a number of arguments for the assimilation of allegory to symbol. In doing so he ends up proffering a cognitive and an aesthetic, but not a communitarian (hermeneutic), source of the self. I expect he does so because of certain (Christian) assumptions of a not Adornonian but Hegelian 'positive dialectic', in which dialectical movement is governed and finally subsumed by the universalist moment of reason. None the less for Taylor, a self-conscious communitarian and hermeneutician, this is a very strange conclusion indeed. The result is a failure systematically to think through the potential sources of the 'we'.

Habitus, habiter, habits

Why do even these most muscular attempts to derive the 'we' from the 'I', to derive community from the individual, by even the most gifted of thinkers, ultimately fail? Why do such analyses end up with the same atomized, abstract phenomena that they began with? Why indeed? One may begin to look for an answer to such failure in perhaps the sort of questions that such analysts are in the first place posing. Perhaps instead the only possible way is to begin with self that is already situated in a matrix of background practices. And such is surely Pierre Bourdieu's starting point in his notion of 'habitus'. Bourdieu has been often likened to Anthony Giddens as a theorist of 'structuration'.[75] At first glance this seems indeed to be true. Bourdieu's 'habitus' as effectively a social actor is involved in the production or construction of social structures. There is further in Bourdieu a 'duality of structure' in which structures are not only the outcome but the reflexive medium of action. Bourdieu had in his early work severely criticized the overly structural approach of Lévi-Strauss from, it seemed, the standpoint of agency. Later, his *Distinction* could serve as implicit critique of overly actionalist conceptions such as in rational-choice theory. Bourdieu's actors in *Distinction* are after all collective as much as individual. They act through the mediation of already structured class-related taste categories as they engage in 'classificatory struggles' for cultural hegemony.[76]

Bourdieu himself has protested against this likening to Giddens, maintaining that his idea of 'habitus' has been radically misunderstood. But is this protest of Bourdieu's to be taken at face value? One way to approach this, possibly, is to begin with Bourdieu's idea of reflexivity. In his recent *Invitation to Reflexive Sociology* Bourdieu speaks of reflexivity in terms of the systematic uncovering of the unthought categories which themselves are preconditions of our more self-conscious (in this case, sociological) practices.[77] What can be meant by this? Let us note to begin with that – unlike in Beck and in Giddens – reflection is not on social structure, that is, it is not on institutional (or other structural) rules. Reflexivity is instead on 'unthought categories', which are not as readily accessible to us as are social structures. Yet these unthought categories are also not, Bourdieu assures us, in principle *in*accessible to the conscious mind as is the Freudian unconscious.[78]

What is Bourdieu getting at? He wants to understand the relationship between the conscious self and the unthought categories neither as (in Beck and Giddens) a subject–object monitoring relation, nor (as in Freud) an object–subject *causal* relation, in which cause is, so to speak, kept secret from effect. What he is getting at, or at least what he is suggesting for present purposes, is a *hermeneutic* relationship, in which the unthought categories are not causes but are to be hermeneutically interpreted. In which the unthought categories are also ontological foundations of practical consciousness. But let us not stop there, but instead proceed on to hermeneutic interpretation of the unthought categories. Bourdieu in effect does this interpretation for us. But first what are these categories which are also not social structures? They are, in the first instance, classificatory categories, on the lines very much of Durkheim and Mauss's *Primitive Classifications*.[79] Durkheim and Mauss observe that the framework for their classifications is the

Aristotelian (and Kantian) categories of logic. But Bourdieu's classificatory categories are not as immediately accessible as the latter; instead they are 'taste' categories, understood on the model of Kant's aesthetic judgement.[80] Now Bourdieu's *Distinction* seems *prima facie* to be a study in the social stratification of consumption. It is, however, much more than this. It is a sociology not just of taste in the strict sense but more generally of the whole range of our most immediate habits and practices. It is a sociology of our unthought, though bodily inscribed, categories. It is in short a sociology of the ontological foundations – in categories of habit – of conscious action.

But Bourdieu wants to interpret the unthought even further. He talks of habitus, most proximally, not in terms of classificatory categories, but of classificatory 'schemata'. This is significant because 'schemata' are more supple than categories, much less fixed. Schemata are in fact more immediate than the least mediated categories. They are difficult to distinguish in nature from the particular cases and practices they putatively subsume. Schemata are, in fact, that contradiction in terms, of 'unmediated (or immediate) mediators'.[81] But the habitus and classificatory schemata can be interpreted yet further and even more immediately as 'predispositions', as 'orientations'. These are even more immediate than classificatory schemata. 'Predispositions' and 'orientations' are the learned, yet unthought, techniques of the body – such as swimming, ways of walking, playing tennis – which for Marcel Mauss too would be foundational for conscious conduct.

This takes us back to Kant's *Critique of Judgement*, which lends itself, it becomes clear now, to a second and radically different reading. Aesthetic reflexivity or 'mimetic reason', *à la* Adorno or Nietzsche, could understand the critique of judgement in terms of the critique by the particular of the universal. But instead of this reversal of this famous metaphysical hierarchy of the concept versus the aesthetic, Bourdieu suggests a step outside of metaphysics altogether and a reading of the third critique simply as judgement via the subsumption of a particular by a particular: the subsumption by 'predispositions', by 'orientations', by 'habits', of routine practices and background activities. The point here is that predispositions and habits are themselves background practices, are themselves routine activities. We are at this point a great distance away from the world of 'structure' and 'agency'. Bourdieu's 'logic of practice' has little to do with structure. In his early critique of Lévi-Strauss, he understood the 'rules' of structure as things the anthropologists imagined they had discovered which regulated the processes of *la pensée sauvage*. On the contrary, claimed Bourdieu, the 'indigènes' were fully aware of the structures and used the rules instead as 'alibis', as legitimations. 'Rules' or structures don't even figure in structuring the habitus; in their place are 'habits' and 'predispositions' which by definition are counterposed to rules much in the same sense as Max Weber's notion of traditional action is to rational action.[82] Habitus is just as far away from 'agency'. The theory of agency speaks the language of the 'unit act', 'habitus' the language of ongoing activities. Action theory posits, at least implicitly, a disembedded, cost-minimizing and benefit-maximizing, preference-scheduled actor. Habitus exists only as situated in its 'world'. Action theory is often 'constructivist', in which agency is the motive force behind structure as for example in 'actor-networks'. Habitus, in contrast, assumes a certain 'thrownness' into a web of already existing practices and meanings.

Bourdieu's reflexive sociology has been especially influential for the 'reflexive anthropology' of Clifford, Rabinow, Marcus and others.[83] And now we can see how. Reflexivity in the sense of Bourdieu and the anthropologists operates in a fully different terrain than cognitive (Beck, Giddens) and aesthetic (Adorno, Nietzsche) reflexivity. In both cognitive and aesthetic reflexivity, a subject is presumed, outside of a world, for whom the world is (conceptually or mimetically) mediated. Reflexive anthropology entails breaking with the objectivism, the realism of Lévi-Strauss and of functionalism, and instead on a partial fusion of horizons with the world of one's 'respondents'. It means learning through habitus, of similar roots to 'habiter',[84] in which truth is neither conceptual nor mimetic, but becomes evident through shared practices. Reflexive anthropology (and sociology) means that we see our own concepts not as categories but as interpretive schemata, as predispositions and orientations, as our own habits. Reflexive human science depends on the emergence of a translation between our schemata and those of our respondents. It entails that we understand reflexively that our 'concepts' are only another set of (by Western accident) privileged schemata. Reflexive human science would need to understand itself as just another 'ethnomethodology'. Thus the notion of reflexivity here is polar opposite to that of Beck and Giddens. For Beck and Giddens it tends to involve the bracketing of the life-world to arrive at individualized, subject–object forms of social knowledge. For reflexive anthropology it involves bracketing subject–object knowledge and situating knowers in their life-world.

Conclusions: reflexive community and the self

We have already outlined basic elements of a notion of community. Community must in a very fundamental sense be in a 'world', or 'worlded'. Even reflexivity in the context of community must be 'in-the-world'. Neither everyday nor human-scientific knowledge is a matter of a relationship between a knowing subject and the world as it is in epistemology.[85] Communal knowledge is instead hermeneutic knowledge and the latter is only possible when the knower is in the same world as and 'dwells among' the things and other human beings whose truth she seeks. Community does not involve chronic problematization of the signifier, but is instead rooted in shared meanings and routine background practices. The shared practices here have ends or a 'telos' that guide them and are set internal to the practice. They involve other human beings, the things and tools (*Zeuge*) worked with and the things that are made. These practices are guided not by rules but by schemata, by *Sitten*, which can range from the 'mysteries' of the medieval crafts to the customs and practice of the sociological imagination. These practices involve an immediate investment of affect in the tools – including the signs – worked with and the other human beings with whom the practices are shared. Everyday activities in the 'we' are about the routine achievement of meaning: about the production of substantive goods, and guided by an understanding of more generally what is regarded as substantively good by that community. The substantively good is not encountered by communal beings as an 'imperative', divorced from the mundane and the everyday. It is instead already present in the world of meanings and practices into which human beings are thrown when they become part of the 'we'. The meanings and practices incorporating the substantive good are learnt, but then become unconscious as if inscribed on the body.

Communities are not about shared *interests*. Political parties and social classes – which have interests in common – are not communities. Political parties are typically aggregations of the interests of a plurality of interest groups, most of whom are not themselves typically communities but atomized collections of individuals. Political parties do have some communal bases. For example, the Sikh community might tend to support the British Labour Party. But the relationship even here between party and ethnic collectivity is hardly 'communal'. Social classes, also a basis of political parties, are not communities but rather interest groups. The middle class by

Table 1 *Aspects of the three sorts of reflexivity I have outlined in this chapter. Cognitive reflexivity is more or less consistent with how I understand the positions of Beck and Giddens. Aesthetic reflexivity is addressed on pp. 135–146, and hermeneutic reflexivity on pp. 143–168*

| | Type of reflexivity | | |
	cognitive	aesthetic	hermeneutic
	'the I' (ego)	'the I' (desire)	'the We'
	{ utilitarian individualism	{ expressive individualism	community
	Enlightenment modernity	aesthetic modernism	tradition
mode of talk	discourse	deconstruction	silence
paradigmatic figures	Descartes/ Bentham	Baudelaire/ Nietzsche	Goethe/ Heidegger
story-telling	narrative	allegory	symbol
access to truth	conceptual	mimesis	through situated practices
mode of social regulation	norms	anything goes	habits *Sitten*
temporality	narrative	the event	tradition
	Zivilisation		*Kultur*
	identity	difference	ontological foundations
	the social		culture
	transcendental ethics	*ethique aesthetique*	ethics of care
	risk	insecurity	care
	the subject	the object	background practices
privileged semiotic element	the referent	the signifier	the signified (meaning)
	action (unit act)		conduct (activities)
spatial mode	geometrical grid	the boulevard	place
ethical mode	norms		values

Table 1 *Continued*

	Type of reflexivity		
	cognitive	*aesthetic*	*hermeneutic*
	interests		needs
	proceduralism		substantive goods
	universalist ethics	ethics of non-identity	particularistic ethics
		ethics of the other	ethics of the same
mode of understanding	realism	deconstruction	hermeneutics
	propositional truth	power/ knowledge	disclosive truth
	epistemology		ontology
mode of dialectics	totality	determinate negation	*Sittlichkeit* (ethos)

many accounts may be so atomized as often not even to perceive shared interests. Middle classes have instead typically been able to pursue their interests on a familial basis. The working class has had typically to pursue collective (not communal) action. In some sectors – for example mining – very strong *communal* sentiments have underlain a typically very great propensity for collective strike action and solidarity. But this is not typically solidarity for the class as a whole.

Communities are not about shared *properties*. Groups of individuals can share sets of properties or characteristics, but yet be completely atomized in regard to one another. On a recent bus tour I took of the San Francisco Bay Area, our (black) bus driver and tour guide narratively pointed us tourists to the neighbourhoods and shops of the 'Chinese community' and the watering holes of the 'homosexual community'. He then spoke to us about how all of this was understood in the 'heterosexual community'. San Francisco's heterosexuals, though they share the property of primarily or exclusively engaging in heterosexual relations, do not in our sense form a community. They might participate in a Bay

Area 'imagined community', or even imagine themselves, against a perceived homosexual menace, to constitute a community, but there are nowhere near enough shared meanings and practices to be a community. San Francisco's homosexual and Chinese denizens are a lot closer to these criteria of community. These are also in certain respects, we shall see, reflexive communities.

'Lifestyle enclaves', like niche markets, share properties but they are not communities. Lifestyle enclaves and niche markets are possible only when consumption is disembedded from the guidance of communal mores. As consumption is individualized from communal guidance it can: 1) remain individualized; 2) be regrouped (through the sign economies of the information and communication structures, through for example marketing and advertising) as niche markets and lifestyle communities; 3) become 'positional consumption' of never-ending oneupmanship of keeping ahead of the Joneses; 4) take the creative turn of the 'romantic imaginery', as disembedding from communal regulation makes possible the modern phenomenon of daydreams[86]; 5) disembedded from *Sitten*, be understood in characteristically modern fashion in regard to 'needs'; 6) set free, can find itself bonded with 'spectacle' and 'sign-value'; or 7) enter the instrumental rationality of 'calculating hedonism'.

Each of these forms of modern consumption (can consumption be conceived of in the absence of modernity?) is possible only in the absence of communal regulation. But a lifestyle enclave such as Berlin's Winterfeldplatz does begin to be a community as the same individuals meet in the same cafés on Sunday mornings, after being out all night on Saturday, and drink *Sekt* on the square. As these same people shop in the Flohmarkt and buy their pasta, fish and cheese from Winterfeldplatz market stalls on Wednesdays and Saturdays. When a certain style of dress, similar time-space trajectories, similar neologisms start systematically to repeat themselves. When it turns out that some Winterfeldplatz regulars have stalls in the market, others have opened up or work in small businesses in the area, a certain number have connection with the Berlin S&M scene, many with Schöneberg's very integrated gay scene, as others are active in the area's avant-garde rock scene. Thus Berking and Neckel can justifiably in their qualitative sociology of this Berlin district speak of Winterfeldplatz in terms of forms of post-traditional '*Vergemeinschaftungen*'.[87] *Vergemeinschaftungen* would need to be translated as 'communalization', but it means a lot more. And it would apply to certain 'taste communities' but not others. People who read the same newspaper or watch the same soap opera share only an imagined community. To be in a taste community, which takes on the facticity of community, entails shared meanings, practices and obligations. It entails the transgression of distinction between consumer and producer. Take, for example the Janes Addiction fans that follow the group's gigs around the UK and meet up again at performances on the European continent; who 'dress the dress', read and write letters to and sometimes edit the fan mags. This is a community – as is the core of the travelling support of Leeds, Manchester United or Arsenal.

'Reflexive community' can be instructively understood in regard to Pierre Bourdieu's notion of the 'field'. Here for Bourdieu in traditional society there are no fields, but there is community. In modernity however there is the differentiation of a number of 'delimited' (religious, political, legal, scientific, artistic, academic, sociological) fields from what then becomes the general, 'social field'. The social field, though it is divided into class fractions, is atomized, and the only sorts of community to be found there are imagined communities. 'Real' modern communities, which are also reflexive communities, are to be found in the delimited fields. In for example the sociological field, are found all our characteristics of community – the shared meanings and practices, the affective involvement with the 'tools' and product, the internalist generation of standards, telos, and ends, the felt obligations, the guidance by *Sitten*, the characteristic habitus of the field. Social actors in a field are as much producers of a cultural product as consumers. The same is true of the Manchester United supporters or the Janes Addiction core fans. That is, the cultural good produced in a given specialist field that we receive in the social field is produced as much by the supporters as by the players. The same would be true of the core membership of the ecological community, not of the pressure groups which are interest associations but of the social movement. The latter crucially define what sort of way ecology as a cultural product is received in the social field. These communities are reflexive in that: first, one is not born or 'thrown', but 'throws oneself' into them; second, they may be widely stretched over 'abstract' space, and also perhaps over time;[88] third, they consciously pose themselves the problem of their own creation, and constant re-invention far more than do traditional communities; fourth, their 'tools' and products tend to be not material ones but abstract and cultural.

There is of course another kind of reflexive community that cannot be assimilated into the Bourdieuan fields. This sort of community is defined by the fact that it cannot be assimilated, full stop.

What I am referring to is 'diasporic' communities, which are not reflexive in the sense that one does not choose to join them, but one is thrown into them. By 'diasporic', I am not referring to the American 'melting pot' of say Irish or Jewish 'communities'. That is, once 'melted', an ethnicity is no longer a community but just an ethnic interest group, raising money and espousing policy favourable to Israel or Sinn Fein. Diasporic communities are not melted but instead maintain what Salman Rushdie calls a collective 'being-in-the-world' which is grounded as, say, Muslim Indian. Yet they are reflexive in two senses. First in the sense that, as diasporic, theirs is a sort of 'mobile' being-in-the-world, which lends to it a certain mediation in regard to the 'original' ethnie in country of origin. Second, such community is reflexive because, like Simmel's 'stranger' and like Mannheim's *freischwebende Intellektuel*, the diasporic self is straight away aware of heterodoxy and aware of the possibility of a de-worlded position *au dessus*, as it were, *de la mêlée*. But unlike the stranger and Mannheim's intellectual, the diasporic self decides *not* to move into the position of subject as opposed to object, but to remain in his or her ethnie's being-in-the-world. The diasporic self of the ethnic minority community (and this would be the case for the 'diaspora-by-night' of the gay community) is thus a bit like the reflexive anthropologist, whose classificatory habits clash and mesh and to a certain extent inter-translate with those of the foreign (heterosexual) other.

Community, I have underscored throughout, is first and foremost a matter of shared meanings. The question then is: is reflexive community possible in our time-space distanciated societies, in which meaning is by definition emptied out? Perhaps the place to look for hints of an answer as to how meaning in modernity is possible, is to the aesthetic realm. The aesthetic dimension has found voice, through for example Simmel, who juxtaposed outer spheres of an increasingly meaningless social ('das Soziale'), and 'inner spheres' of a life-enhancing meaning-creating subject. And sociologists today have observed that this aesthetic-expressive meaning-creating subject, with origins in aesthetic modernism, has now become ubiquitous in all the social strata and in everyday life, in the expressive individualism of what Gerhard Schulze insightfully chronicles as the *Erlebnisgesellschaft*. Niklas Luhmann, in his *Love as Passion*, has taken this meaning-creating modern subject and transformed it into the transcendental expressive inter-subjectivity of the love relationship, characterized by intensified semantic interchange, whose very density constitutes itself as an 'autopoetic system' set off *vis-à-vis* the environment.[89] And indeed Luhmann's understanding has far greater truth content than the post-structuralist semiotic metaphysics of desire. That is, love and sexual relationships have very little to do with the 'free play of the signifier', and a lot more to do with the intensity of semantic interchange, that is of the interchange of meanings, of 'signifieds'. It is only when the relationship breaks down that we move into the subject–object mode, that we ask ourselves what has gone wrong – that we take the signifier as problematized, and wonder what she meant by that last faxed letter. It is only when things *really* have broken down that we bring in the 'expert-system', either as a set of legitimating arguments for our side of the dispute, or, worse, as professionals in the flesh. The very sad fact that we in modernity tend already, chronically, and preventively to use expert-systems tends in anticipation to create a semantic deficit in intimate relationships.

But even the emotional relationship of high-density semantics is hardly a community. Besides, this sort of relationship is overloaded with semantic affect and is inherently unstable. It is 'cocooned' from the wider community, and, worse, it can be just one more iteration of the solipsism of the contemporary expressive 'I', for whom both substantive and procedural goods have disappeared, and all that is left is the narcissistic self-grounding, not in the Cartesian 'I think therefore I am', but in Beck's 'I am I'. Bellah and his colleagues usefully juxtapose this intersubjective solipsism to classical friendship described by Aristotle, in which friendship rested in obligations not just between friends but to a wider community of practice, of shared activities with particular standards and ends.[90] And perhaps this is a clue to the question of meaning in contemporary reflexive communities. That is, we should not so much ask the question of the creation of meaning but look for the meaning that is already there. A number of German thinkers have contrasted two notions of 'experience', *Erlebnis*, which is subjective, and *Erfahrung*, which is more public and also connotes, for example, being 'experienced' in say a trade. The point is that perhaps we already live in what is not just an *Erlebnis-* but also an *Erfahrungsgesellschaft*. The point is that perhaps in various subcultures, in various practices that we reflexively commit ourselves to, the meaning is already there, already inscribed in the practices.

Where, however, does all this leave the 'self'? Is the self possible in the context of a genuine communitarianism? Some political philosophers like MacIntyre seem to lose the self, it seems, in a Thomist absorption in the communal practices. Others, like Charles Taylor, perhaps partly because his Hegelian conceptions operate through not a negative but a 'positive' dialectic, seem overly to assimilate the community to the self. It is not, on the other hand, at all satisfactory only to allude vaguely to a 'dialectic' of self and community or to speak of a theory of community that 'leaves space' for the self. What is needed is a notion of involvement in communal practices out of which the self grows. And perhaps a clue here is found in Seyla Benhabib's call not for an ethics based in transcendental subjectivity or intersubjectivity but instead for a situated ethics grounded in 'care'. What she is looking for is not a situationist ethics like earlier existentialist moralists such as Rollo May, nor a standpoint ethics, on the lines of some feminists' standpointist epistemologies, but a situated ethics, and ethics firmly situated in a *Sittlichkeit*, in a world.[91]

The notion of *care* is crucial in the present context. We know that in the very late Foucault's 'subjectivist turn', one of the two volumes he wrote on sexuality was entitled 'the care for the self'. Much more explicitly and systematically Heidegger, of course, establishes the closest of bonds between the phenomenon of care and the self. In fact for Heidegger the self is unthinkable outside of care. Division One of *Being and Time* thematizes the world, much in the sense of the above view of shared meanings and practices. Division Two, however, thematizes care and the self. But already in Division One Heidegger has implicitly introduced care. That is, first the relationship in-the-world between human beings (*Dasein*) and things is understood in terms of 'concern'. Now the German for care is *Sorge*; for the tools and things in Heidegger's 'workshop', 'concern' is *besorgen*, and the 'solicitude' for other human beings of being-in-the-world is *fürsorgen*.[92]

So at least implicitly care (*Sorge*) for the self in Heidegger arises out of the same logic as *besorgen* (concern) for things and *Fürsorge* (solicitude) for other human beings. Now *besorgen*-type care for the tools, the signs, the product and the referential whole of the workshop, that is, care for 'entities', is connected with the fact that entities reveal themselves for situated human beings. They reveal themselves in their unfolding, in their becoming. And 'care' entails that *Dasein* must have respect for that becoming; that it must matter to *Dasein*. The same can be said for the development of other human beings in *Fürsorge*. *Sorge*, the third type of Heideggerian care, is the one closest to Foucault's care for the self. Here care no longer relates to beings absorbed in, and as absorption in, the meanings and practices of the world, but to the radical thrownness of *Dasein* into the uncanniness, into the isolation of *Dasein*'s 'being-towards-death'. A radically individuated, Kierkegaardian temporality emerges in the structure of care for the self. But for Heidegger *Sorge* and the authentic self bound up with this uncanny and radical individuation must first be involved with and care for things and other human beings in everyday communal practices.[93]

To develop this line of thought further is beyond the scope of the theoretical sociology of reflexivity which is the theme of this book. What I wanted to point to was just one possibility of developing a notion of the self consistent with involvement in the 'we'. Let me append finally a coda with a very few self-reflections on my own method in this book. The thrust of my argument has been in support of hermeneutic reflexivity and community, against the individual-ization theses of both aesthetic and especially cognitive reflexivity. This can be accounted for, first with a justification and then with an explanation. By way of justification let me say that in fact I think that there are three very important sources of the contemporary self, which are analytically separable as cognitive, aesthetic and hermeneutic-communitarian 'moments'. And that these exist in us in an often contradictory and irreconcilable way. I don't imagine that this can be remedied a great deal, and am not certain that it should be. The majority of us will most probably have to live with these contradictions. My concentration on the hermeneutic or communitarian dimension has been largely because – in our present age of cognitive-utilitarian and aesthetic-expressive individualism – it is the one I feel is most in need of some sort of operation of retrieval.

The good news about the sort of hermeneutics of retrieval I am advocating is that it does give substantial purchase on the phenom-enon of community. The bad news is that it has typically done so – in Heidegger, in philosophical communitarians like MacIntyre and Taylor, in sociological communitarians like Bellah and Daniel Bell, in the sociological hermeneutics of the ethnomethodologists – through assuming away power, through the unjustified and by implication politically conservative presumption of consensus. What seems to be needed is a radical hermeneutics. Yet I do not believe that contemporary critical hermeneutics or critical socio-linguistics has been of sufficient help in this context. The tendency of both is to think in terms of subject–object notions of truth, and to interpret discourse and practice in terms of underlying ideological structures. The tendency is to speak of practices which are not at the same time *Sitten* or routine background activities but which instead are, in some substantial sense, rule-bound. In this sense critical hermeneutics is a hermeneutics not of retrieval but of suspicion.

Maybe the place to turn again is to Bourdieu, who, as we showed at length above, gives us a hermeneutics of retrieval at whose core is not consensus but power. That is, Bourdieu's 'fields' are peopled not by the structures, agents, discourses, ideologies, subjects and objects of the hermeneutics of suspicion but instead by habits, unconscious and bodily practices and categories of the unthought. Yet power is there in the Bourdieuan framework of classes and class fractions which are struggling for hegemony. But what is struggled over is vastly different than in the hermeneutics of suspicion. What is struggled over is not ideas as discursively redeemable validity claims. It is instead the background assumptions (taste categories, the most immediate classificatory categories) which are the ground for such rational speech acts. What is struggled over is not ideology, which itself is rule-bound and normatively structured and discursively articulated: it is instead the habits, the *Sitten*, which are the ontological foundations of ideology. Ideology is comprised of *judgements*, though of false judgements, to which critical hermeneutics counterposes the valid or true judgements. The perhaps not critical but *radical* hermeneutics of retrieval will instead look at the grounding of ideology itself in a set of *pre*-judgements, in a set of *Sitten* which also offer access to truth. Who is doing the struggling in Bourdieu's view is not class (or class-fraction) conceived as a collective actor, with its attached assumptions of consciousness and the abstract unit act. It is class as a collective habitus, as a set of routine activities, as a *form of life*. It is not class as an organized actor with conscious goals. Instead of a logic of consciousness it is a 'logic of practice', and it takes place not through institutional organization but through the force of shared meanings and habits. At issue is finally not a question of the 'structures' being present in the practices, and that is because these shared meanings and *Sitten* are not structures at all.

The classes-in-struggle in reflexive modernity are, as I suggested above, determined by their place in not the mode of production but the 'mode of information'. And this sort of structural location also partly explains the nature of this book. That is, Bourdieu's 'social field' is becoming increasingly the same thing as this informational and communicational field. And the sociologist, previously marginalized and 'above' the social like Mannheim's free-floating intellectual, is now smack dab in the middle of the new

Kulturgesellschaft.[94] As the middle class grows, as the proportion of the population grows who work inside the information and communication-structures, so at the same time does the scope of the expert-systems grow. That is, Bourdieu's specialist fields or Giddens's expert-systems now no longer either dominate or liberate the masses. Instead they *are* the masses. In the UK and USA probably some 25 per cent of the work-force is active in expert-systems. The sociologist, previously the objective student of the masses, finds himself or herself in just another expert-system alongside, and in the same world as, the masses now peopling the other expert-systems.

This location, no longer at the margins but at the heart of an increasingly cultural society, at the heart of the *Kulturgesellschaft*, means not just that the sociologist is in largely the same world as his or her respondents. It also means there is a growing displacement of the object of the human sciences from the social to the cultural. This is registered in the recent explosion of cultural studies (in the broadest sense of the term), in student numbers, Ph.D.s, books, journals and magazines. Just as the nineteenth-century separation of the social from the polity heralded the turn-of-the-twentieth-century birth of sociology in the advanced countries, so does the later twentieth-century growing superimposition of the information and communication (I&C) structures, which are *cultural* structures, on the social herald the turn-of-the-twenty-first-century birth and pervasion of cultural studies. This is reflected for example in the transformation of structuralism, which from Marx via Durkheim through Parsons essentially was a question of *social* structuralism; whilst from the 1960s in, for example, Lévi-Strauss, Barthes, Lacan and Foucault, it became a linguistic or *cultural* structuralism. Giddens's and Beck's theories of reflexive modernization also point to and reflect this same sort of decline of social structures. Only they don't sufficiently take into account the newer importance of cultural structures.

There are two ways that we can understand the 'implosion' of the social field into, on the one hand, the I&C structures and, on the other, into the mass expert-systems of the mass specialist fields. Either we can presume that now everybody is even further individualized, further atomized, as at one time the isolated (expert) sociological observer was. Or we can see chances open up for new forms of the 'we' – grounded in the expert-systems, founded on the I&C structures – which are vastly different from traditional communities. In turn these new cultural communities offer possibilities of even more intensified reflexivity. That is, these new communities are hardly 'irrationalist'. They entail a reflexivity that is much more enhanced than that merely on social structures. They entail a reflexivity and understanding of the unthought categories, of the far less accessible *Sitten*, of the shared meanings that are the basis of community. They involve in short a hermeneutic reflexivity. And this hermeneutic reflection is not solely a matter of 'choice'. It is partly something to which we are fated by the increased hegemony of the cultural structures.

But new community involves not just heightened reflexivity but at the same time its opposite in the substantial intensification of contingency. The very 'groundless ground' of reflexive community has been captured by two important cultural theorists in very different contexts through the poet William Carlos Williams's phrase 'pure products of America gone crazy'. The first of these was the reflexive anthropologist James Clifford. The second was popular culture commentator Greil Marcus in his *Dead Elvis*.[95] Now Elvis Presley was a 'pure product of America' (the ground) to be sure. And he was a pure product 'gone crazy' (the groundless). *Dead Elvis*, or Elvis dead, represents even more poignantly this contradiction, of a groundless ground, of a being-in-the-world which is simultaneously radically contingent. Of being-in-the-world as *fortuna*. But how different from this is the sociologist, the cultural analyst, now grounded in the world, now grounded in reflexive communities inside the expert-systems, inside the information and communication structures, which themselves are cast adrift? Are we too not the groundless ground, the groundless community? Too often we, inside the expert-systems, 'we' constituting informed public opinion, will look askew at the 'neo-tribalism' of say, the anomic eastern German new Nazis of the terraces. Perhaps we would do better to redirect our gaze on a much less marginal phenomenon. Perhaps we would do better to redirect our gaze somewhat closer to home. Perhaps we could come to gain the courage to pose the radically important and radically difficult questions: that is to ask ourselves if it is perhaps not also we who are the neo-tribes.

NOTES

This contribution owes special debt to a number of discussions at crucial points during its conception – to discussions with Alistair Black, Dede Boden, Mick Dillon, Celia Lury, Shane O'Neill, Hermann Schwengel, Nick Smith and the participants in my M.A. and Ph.D. seminars in the Sociology

Department at Lancaster University. I am particularly indebted to Diane Faichney and Karen Gammon who, in the context of a crisis of computers, heroically typed and organized the manuscript, while at the same time doing a lot of the running of Lancaster's large and unwieldy Graduate Studies programme.

1   A. Touraine, *L'après-socialisme*, Paris: Grasset, 1980.
2   B. Anderson, *Imagined Communities*, London: Verso, second edition, 1991, pp. 32–3.
3   M. Landmann, 'Georg Simmel und Stefan George', in H. J. Dahme and O. Rammstedt (eds), *Georg Simmel und die Moderne*, Frankfurt: Suhrkamp, 1984, pp. 147–52.
4   U. Beck and E. Beck-Gernsheim, *Das ganz normale Chaos der Liebe*, Frankfurt: Suhrkamp, 1990, pp. 11–12; A. Giddens, *Modernity and Self-Identity*, Cambridge: Polity, 1991, pp. 7–8.
5   U. Beck and W. Bonss, 'Verwissenschaftlichung ohne Aufklärung?', in U. Beck and W. Bonss (eds), *Weder Sozialtechnologie noch Aufklärung?*, Frankfurt: Suhrkamp, 1989, pp. 7–45 (p. 19).
6   S. Lash, 'Reflexive modernization: the aesthetic dimension', *Theory, Culture and Society*, vol. 10, no. 1, 1993, pp. 1–24.
7   A. Giddens, *The Consequences of Modernity*, Cambridge: Polity, 1990, pp. 112–13, 131–2.
8   R. D. Laing, *The Divided Self*, London: Tavistock, 1960.
9   H. L. Dreyfus, *Being-in-the-World*, Cambridge, Mass.: The MIT Press, 1991, pp. 228–30.
10 Giddens, *The Consequences of Modernity*, pp. 83–4.
11 S. Lash and J. Urry, *Economies of Signs and Space*, London: Sage, 1993, chapter 6.
12 M. Poster, *The Mode of Information*, Cambridge: Polity, 1990.
13 K. Koike, *Understanding Industrial Relations in Modern Japan*, London: Macmillan, 1988, pp. 182–8; M. Aoki, *Information, Incentives and Bargaining in the Japanese Economy*, Cambridge: Cambridge University Press, 1988, pp. 7–13.
14 R. Dore, *Taking Japan Seriously*, London: Athlone, 1987, pp. 173–91.
15 M. Sako, 'Neither markets nor hierarchies: a comparative study of the printed circuit board industry in Britain and Japan', paper, Comparing Capitalist Economies: the Governance of Economic Sectors, Colloquium, Madison, Wisc. May 1988.
16 M. Aoki, 'The participatory generation of information rents and the theory of the firm', in M. Aoki, B. Gustaffson and O. Williamson (eds), *The Firm as a Nexus of Treaties*, London: Sage, 1990, pp. 26–52 (pp. 28–9).
17 J. Hoffmann, 'Innovationsforderung in Berlin und Baden-Württemberg – zum regionalen Eigenleben technologie-politischer Konzepte', in U. Jürgens and W. Krumbein (eds), *Industriepolitische Strategien*, Berlin: Sigma, 1991, pp. 64–97 (pp. 75–6).

18 W. Bernschneider, G. Schindler and J. Schüller, 'Industriepolitik in Baden-Württemberg und Bayern', in ibid., pp. 57–73.

19 B. Lutz and P. Veltz, 'Maschinenbauer versus Informatiker – gesellschaftliche Einflüsse auf die fertigungstechnische Entwicklung: Deutschland und Frankreich', in K. Duell and B. Lutz (eds), *Technikentwicklung und Arbeitsteilung im internationaler Vergleich*, Frankfurt: Campus, 1989, pp. 215–72 (p. 261).

20 W. Streeck, 'Organizational consequences on neo-corporatist cooperation in West German labour unions', in G. Lehmbruch and P. Schmitter (eds), *Patterns of Corporatist Policy-Making*, London: Sage, 1982, pp. 29–82.

21 W. Streeck, J. Hilbert, K. van Kevelaer, F. Maier and H. Weber, *Steuerung und Regulierung der beruflichen Bildung*, Berlin; Stigma, 1987.

22 Lutz and Veltz, 'Maschinenbauer versus Informatiker', pp. 226–8.

23 B. Casey, 'Recent developments in the German apprenticeship system', *British Journal of Industrial Relations*, vol. 29, 1991, pp. 205–22.

24 R. Bellah, R. Madsen, W. Sullivan, A. Swidler and S. Tipton, *Habits of the Heart*, Berkeley: University of California Press, 1985, p. 48.

25 A. MacIntyre, *Whose Justice? Which Rationality?*, London: Duckworth, 1988, pp. 124–30; Charles Taylor, 'The diversity of goods', in his *Philosophy and the Human Sciences*, Philosophical Papers, 2, Cambridge: Cambridge University Press, 1985, pp. 230–47.

26 M. de Jong, K. Machielse and P. de Ruitjer, 'Producer services and flexible networks in the Netherlands', in H. Ernste and V. Meier (eds), *Regional Developments and Contemporary Industrial Response*, London: Belhaven, 1992, pp. 147–62; S. Sassen, *The Global City*, Princeton: Princeton University Press, 1991.

27 R. Walker, 'Is there a service economy? The changing capitalist division of labor', *Science and Society*, vol. 49, 1985, pp. 42–83.

28 T. Malsch, 'Arbeit und Kommunikation im informatisierten Produktionsprozess', International Institute of Comparative Social Research/Labour Policy. Berlin: Wissenschaftszentrum, 1987.

29 W. J. Wilson, *The Truly Disadvantaged*, Chicago: University of Chicago Press, 1987.

30 M. A. Hughes, 'Formation of the impacted ghetto: evidence from large metropolitan areas 1970–1980', *Urban Geography*, vol. 11, 1990, pp. 265–84.

31 P. Bourgois, 'In search of respect: the new service economy and the crack alternative in Spanish Harlem', Working Conference on Poverty, Immigration and Urban Marginality, Maison Sugar, Paris, 10–11 May 1991.

32 H. Ganssmann, 'Ein Versuch über Arbeit', unpublished paper, Freie Universität Berlin, Institut für Soziologie, 1990.

33 T. Luke, 'New world order or neo-world orders: power, politics and ideology in the informationalizing global order', Theory, Culture and

Society, 10th Anniversary Conference, Champion, Pennsylvania, 16–19 August 1992.

34   G. Esping-Andersen, *The Three Worlds of Welfare Capitalism*, Cambridge: Polity, 1990.

35   Luke, 'New world order'.

36   F. Jameson, *Late Marxism: Adorno, or the Persistence of the Dialectic*, London: Verso, 1990.

37   G. Schulze, *Die Erlebnisgesellschaft: Kultursoziologie der Gegenwart*, Frankfurt: Campus, 1992.

38   F. Nietzsche, 'Über Wahrheit und Lüge im aussermoralischen Sinne', in Nachgelassene Schriften, 1870–3, *Nietzsche Werke*, III, 2, Berlin: de Gruyter: 1973, pp. 367–84. I am indebted to Alistair Black on this point.

39   P. Bürger, 'Das Vermittlungsproblem in der Kunstsoziologie Adornos', in B. Lindner and W. M. Lüdke (eds), *Materialien zur ästhetischen Theorie: Theodor W. Adornos Konstruktion der Moderne*, Frankfurt: Suhrkamp, 1980, pp. 169–85, p. 177.

40   G. W. F. Hegel, *Philosophy of Mind*, Oxford: Clarendon, 1971, p. 293.

41   D. Kliche, 'Kunst gegen Verdinglichung: Berührungspunkte im Gegensatz von Adorno und Lukács', in Lindner and Lüdke (eds), *Materialien zur ästhetischen Theorie*, pp. 219–60.

42   B. Lindner and W. M. Lüdke, 'Kritische Theorie und aesthetisches Interesse', in Lindner and Lüdke (eds), *Materialien zur ästhetischen Theorie*, pp. 11–39.

43   K. Eder and A. Kluge, *Ulmer Dramaturgien: Reibungsverluste*, Munich: Hanser, 1981.

44   Jameson, *Late Marxism*, pp. 145–6.

45   S. Lash, 'Discourse or figure?: Postmodernism as a regime of signification', in Lash, *Sociology of Postmodernism*, London, Routledge, 1990; C. Lury, *Cultural Rights*, London: Routledge, 1993. I am indebted to discussions with Celia Lury on these points.

46   U. Eco, *A Theory of Semiotics*, Bloomington, Ind.: Indiana University Press, 1976.

47   U. Sonnemann, 'Geschichte gegen den Strich Gebürstet', in P. Bulthaup (ed.), *Materialien zu Benjamins Thesen 'Über den Begriff der Geschichte'*, Frankfurt: Suhrkamp, 1975, pp. 231–53.

48   M. Hansen, 'Mass culture as hieroglyphic writing: Adorno, Derrida, Kracauer', *New German Critique*, no. 56, 1992, pp. 43–75.

49   I am indebted to Mick Dillon for discussions of Machiavelli and *fortuna*.

50   See in general the articles collected in Beck and Bonss (eds), *Weder Sozialtechnologie nach Aufklärung*.

51   M. Featherstone, *Consumer Culture and Postmodernism*, London: Sage, 1991, chapter 6.

52   D. Willer and J. Willer, *Systematic Empiricism*, Englewood Cliffs: Prentice-Hall, 1973.

53   Z. Bauman, *Modernity and Ambivalence*, Cambridge: Polity, 1991.

54 P. Lawrence, *Georg Simmel*, Sunbury-on-Thames: Nelson, 1976, p. 21.
55 Z. Bauman, *Modernity and the Holocaust*, Cambridge: Polity, 1989.
56 Jürgen Habermas, *The Philosophical Discourse of Modernity*, Cambridge: Polity, 1987, pp. 181–3.
57 Cited in E. Cassirer, *Kant's Life and Thought*, New Haven, Conn.: Yale University Press, 1981, p. 275.
58 Ibid., pp. 280–8.
59 Bauman, *Modernity and Ambivalence*, p. 192.
60 R. Rorty, 'Cosmopolitanism without emancipation: a response to Lystand', in S. Lash and J. Friedman (eds), *Modernity and Identity*, Oxford: Blackwell, 1992, pp. 59–72.
61 A. Smith, *The Ethnic Origins of Nations*, Oxford: Blackwell, 1986.
62 H. Cixous, 'The laugh of the medusa', in S. Lash (ed.), *Post-Structuralist and Post-Modernist Sociology*, Aldershot: Edward Elgar, 1991, pp. 268–87.
63 J. B. Thompson, *Critical Hermeneutics*, Cambridge: Cambridge University Press, 1981; J. Milbank, *Theology and Social Theory*, Oxford: Blackwell, 1990.
64 J. Fiske and J. Hartley, *Reading Television*, London: Methuen, 1978.
65 D. Hebdige, *Subculture: the Meaning of Style*, London, Methuen, 1979.
66 S. Hall and T. Jefferson (eds), *Resistance through Rituals*, London: Hutchinson, 1976.
67 M. Heidegger, *Sein und Zeit*, sechzehnte Auflage, Tübingen: Max Niemeyer Verlag, 1986, pp. 76–82.
68 P. Dews, *Logics of Disintegration*, London: Verso, 1987.
69 Heidegger, *Sein und Zeit*, p. 68.
70 Dreyfus, *Being-in-the-World*, pp. 141–9.
71 J. Habermas, *The Theory of Communicative Action*, vol. 1, London: Heinemann, 1984, pp. 189–90.
72 M. Stubbs, *Discourse Analysis*, Oxford: Blackwell, 1983.
73 Heidegger, *Sein und Zeit*, pp. 73–4.
74 C. Taylor, *Sources of the Self*, Cambridge: Cambridge University Press, 1989; C. Taylor, *Hegel*, Cambridge: Cambridge University Press, 1975.
75 S. Lash, 'Pierre Bourdieu: cultural economy and social change', in C. Calhoun, E. LiPuma and M. Postone (eds), *Bourdieu: Critical Perspectives*, Cambridge: Polity, 1993, pp. 193–211.
76 P. Bourdieu, *Distinction*, London: Routledge, 1984, pp. 472–3.
77 P. Bourdieu, *An Invitation to Reflexive Sociology*, Cambridge: Polity, 1992.
78 Bourdieu, *Distinction*, pp. 170–2.
79 See the excerpt reprinted in S. Lash (ed.), *Post-Structuralist and Post-Modernist Sociology*, pp. 3–34.
80 Lash, 'Reflexive modernization: the aesthetic dimension', p. 9.
81 Bourdieu, *Distinction*, p. 466.
82 P. Bourdieu, *Outline of a Theory of Practice*, London: Routledge, 1977, pp. 29–30.

83 See, e.g., J. Clifford, *The Predicament of Culture*, Cambridge, Mass.: Harvard University Press, 1988.

84 H. Dreyfus and P. Rabinow, 'Can there be a science of existential structure and social meaning?', in C. Calhoun et al. (eds), *Bourdieu: Critical Perspectives*, pp. 35–44.

85 See the critique of realism in *Sein und Zeit*, pp. 200–10.

86 C. Campbell, *The Romantic Ethic and the Spirit of Modern Consumerism*, Oxford: Blackwell, 1987.

87 H. Berking and S. Neckel, 'Die Politik der Lebensstil in einem Berliner Bezirk: zu einegen Formen nachtraditioneller Vergemeinschaftungen', *Soziale Welt*, Sonderband 7, 1990, pp. 481–500.

88 Anderson, *Imagined Communities*, pp. 170–8.

89 N. Luhmann, *Love as Passion*, Oxford: Polity, 1986.

90 Bellah et al., *Habits of the Heart*, p. 115.

91 S. Benhabib, *Situating the Self*, Cambridge: Polity, 1992.

92 Heidegger, *Sein und Zeit*, pp. 106, 121.

93 See *Sein und Zeit*, Division II, Part 1.

94 H. Schwengel, 'British enterprise culture and German *Kulturgesellschaft*', in R. Keat and N. Abercrombie (eds), *Enterprise Culture*, London: Routledge, 1990, pp. 136–50.

95 Clifford, *Predicament of Culture*, pp. 3–6; G. Marcus, *Dead Elvis*, London, Penguin, 1991.

4   Replies and Critiques

Self-Dissolution and Self-Endangerment of Industrial Society: What Does This Mean?

Ulrich Beck

An elementary thesis of reflexive modernization states this: the more societies are modernized, the more agents (subjects) acquire the ability to reflect on the social conditions of their existence and to change them in that way. That thesis is varied in this book and thought through in its consequences for the theories of social change in the areas of culture and tradition (Giddens), aestheticization and the economy (Lash), and politics and sub-politics (Beck). In this way, the controversy between modernists and postmodernists is overcome in a third way: reflexive modernization.

What that concept means, however, is certainly also controversial, even among the authors of this book. These differences and contrasts can be worked out as answers to four questions:

First, who is the *subject* of reflexive modernization? The answers here vary: individual and collective agents are the primary subject of reflexive modernization or scientists and ordinary people, institutions and organizations, all the way to structures.

Second, what is the *medium* of reflexive modernization? The answer appears obvious: knowledge in its various forms – scientific knowledge, expert knowledge, everyday knowledge. In fact, however, quite the opposite is asserted (by me): non-knowledge, inherent dynamism, the unseen and the unwilled.

Third, what are the *consequences* of reflexive modernization? This seems less disputed. Giddens focuses on 'disembedding' and 're-embedding', Beck on individualization, while Lash concentrates on aestheticization and community formations, but this of course also includes reactions in the spectrum from esotericism, religious movements, new social movements or neo-nationalism, all the way to the invention of the political after the end of the East–West conflict.

A fourth question as well – what is considered the *motor* of reflexive modernization? – is answered by us authors without controversy (if I see things properly): not a new modernization, but the known one in the model of Western (capitalist, democratic) industrial society, which – as Giddens shows in his book *The Consequences of Modernity* – is becoming global or, simply, reflexive.

For the question of the agents (subjects), the accents are placed differently in the various theory sketches. In emphasizing the aesthetic dimension, Lash appears to have his eye more on individual (and social) agents, while Giddens deals additionally and centrally with the role of 'expert systems' and 'institutional reflexivity'. For me, in turn, structures also play a central part, in the sense that structures change structures, by which action is made possible, indeed compelled.

What this means will perhaps become clearer with the strongly contrasting answers to the second question. Unlike Giddens and in contrast to Lash, I assert the thesis, at first glance paradoxical enough, that it is not knowledge but rather non-knowledge which is the medium of 'reflexive' modernization. To put it another way: we are living in the *age of side effects*, and precisely this is what is to be decoded – and shaped – methodologically and theoretically, in everyday life or in politics. I must therefore again take up and deepen a distinction which I have already mentioned and explained above.

The distinction between reflection (knowledge) and reflexivity (self-dissolution)

There is a beautiful image for the intellectual metaphor of reflection, which has been so central ever since the Enlightenment: seeing with an added eye (Johann Gottlieb Fichte). It is definitely in accordance with this when Alvin Gouldner speaks of 'reflexive sociology' and Jürgen Habermas of the 'communicative society'. In talk of the 'self-referentiality of the systems' (Luhmann), on the other hand, the different aspect of the relationship to the self occupies the centre of attention. On this contrast between consciousness and nonconsciousness, Bourdieu occupies a mediating position. He conceives of reflexivity as systematic reflection on the unconscious presuppositions (categories) of our knowledge.

Giddens also shows how the reflexivity and circularity of social knowledge can unpredictably change the conditions of action. Scott Lash distinguishes between cognitive, moral and aesthetic reflection.[1] To that he connects the objection to Giddens and myself that we base our argumentation on a cognitively foreshortened understanding of reflection. This is accurate in one respect, simply because so far only Lash has worked out the indubitably important aesthetic dimension of reflexive modernization. At the same time, however, this objection misses the central distinction between reflection (knowledge) and reflexivity (unintentional self-dissolution or self-endangerment) which is the basis of my argument. Putting it another way, it is precisely the distinction between cognitive, moral and aesthetic dimensions of reflexive modernization which makes it clear that Lash speaks exclusively of (more or less conscious) reflection, and misunderstands the problematic of unconscious, unintended reflexivity in the sense of self-application, self-dissolution and the self-endangerment of industrial modernization.

In pointed terms, the 'reflexivity' of modernity and modernization in my sense does not mean reflection on modernity, self-relatedness, the self-referentiality of modernity, nor does it mean the self-justification or self-criticism of modernity in the sense of classical sociology; rather (first of all), modernization *undercuts* modernization, unintended and unseen, and therefore also reflection-free, with the force of autonomized modernization.

The classical premise of the reflection theory of modernity can be simplified down to the initially stated thesis: the more societies are modernized, the more agents (subjects) acquire the ability to reflect on the social conditions of their existence and to change them in that way. In contrast to that, the fundamental thesis of the reflexivity theory of modernity, crudely simplified, runs like this: the further the modernization of modern societies proceeds, the more the foundations of industrial society are dissolved, consumed, changed and threatened. The contrast lies in the fact that this can quite well take place without reflection, beyond knowledge and consciousness.

Viewed in the cold light of day, aren't those completely different theories? What do they have in common? My first answer at least is one main consequence. Both argue that in reflexive modernity, individuals have become ever more free of structure; in fact they have to redefine structure (or, as Giddens puts it, tradition) or, even more radical, reinvent society and politics.

My second answer is that the theory of reflexivity (under certain conditions) includes the reflection theory of modernization – but not vice versa. Reflexive modernization in the sense of cognitive theory ignores (if I interpret it correctly) the possibility that the transition into another epoch of modernity could take place unintended, unseen and bypassing the dominant categories and theories of industrial society (including its social science controversies).

An additional difference is connected to this. The cognitive theory of reflexive modernization is optimistic at its core – more reflection, more experts, more science, more public sphere, more self-awareness and self-criticism will open up new and better possibilities for action in a world that has got out of joint. This optimism is not shared by the theory of the reflexivity of modernity; neither does it share the pessimism of the opposite position, for instance, Adorno and Horkheimer's *Dialectics of Enlightenment*. The theory suggested by me is neutral and more complex with respect to this; it takes up and takes on the 'ambivalence of modernity' (Bauman). Its argument runs: reflexivity of modernity can lead to reflection on the self-dissolution and self-endangerment of industrial society, but it need not do so. Even opposite extremes (and intermediate or hybrid forms) are conceivable – and real – in Europe after the cold war: the banality of violence, esotericism, neo-nationalism, wars.

Of course it would be false to equate this – crude – contrast between reflection and reflexivity with the differences between Giddens, Lash and myself. All three authors deal with both aspects. Yet important controversial points and differences do seem localizable here to me. This is true, first, on the axis of the consciousness/non-consciousness (or the autodynamism) of 'reflexive' modernization, and, second (and very closely connected to it), on the axis of rupture versus continuity *within* modernity. Both points of view lead into this question: how radically does the respective author assert that modernity in the plan of industrial society abolishes the foundations of industrial society and its institutions?

The paradigm according to which I answer this question is the ecological crisis. As we know, the latter is produced by abstracting from the question, that is, by unchecked economic growth. If one aims only at growth and screens out ecological questions and consequences, then that intensifies the ecological crisis (not necessarily in people's consciousness or in the public sphere).

But here another difference immediately stands out. In contrast to the ecology debate, the talk of the reflexivity of modernity does not aim at self-destruction, but rather the self-alteration of the foundations of industrial modernization. Whether the world will perish is not only completely open but also completely uninteresting sociologically. For a sociology of industrial progress, only the threatening downfall is the topic, but a great one that has so far scarcely been opened up.

Thus, this is not a theory of crisis or class, not a theory of decline, but rather a theory of the unintended, latent disembedding and re-embedding of industrial society due to the success of Western modernization.

In methodological terms, this means the self-application of modernization to (industrial) modernity. As a diagnosis of the times this means that the reflexivity of modernity produces not only cultural crises of orientation, as the communitarians allege, but, centrally and more extensively, deep-seated institutional crises in late industrial society. Key institutions (such as political parties and labour unions, but also causal principles of accountability in science and law, national borders, the ethic of individual responsibility, the order of the nuclear family, and so forth) all lose their foundations and their historical legitimacy. Reflexivity of modernity is tantamount then to the prognosis of difficult-to-resolve value conflicts on the foundations of the future.

Here lie antitheses to the classical – or in my terms, simple – sociology of modernity and modernization, on the one hand, but also to the conceptions of Giddens and Lash in this book on the other.

Self-endangerment of modernity – what does that mean?

Now, of course, this argument of self-endangerment is neither as original nor as unambiguous as it pretends to be. It is certainly already found in classical sociology. First of all, Ferdinand Tönnies, for instance, but in the present Jürgen Habermas, Daniel Bell and, with renewed vehemence, the 'communitarians' assert and elaborate the thesis of the *loss of community* (often with the nostalgic accent characteristic of cultural pessimism).

Second, it was asserted early and extensively that differentiation may (under certain conditions) produce *dis*integration and in consequence anomie, violence and suicide (the leading role here is played by the early studies of Durkheim).

Characteristically, however, both self-endangerment arguments are presented in limited fashion in classical sociology. The secondary problems, so the argument goes, do not impact on the institutions, organizations and subsystems; they do not threaten the latters' claims to monitor and regulate, nor the self-referentiality and autonomy of the subsystems.

This is based, on the one hand, on the two-world theory of individual and system, organization and private life-world, which are conceived as essentially autonomous of one another. On the other hand, the diagnosis of disintegration and loss of community in classical sociology is grounded 'ecologically', as it were. The starting point is the assumption that modern societies use up 'resources' – culture and nature – on which they depend without being able to see to their preservation or renewal. But these types of self-endangerment – here is where the optimistic faith in progress resides – can be foisted off on the environment. Optimization within one sphere of action triggers difficult-to-handle secondary problems in other spheres of action, but not in the system itself.[2]

Now this preordained harmony of control is of course the fairy tale, the innocent faith, of the sociology of simple modernization. More or less all three authors of this book break with that, if I see things correctly. But how this happens, and what consequences for the sociological theory of modernity are drawn from it, point to quite different accentuations and antitheses.

In a first variant interpretation, self-endangerment is replaced by self-modification. The diagnosis is not decline but rather a change of scene or, more precisely, a play of two interacting realities. The old and familiar reality of the distributional struggle over desired 'goods' now competes with the new reality of the risk society. The latter reality is essentially a definitional struggle over the new 'bads', yet this newly discovered reality interacts with the old conflict in confusing and contradictory ways. This is the present drama of the risk conflict.

In the alternation between news of pollution and unemployment, one can study today how these two scenarios replace and subvert one another, how the parts are 'played' simultaneously and in opposition in the institutions that were apparently designed and equipped only for the old position struggles. Here it is as if there was a performance of a mixture of Marx and Macbeth, or of the collective bargaining talks in the public sector and Goethe's 'Sorcerer's Apprentice'.

Second, a variation of the same thing can be observed and illustrated in the erosion of male and female roles. At first sight the argument sounds familiar: equality of women in the labour market is abolishing the familial foundation of industrial society. But that only means that the basis of the division of labour and its certitude is crumbling. Here the 'classical' roles of men and women mix and subvert one another. That should not be equated with destruction (as in the ecological crisis) but not with the displaced scenarios of the wealth–risk conflict either. Instead it means loss of certainties, insecurity, deciding, negotiation, and thus communication and reflection as well.

Now the hard core of the reflexivity argument begins. This theory contradicts the wide-eyed attitude of simple modernization, its instrumental optimism regarding the predetermined controllability of uncontrollable things. A whole chain of arguments can be forged from this.

First – and rather sweepingly – the globalization of 'side effects' in the nuclear state and in the creeping ecological catastrophes (the ozone hole, climatic changes, and so on). As Günther Anders, Hans Jonas, Karl Jaspers, Hannah Arendt, Robert Jungk and many others have impressively shown, the possibility of intended and unintended collective suicide is in fact a historical novelty which blows apart all moral, political and social concepts – even that of 'side effect'. But this destructive power of modern mega-technologies which were discovered and developed only in the second half of this century, since it encompasses even as yet unborn generations, makes talk of 'externalizability' a joke, a syndrome of the prevailing 'apocalypse-blindness' (Günther Anders).

Second, the assumption of externalizability in classical sociology has been called into question by a variety of cumulative and boomerang effects. 'Side effects' devalue capital, cause markets to collapse, confuse agendas and split apart staffs, management, trade unions, parties, occupational groups and families. This applies even to costs in the narrower sense, in view of legal reforms that redistribute burdens of proof or the constraints of insurance protection and the like. The question of how the constructions of externalizability disintegrate can certainly remain open for now.

Third, the individuals carry the 'secondary problems' back into the plants and organizations in their consciousness. To the extent that the ecological issue has become established and taken for granted in a society, even the inner circles and centres of the modernization agents in business, politics and science can no longer shield themselves against it. If one starts with the view that 'organizations' are essentially the achievements and products of interpretations by individuals in social interactions, then it becomes clear that only a metaphysics of the system can protect the differentiated subsystems against the reflexive action of the self-endangerments they provoke. Externalizability is therefore a faith, perhaps *the* faith, of the sociology of simple modernization and it disintegrates and becomes absurd along with the growth of the side effects and their perception.

Fourth, this argument broadens, and applies also in the case of the equating of modernization with scientization or, as Giddens says, the dominance of the 'expert-systems'. The sociology of simple modernization combines two types of optimism: linear scientization and faith in the anticipatory controllability of side effects – whether these be 'externalized' or worked out by surges of 'more intelligent' automation and transformed into economic booms. Precisely this double optimism of control is what is contradicted by historical experience and, along with it, the theory of reflexive modernization (in my sense).

For one thing, one type of scientization undermines the next. There is growth – of obligations to justify things *and* of uncertainty. The latter conditions the former. The immanent pluralization of risks also calls the rationality of risk calculations into question. For another thing, society is changed not just by what is seen and intended but also by what is unseen and unintended. The side effect, not instrumental rationality, is becoming the motor of social history.

In conclusion, this argument can be clarified once again in an analysis of an objection that Scott Lash has formulated against my concept of 'reflexive modernization'. Risks, he agrees with me, are an attempt to make the incalculable calculable. Events that have not yet occurred become calculable (at least economically) through the insurance principle. Since the dialectic of risk and insurance is developed and spread in the phase of classical industrial society, that is to say, simple modernity, and the anticipation of consequences is without a doubt a result of highly developed institutional reflection, then in his argument the differentiation criteria between simple and reflexive modernity do not apply.[3]

That objection, however, is based upon the aforesaid confusion of reflection with reflexivity. Industrialism in its advanced stage in the second half of the twentieth century is increasingly producing effects that can no longer be encompassed or covered by the calculus of risk and insurance. Rather, these latter confront the technical and social institutions of the 'precaution state' (F. Ewald) with threats that nullify, devalue and undermine all calculations to their very foundations. To put it ironically, the self-reflection of late industrial society on the pattern of risk remains and blinds us to the confrontation with incalculable threats, which are constantly euphemized and trivialized into calculable risks. It also blinds us to the institutional crisis, the loss of faith and its consequences and the disturbances for law, politics, the economy and what seems to be privacy, which are made permanent in this way.[4]

To put it another way, there is no automatic transition from the unsettling of classical industrial society to the reflection of this self-dissolution and self-modification. Whether the disembedding and re-embedding of the structures of industrial society will lead at all to a public and scientific, policy-creating self-reflection on this epochal change, whether this will seize and occupy the mass media, mass parties and the organized agents, whether this will become the object of general controversies, conflicts, political elections and reforms, is an empirical question; we must wait for its answer; it depends on many conditions and initiatives that cannot be decided in advance and forecast theoretically.

The analytical core of the theory states quite amorally and free of hope that the reflexivity of modernity produces fundamental shocks, which are either grist for the mills of neo-nationalism and neo-fascism (specifically when the majority calls for and reaches for the old rigidities as certainties disappear), or at the opposite extreme, can be used for a reformulation of the objectives and foundations of Western industrial societies. These include the hope – to borrow a phrase from Zygmunt Bauman – that reflexive modernity can become a 'homeland of incompleteness'.

Summary[5]

How then do the epochs and theories of simple (orthodox) and reflexive modernization (in my sense) differ? Five contrasts and clusters of features delineate the horizon.

First, with respect to life situation, life conduct and social structure: large-group categories and class theories are essentially different from theories of the individualization (and intensification) of social inequality.

Second: the problematics of the functional differentiation of 'autonomized' spheres of action are replaced by the problematics of the functional coordination, networking and fusion of differentiated subsystems (as well as their 'communicative codes').

Third: the linearity models (and atavistic beliefs in control) characteristic of the faith in progress from perpetual modernization are replaced by multiple and multi-level argumentation images of the self-modification, self-endangerment and self-dissolution of the foundations of rationality and the forms of rationalization in the (power) centres of industrial modernization. How? As uncontrollable (side) effects of the triumphs of autonomized modernization: uncertainty returns.

Fourth: while simple modernization ultimately locates the motor of social transformation in categories of instrumental rationality (reflection), 'reflexive' modernization conceives of the motive force of social change in categories of the side effect (reflexivity). What is not seen, not reflected upon, but externalized instead adds to the structural rupture which separates industrial society from risk society, which separates it from the 'new' modernities of the present and future.

Fifth: beyond left and right – the spatial metaphor which became established along with industrial society as the ordering of the political – political, ideological and theoretical conflicts are beginning, which (for all their tentativeness) can be captured in the axes and dichotomies of certain–uncertain, inside–outside and political–apolitical. Thinking these through in their cultural, social, political and economic dynamism exceeds the scope of this book, but it should none the less become an essential object of future studies and debates.

NOTES

1 S. Lash, 'Reflexive modernization: the aesthetic dimension', *Theory, Culture and Society*, vol. 10, no. 1, 1993, pp. 1–24. In German, 'Ästhetische Dimensionen reflexiver Modernisierung', *Soziale Welt*, vol. 2, 1993.
2 Johannes Berger, 'Modernitätsbegriffe und Modernitäts Kritik', *Soziale Welt*, vol. 3, 1988.
3 Lash, 'Ästhetische Dimensionen', p. 264.
4 On this point see my *Ecological Politics in the Age of Risk*, Cambridge: Polity, 1994 and *Ecological Enlightenment*, New York: Humanity Press, 1994.
5 See pp. 1–55 above.

Risk, trust, reflexivity

Anthony Giddens

Writing this response has put me in something of a quandary. I could use the whole of the space available to me to debate any one of several key ideas discussed by my two colleagues, including especially the notion of reflexive modernization. Yet both of their contributions are rich in original ideas and provocative assertions; it would be too limiting to confine myself to a single theme, no matter how substantive the depths to be plumbed there. So I have decided to disentangle a number of strands that run through our various discussions and to write briefly about each. I hope it won't be too irritating for the reader if I do so in a numbered sequence of points. Because of limited space available, these are liable to sound like dogmatic assertions, but I hope that they will prove of some interest nevertheless.

(1)   The background to all three papers, I take it, is that we live today in a world which the leading figures of the Enlightenment, whose work was at the origins of social science today, did not anticipate. Such thinkers believed, quite reasonably, that the more we get to know about the world, as collective humanity, the more we can control and direct it to our own purposes. Increasing knowledge produced about the social and natural worlds would lead to greater certainty about the conditions under which we lead our lives; and would thereby subject to human dominance what was once the domain of other influences.

The connections between the development of human knowledge and human self-understanding have proved more complex than such a view suggests. Characteristic of our lives today is what one might call 'manufactured uncertainty'. Many aspects of our lives have suddenly become open, organized only in terms of 'scenario thinking', the as-if construction of possible future outcomes. This is as true of our individual lives as of that of humankind as a whole. On the one side, we can easily discern many new opportunities that potentially free us from the limitations of the past. On the other, almost everywhere, we see the possibility of catastrophe. And in many instances it is difficult to say with any degree of surety in which direction things will move.

A sceptic might ask, is there anything new here? Hasn't human life always been marked by contingency? Hasn't the future always been open and problematic? The answer is 'yes' to each of these questions. It is not that our life-circumstances today have become less predictable than they used to be; rather the origins of unpredictability have changed. Many of the uncertainties which face us today have been created by the very growth of human knowledge.

The explanation for this state of affairs is not, as is often thought, to be found in the methodological scepticism of modern knowledge, important though that is. The main factor involved is precisely institutional reflexivity, a term which I favour over reflexive modernization. Reflexive modernization tends to imply a sort of 'completion' of modernity, the bringing into view of aspects of social life and nature that were previously dormant. There is, as it were, a clear 'direction' of development supposed here.

Yet such a situation is not really found today. Instead, we face more confusing circumstances in which – as the protagonists of postmodernism have stressed – there are no longer clear paths of development leading from one state of affairs to another. A social universe of expanded reflexivity is one marked by the rediscovery of tradition as well as its dissolution; and by the frequently eccentric disruption of what for a time seem established trends. This does not mean – as some followers of postmodernism say – that the world becomes inherently refractory to human attempts at control. Such attempts at control, in respect, for example, of high-consequence risks, remain necessary and feasible; we must recognize, however, that these endeavours will be subject to many fracturings, whether for good or for ill.

(2)   Some of the most apparently arcane disputes of philosophy, which on the face of things seem unresolvable, today reflect quite mundane matters with which lay actors (in some sense or another) cope. This is again an expression of institutional reflexivity. The specific authority which science once enjoyed, which turned it into a sort of tradition, could only be protected in so far as there was an insulation dividing scientific expertise from the diverse forms of knowledgibility of lay populations. The possession of esoteric knowledge, of course, still guarantees a certain 'protection' for the technical expert against the probings of lay individuals. But this dividing line is no longer a generalized one, sealing off science as a whole from the 'local knowledge' of laypersons. The very specializ-

ation which expertise undergoes makes it obvious to everyone that there can be no 'experts of all experts', but that all expert claims to knowledge are not only very specific but also liable often to be internally contested.

The fact that experts frequently disagree becomes familiar terrain for almost everyone. More than this, however, the claim to universal legitimacy of science becomes much more disputed than before. All kinds of cult, folk knowledge and traditional orientations return to claim some sort of hegemony alongside the realms of orthodox science. This again is not easily contained within a concept of reflexive modernization. The many tensions that develop between (diverse interpretations of) science and alternative forms of knowledge-claim are more disruptive than would be the case if this were just a matter of science 'coming to understand itself better'.

(3)   Risk and trust, as well as their various opposites, need to be analysed together in conditions of late modernity. The 'first global society' is certainly unified in a negative way, as Beck says, by the generating of common risks. The 'goods' created by industrial development become besmirched by a very obvious range of 'bads'. This society, nevertheless, is not *only* a 'risk society'. It is one where mechanisms of trust shift – in interesting and important ways. What can be called *active trust* becomes increasingly significant to the degree to which post-traditional social relations emerge.

Active trust is trust that has to be energetically treated and sustained. It is at the origin of new forms of social solidarity today, in contexts ranging from intimate personal ties right through to global systems of interaction. I agree with Beck when he argues that 'individualization' (in his sense of that term) is not the same as egoism. It is a mistake to connect such individualism too closely to the celebrated 'me generation'. New forms of social solidarity might often be less based upon fixed localities of place than before, but they can be very intense and perhaps durable.

We need therefore to question today the old dichotomy between 'community' and 'association' – between mechanical and organic solidarity. The study of mechanisms of social solidarity remains as essential to sociology as it ever was, but the new forms of solidarity are not captured by these distinctions. For example, the creation of 'intimacy' in post-traditional emotional relations today is neither the *Gemeinschaft* nor *Gesellschaft*. It involves the generating of 'community' in a more active sense, and community often stretched across indefinite distances of time-space. Two people keep a relationship going even though they spend much of their time thousands of miles away from one another; self-help groups create communities that are at once localized and truly global in their scope.

In the profound transformations happening now in personal life active trust is necessarily geared to the integrity of the other. Such integrity cannot be taken for granted on the basis of a person's incumbency of a particular social position. Trust has to be won and actively sustained; and this now ordinarily presumes a process of mutual narrative and emotional disclosure. An 'opening out' to the other is the condition of the development of a stable tie – save where traditional patterns are for one reason or another reimposed, or where emotional dependencies or compulsions exist.

In larger organizational contexts, active trust depends upon a more institutional 'opening out'. The 'autonomy' involved here can be understood in terms of responsibility and bottom-up decision-making. Some suppose that the changes now affecting – and breaking down – hierarchical, command systems in the economic and political spheres are the result of technological innovations – in particular, of the introduction of computerization and information technology. But the prime influence again is the expansion of institutional reflexivity, developed against the general backdrop of a post-traditional order. Today, in many situations, we have no choice but to make choices, filtering these through the active reception of shifting forms of expert knowledge; in such circumstances, new forms of organizational solidarity tend to replace the old.

Even in the domain of expert systems active trust becomes more prominent. This happens partly because of the divisions within, and contestations of, expertise noted earlier. Wherever there is scepticism, wherever there is an awareness of the disputes that divide expert authorities, mechanisms of active trust proliferate. As Beck notes, new forms of regulation affecting expert systems form a major area of confrontation in the area of 'sub-politics'.

(4) In some circumstances, burgeoning reflexivity is emancipatory. In other respects, and in a diversity of contexts, it produces the contrary: an intensifying of stratification. Lash is quite right to emphasize this point. Increasing freedom for some regularly goes along with, or is even the cause of, greater oppression for others. Such an observation holds true for earlier phases of social development as well; here, though, we have to make specific reference to the dialectical and contradictory nature of globalizing influences. Thus

an impoverished group may live alongside one that is much more wealthy in, say, two adjacent city neighbourhoods; the deprivations of the one might be causally related to the affluence of the other, but not as a direct connection, not even perhaps as mediated only through the national society.

Poverty was never easily defined, but becomes much more complex than it used to be when we consider the risk environments implied in institutional reflexivity. The more the demand to 'make one's own life' becomes acute, the more material poverty becomes a double discrimination. Not only is there lack of access to material rewards, the capacities for autonomy enjoyed by others may become crushed. Some of the principal dynamics of stratification thereby are altered. Class relations, for instance, while they may be in some respects accentuated, become thoroughly permeated by the influence of 'biographical decision-making'. Class groups still sometimes form communities, but like other communities become less linked to local and fixed forms of solidarity. Life chances that are enhanced in some ways may produce perverse consequences in others. Thus women today are leaving marriages in large numbers, in an active fashion rather than as the passive victims of circumstance. Yet this very assertion of autonomy has the consequence of plunging many women, as lone heads of households, into poverty.

On the larger scale, globalization cannot today simply be understood as Westernization. There is no longer any appropriate term for 'developing societies' and the idea of 'development studies' loses its cogency. On all sides, even in the poorest areas of the globe, we see mixed processes of development, underdevelopment and overdevelopment. In the societies of the industrialized world, characteristics previously associated with 'underdevelopment' become commonplace. Cultural diasporas, as Lash observes, are no longer confined to the rich. In dress, in religious or political orientation, in music, people in the poorest ghettos link themselves to transnational 'communities of taste' in an active way.

(5)   Beck has provided a compelling analysis of ecological crisis of late modernity. In a world where talk of 'crisis' has long lost any capacity to alarm, ecological problems expose all those difficulties that an apparently triumphant capitalism brings in its train. Since ecological issues are about the 'environment' it would seem as though they could be understood in terms of the need to 'protect the earth'. In fact, partly through the impact of Beck's work, it has

become apparent that questions of ecology are markers of a host of other problems that face us.

In the first instance, of course, there is the basic issue of survival or global security. The 'bads' which afflict us as high-consequence risks have to be limited as far as possible. It does not need much insight to see how difficult this is likely to be. Industrialization and technological development – with all their attendant misfortunes as well as benefits – developed under the aegis of the Western societies. Why should the 'less developed' societies now embarking upon large-scale industrialization processes limit their economic growth in order to help solve problems created by the rich? The pervasiveness of global poverty, and the urgent demand for global justice, are self-evidently bound up with ecological dilemmas. Viewed in an appropriate way, the ecological crisis brings these problems into sharp focus.

As I emphasize in my contribution to this book, ecological questions have to be understood in terms of the 'end of nature' and de-traditionalization. In both instances what was, or appeared to be, external to human social life becomes the outcome of social processes. Although ecology seems to be wholly about 'nature', nature in the end has very little to do with it. De-traditionalizing influences are often just as important as the socialization of nature in producing this effect, or more important. Take as an example the factors affecting women in relation to conception and childbirth. As a result of the development of modern reproductive technologies, many traits that used to be 'naturally given' have become matters for human decision-making. Reproduction no longer has any necessary connection with sexuality. Virgin birth is now possible; single individuals and same-sex couples can have children of their own. Parents can choose the sex of a child.

Yet a much more fundamental influence on 'nature' than these technological factors was the movement towards small families which occurred in most Western countries at some point in the nineteenth century. Before this transition – a break with pre-existing traditions – the conditions of life for many women were established by the routines of the successive pregnancies and the duties of childcare. The coming of small families was actually the condition of the development of 'sexuality' in its current form, the principal dividing line which began to separate sexual activity thoroughly from reproduction.

Wherever what used to be settled by 'nature', whether this be the 'environment' or tradition, becomes a matter of decision-making, new ethical spaces are opened up and political perplexities created. In these spaces the tensions between dialogue and the assertion of moral certitude frequently become acute. Fundamentalisms can arise in all the arenas opened up by the transformation of nature and tradition. I take fundamentalism to mean not a 'return to the past', or 'an insistence upon first principles', but a defence of the formulaic truth of tradition. We can speak in this sense not only of religious fundamentalism but of fundamentalisms of nationalism, ethnicity, the family and gender – among others.

Fundamentalisms are not necessarily primitive. Fundamentalism is in genuine dialogue with modernity. The principle of radical doubt, after all, can be turned back against itself; and doubt as a behavioural principle creates many perplexities in everyday life, from which fundamentalism can offer safe havens. In so far as they cultivate the terrors which difference in all its forms can inspire, however, fundamentalisms become dangerous. In such a guise, fundamentalism is more than just a refusal of dialogue; it demonizes the alien in a world – as Beck has put it – where 'there are no others'. There are connections here between the 'male funda-mentalist' who wreaks his revenge on women; violence at the abor-tion clinic; and violence between religious, nationalist or ethnic groups at a more macroscopic level.

Dangerous as they may sometimes be, fundamentalisms need to be listened to by those whom they do not persuade. For they take seriously the ethical aridity of fields of action and value that are opened up by technology but which are irreducible to technical decisions. In this context we see some important realignments of political agendas. Consider, for example, the fate of conservatism, which with the apparent demise of the left might seem all-conquer-ing. Understood as neo-liberalism, conservatism has become intern-ally contradictory. The free play of market forces that it advocates is radically de-traditionalizing. Yet conservatism depends for its sup-port upon groups who wish to conserve – to protect traditional ways of life. Conservatism has thus become a mélange of emancipatory impulses and fundamentalisms. The current debate over 'family values' is just one expression of this by now thoroughly tangled web. We reach the seemingly perverse conclusion that the reasoned conserving of traditions and the creation of ethical values today has to be part of a programme of renewed political radicalism.

(6) Beck and Lash each have interesting things to say about the shifting character of politics today. Many complex questions are

raised here and I shall limit myself to a few remarks about democracy. Understood as liberal democracy, democracy has suddenly become highly popular across the world. The popularity of democracy, as we all know, is quite recent. Quite apart from the existence of authoritarian states and state socialist systems around the world, in most Western countries until relatively recently democracy was not among the foremost values promoted by either right or left.

There are two contrasting ways in which one might try to understand the spread of democratic institutions. One is what might be called, tongue in cheek, the *fragile-flower* theory of democracy. According to this view, democracy is a tender plant that needs to be regularly watered if it is to sustain itself. It also needs a rich soil: it has to be nurtured over a long period through the long-term development of a civic culture.

The fragile-flower theory sees processes of democratization in the current period – to shift metaphorical gears a bit – in terms of a process of catching up. The virtues of democracy have become more universally apparent now that socialism has failed and authoritarian regimes, for one reason or another, have started to crumble. The ideas set out by Francis Fukuyama provide a celebrated source for this sort of view. Fascism has more or less disappeared and socialism has disintegrated. Everyone begins to appreciate the superiority of multi-party democracy, combined with entrepreneurial capitalism, as the only system which mixes freedom and economic efficiency in a tolerable fashion. The problem for states emerging from a background of authoritarian government is to enrich the ground upon which democracy can be nurtured. The construction of democratic forms of government is a complex and necessarily protracted process. What is involved essentially, however, is allowing the retarded countries to catch up with their more advanced counterparts where liberal democracy is already firmly established and its roots deep.

The fragile-flower theory faces various objections. First, some societies in the past have moved very rapidly from authoritarian, even fascist, backgrounds to become functioning liberal democracies: Germany and Japan following the Second World War offer examples. It is not clear that a long-established civic democratic culture is needed to make the institutional changes involved, particularly where there is a distinct break of some sort with the past. Second, as an account of the quite sudden worldwide lurch towards democracy, the fragile-flower theory seems inadequate. Trends towards democratization surely connect with wider developments;

the pressures leading to democratization and the break-up of the command economy in East European countries did not derive simply from an internal collapse of the order; the generalizing of democracy today is not a *sui generis* phenomenon.

Finally, just at the seeming peak of its success, liberal democracy is in some trouble almost everywhere. Corruption has become a public issue in countries as far removed from one another as Brazil, Japan and Italy. The domain of orthodox politics seems increasingly to cross-cut the major problems that dog people's lives. Voters become disaffected and the numbers of those who distrust all political parties increases. The struggles of party politics come to many to seem like a game, which only occasionally touches in an effective way upon real-world problems.

As an alternative interpretation of democratization today, let me offer what I might term the *sturdy-plant* view. Such a perspective does not equate democracy solely with liberal democracy within the nation-state. Processes of democratization stimulate the emergence of liberal democracy where it did not previously exist, yet at the same time also expose its limitations. Democracy in this broader sense is a hardy growth that can develop shoots even in quite infertile ground. It can be quite readily transplanted when the conditions are right, although no doubt it always needs to be cultivated and cared for.

The sturdy-plant theory suggests that there are profound social changes occurring in the current era that do not occur mainly on the level of the state. Rather, such changes reshape and place in question the powers that states hitherto have claimed for themselves. The three contributions to this volume provide clear suggestions about what these changes are and how they might best be understood. The intensifying of globalization empties out local contexts of action, demanding and stimulating the growth of institutional reflexivity. The transformations of everyday life occur in the domains of Beck's 'sub-politics', not in the orthodox political arena. The issue is not only that, as Daniel Bell put it, the nation-state has become too small to solve global problems and too large to deal with local ones; the intricate connections between changes in global and local life start to attack the very integrity of the state.

Democracy, as David Held has shown, is linked to a principle of autonomy. Autonomy is promoted by the capability to represent one's interests and by the possibility of resolving clashes of interest through public dialogue. We see these conditions becoming met, against many resistances, in various sectors of social life outside the formal political sphere. Acknowledging this, in discussing democratization Beck stresses the importance of controlling expertise. We must, he says, dispel the illusion that administrators and experts always know best. Expertise has to be 'demonopolised'. 'Social standards of relevance' should be, and are becoming, more prominent than decision-making within closed circles of experts. Norms of discussion and debate relative to change in the domain of 'sub-politics' should be established and guaranteed.

These points are well taken, even if the institutional arrangements which would be presumed remain somewhat elusive in Beck's discussion. But I would put things in a somewhat different way. As a result of the combined processes of globalization and the transformation of everyday life, we can recognize at least four social contexts within which democratizing processes are at work – although in each of these the familiar tension between opportunity and possible catastrophe applies.

First, we see the potential emergence of 'emotional democracy' in the domains of sexual relations, parent–child relations and friendship. To the degree to which the pure relationship becomes dominant in these spheres, a relation of equals, organized through emotional communication coupled to self-understanding, becomes possible. Emotional democracy, if it does progress, promises a great deal for the reconstruction of civic ethics as a whole. Individuals who are at home with their own emotions, and able to sympathize with those of others, are likely to be more effective and engaged citizens than those who lack such qualities.

Second, there are clear trends towards the replacing of bureaucratic hierarchies by more flexible and decentralized systems of authority. Democratizing processes here are once more tied to institutional reflexivity and clearly exhibit the principle of autonomy. Such changes may of course develop alongside existing, or newly created, procedures of more formal industrial representation. As in other areas we must speak here mainly of a potential rather than an actuality. Most processes of change are dialectical. Those authors who diagnose a more or less wholescale shift from hierarchy to flexibility may very well be quite unrealistic; flexibility for some groups, in some contexts, may signal increasing constraint or oppression for others.

The third context of potential democratization is that of the development of social movements and self-help groups. In many circumstances such movements and groups set themselves up against existing 'authorities', whether these be state officials, professionals or others. Here they can in principle foster the qualities which Beck wishes to see realized in the domain of 'sub-politics'. Quite apart from the issues they pursue, however, such groups can be (although they by no means always are in practice) democratizing as modes of social association. Most sociological work has concentrated upon social movements, but self-help groups are in some respects both more interesting and influential.

Finally, there are important democratizing influences at more global levels of development. We should not understand these as steps on the way to world government, certainly if 'government' is understood as the nation-state writ large. Rather, such tendencies connect in a direct way with the three other domains of potential democratization just referred to. What may appear as 'sub-political' trends can be at the same time 'superpolitical' – the interplay of local context and globalizing consequences is of great importance here. Democratizing tendencies in the global order are likely to draw upon just those characteristics of reflexivity, mobilization and flexibility implied in the changing domains of everyday life. The cybernetic model of social regulation is dead. For the world community this is probably more of a plus than a minus. For it would be difficult indeed to imagine a directive intelligence that could somehow organize social and economic life on a global scale. In the mixture of reflexivity, autonomy and dialogue characteristic of active trust we may eventually generate a cosmopolitan global order where greater justice prevails and where large-scale war has become obsolete.

In all these domains I would speak of the need for utopian realism. Moves towards democratization are real and very pervasive; it is plausible to suppose that they may be developed much further yet. On the other hand, the countervailing forces are many and a strong dose of realism is always necessary.

(7) If liberal democracy is not the end of history in the political sphere, nor is capitalistic production in the domain of economic relations. What might come into being on the other side of capitalism is not socialism, in the sense of the centralized direction of economic life. Rather, we see the possibility of the emergence of a post-scarcity order. Here again we must introduce the notion of utopian realism and speak only of immanent trends. The idea of a post-scarcity system can no longer mean, as some interpreters of

Marx have supposed, a society in which scarcity has been eliminated by endless abundance. Not only will there always be
scarcities associated with 'positional goods'; the ecological crisis
shows us that scarcity is in some respects endemic to human life
upon this earth. A post-scarcity order would rather be one in which
the drive to continuous accumulation has become weakened or
dissolved. Here questions of life politics connect quite directly with
the prospects for global justice.

A post-scarcity order begins to emerge in so far as individuals
actively restructure their working lives, valuing other things
than their sheer economic prosperity. The German 'time-pioneers'
are an illustration. The restructuring of time, the ultimate scarce
resource for the finite human being, introduces flexibilities into the
life-cycle that are unimaginable when a career is simply accepted
as 'fate'. These things are to some degree gender-divided. Until
recently, for many men a lifetime of paid work from the end of
adolescence through to a fixed retirement age was 'fate'. For many
women, on the other hand, 'fate' meant domesticity. While this
role division reinforced patriarchy, it also created a schizophrenic
masculinity. Work became driven by that compulsiveness which
Weber identified. Although this is put in much too crude a way,
we can say that men became cut off from their emotional lives
in ways that had many consequences for themselves as well as
for women. Women in effect became 'specialists in love', while,
apart from 'idle romantics', men more or less ceased to speak of love
altogether.

The large-scale entry of women into the paid labour force,
coupled to the growing 'feminization' of some male careers,
forces adjustments to this situation. The outcome of this double
shift, as in so many other areas of social life now, is still unclear. But
it is worth remembering that the growth ethic was never adopted by
the whole population; many women stood outside, and continued
to live for values other than those implied in 'secularized Puritanism'. A generalizing of some of those values would certainly make
a large dent in the ethic of continuous economic accumulation.

A second cluster of influences promoting the emergence of a
post-scarcity order stems from the well known contradictions of
abundance. Here there is a close connection with ecological concerns. The 'bads' generated by industrialism provide an impetus to
change in and of themselves. No matter how it be interpreted, for
instance, 'responsible growth' necessarily introduces other values
than wholly economic ones. Some of the contradictions of abun-

dance are self-evident. Thus at a certain point the traffic through a
city becomes so cluttered that it is quicker to walk; at that point, and
with such examples before them quite often well before it, city
authorities start to create traffic-free city centres.

A critic might say: surely if there is any possibility of the development of a post-scarcity order, this only applies to the First World?
What about impoverished Third World countries, not to speak of
the poverty that continues to exist within even the most affluent
societies? Yet a post-scarcity order is far from something that
only has relevance to the economically advanced sectors of the
globe. In the first place, it is not an order where economic development comes to a halt; wealth creation will remain necessary
for a long while yet. Even more important, the glimpses of a post-
scarcity system which we see today allow us to envisage a different
way of life for the people of the earth as a whole. We know now that
direct redistribution of wealth, even if it could somehow be
achieved, would be no more than a partial solution to problems
of poverty. The welfare state in Western countries has helped blunt
the polarizing tendencies of classical capitalism. Yet its limitations
have also become apparent. People won't pay taxes beyond a certain level, especially when there is little accounting for where their
money goes. Welfare dependency is a real phenomenon, not a myth
just conjured out of the imagination of the political right – and
so forth.

When we think of the global polity, it is no good any longer
envisaging some kind of gigantic redistributive welfare state. We
have to think in other terms. As has become familiar among those
who work upon 'development' issues, as well as those concerned
with welfare institutions in Western countries, effective measures
taken to counter underprivilege have to be enabling. That is, they
must take account of, and draw upon, the reflexivity of the individuals or groups they address. The issues involved here are as
much a concern of life politics as emancipatory politics. If again we
think in terms of beginnings rather than endings, a post-scarcity
society is a society in which the aim of 'development' precisely
comes under close scrutiny. Here the affluent have a great deal to
learn from the poor; and the West from other cultures which in the
past it has simply threatened with extinction.

(8)   Finally, let me come to the question of aesthetics. I have left
this field until last for a reason. So much of the debate about

postmodernity has been refracted through questions of aesthetics or culture; but to me this situation is an unsatisfactory one. In my opinion, it is worth making a distinction between 'post-modernism' and 'postmodernity'. The first can be taken to refer to changes (supposing they have happened at all) occurring in architecture, art, literature and poetry. 'Postmodernity' then refers to institutional changes affecting the social world today. For me, the question of postmodernity is more interesting than issues of postmodernism. Avoiding at least one of the 'posts' which otherwise tend to tramp across our pages, I prefer the terms 'high modernity' or 'late modernity' to refer to these institutional transitions.

Is there such a thing as aesthetic reflexivity? I don't really think so, or at least I wouldn't put it this way. I am not at all sure that, as Lash puts it, there is 'an entire other economy of signs in space' that functions separately from 'cognitive symbols'. As I would understand institutional reflexivity, it virtually always has some relationship to the emotions; it isn't just 'cognitive' at all. The idea of 'an economy of signs in space' seems to me to resonate quite strongly with the outlook of post-structuralist thought, to which on the whole I am opposed. Signs, no matter how wholly 'non-verbal', never relate to one another; they do so only through human mediation. In an increasingly electronic culture, non-verbal images become commonplace in the organization of day-to-day experience. But there are two ways of interpreting this phenomenon. There is the familiar Saussurean route, elaborated upon in numerous ways in post-structuralist theory. Here the 'economy of signs' simply discloses what is in any case basic to all language: the creation of meaning from non-meaning by the play of difference.

However, there is a quite different point of view, which is the one I hold. Language does not derive from semiotic difference, which cannot generate a satisfactory notion of meaning. Rather, language has meaning only because of the indexical properties of its use. No signs exist without narratives, even those that appear to be wholly iconic. Aesthetic reflection in the current period is paradoxical in that its reflexivity has characteristically been deployed in such a way as to subvert, or place in question, the very narrative forms that it presumes. An understanding of aesthetics developed along these lines, it seems to me, would look rather different from the views which at present tend to rule the roost.

Expert-systems or Situated Interpretation? Culture and Institutions in Disorganized Capitalism

Scott Lash

The continuing convergence of the constantly developing and fundamentally innovative – both in terms of analytic penetration and real-world relevance – work of Ulrich Beck and Anthony Giddens is little short of remarkable. Both having previously addressed the general outlines of the transformation of modernity, the two theorists at the beginning of the 1990s shifted their focus to issues of love, intimacy and self-identity. And now – in this book and elsewhere – both have shifted their attention in the direction of institutional metamorphoses and the political. In doing so Beck and Giddens continue to thematize the ecological dimensions of social change and especially the role of science and expertise therein. In such considerations the two authors have in this book come to strikingly similar conclusions. In these the shift from 'early' or 'simple' modernity to 'late' or 'reflexive' modernity involves a corresponding displacement from 'emancipatory' and centralized politics to 'life politics' or 'sub-politics'. Such a life politics involves the politicization of a number of issues – gender divisions, biotechnology, noxious substances – which are at once global and affect us in the inmost recesses of the private sphere. These issues involve risk, trust and major roles for scientists and professionals, that is in short for expert-systems. In both Beck and Giddens such expert-systems, affecting intimate everyday life but now open to democratic debate and contestation from the lay population, constitute a set of emergent and decentralized effective mini-public spheres for the new politics of reflexive modernity.

Ulrich Beck's and Anthony Giddens's contributions to this book initiate a theoretical departure for each writer. These involve the focus of analysis, the notion of reflexivity and metatheoretical assumptions. In terms of analytic focus both Beck and Giddens have fundamentally displaced their attention to the realm of politics. Regarding reflexivity, what was once a process involving individuals is now primarily a question of institutions and 'institutional reflexivity'. Regarding metatheoretical assumptions, Giddens has effectively drawn on Habermas in looking at expert-systems and institutions as *de facto* public spheres of democratic and rational will formation. Beck has on the contrary been influenced by Zygmunt Bauman's work. And his understanding of reflexive modernity is now as much characterized by 'ambivalence' as by new forms of order.

I shall argue in this response that, despite these significant departures, their analyses remain not so much flawed as partial because of a *scientistic* character of their assumptions. I think that the debates between left and right in social theory in the 1960s and 1970s have been overtaken by new and emergent fault lines – on each side of which you will find both the 'left' and 'right', radicals and effective reactionaries. This division does not replicate the counter-position of modernism versus postmodernism, or positivism versus interpretative analyses, and surely not rationalism versus irrationalism. It does, however, pit rationalistic (cognitivist) or *scientistic* understandings versus culturalist or hermeneutic views. It might help to oversimplify considerably and understand such 'scientism' versus 'culturalism' in terms of a continuum in contemporary theory. This in part represents the distinction between in the broadest sense scientific sociology on the one side and cultural theory on the other. At the science end of the continuum there is the hard realism of an Althusserian Marxist such as David Harvey. Harvey pits his Marxist historical materialism against the 'soft' dialectical materialism of hermeneutic Marxism. For him culture, postmodern or other, is more or less reduced to a causal effect of transnational capital. For Harvey it makes sense only to understand nature instrumentally, and environmental matters as matters almost exclusively for experts. A concern with other sorts of cultural and emotional involvements and responses of laypeople with the natural would be dismissed by analysts such as Harvey as the concerns of back-to-nature communal Romantic dreamers.

At the 'culturalist' end of the spectrum stand such unlikely bed-fellows as Mary Douglas and Jacques Derrida, who reduce the social to the cultural and deconstruct the distinction between tradition and modernity. More towards the middle of the culturalist (or hermeneutic) end of the spectrum stand for example Foucault or Bauman who do work from the distinction of tradition and modernity; who will understand the distinction of the cultural and the social as constituted in the modern; but for whom expert-systems are at their best normalizing discourses, at their worst the political institutions of the Third Reich. Beck and Giddens stand more in the respectable middle of the scientistic or rationalist wing of the spectrum.

The point I want to make, however, is not so much the extent to which theorists are (scientistic) cognitivists or (hermeneutic) culturalists. The point instead concerns everyday lay actors, institutions and politics. It is that the attunement or attitude of everyday life in reflexive modernity is as importantly cultural/hermeneutic as it is cognitivist or scientistic. It is that institutions and politics in late modernity have become increasingly cultural. The point is that a theory such as Beck's and Giddens's virtual neglect of the cultural/hermeneutic sources of the late modern self entails at the same time a neglect of this crucial dimension of politics and everyday life. It means further that their conceptions of 'sub-politics' or 'life politics' focus on the experts with relative neglect of the grassroots. It means for them a concentration on the formal and institutional at the expense of the increasing proportion of social, cultural and political interaction in our increasingly disorganized capitalist world that is going on outside of institutions.

Institutional reflexivity: responsibility, tradition, truth

In previous work Beck, Giddens and I have proffered a rather individualistic notion of reflexivity. Here in reflexive modernization, structural change forces agency to be free from structure, forces individuals to free themselves from the normative expectations of the institutions of simple modernity and to engage in reflexive monitoring of such structures as well as self-monitoring in the construction of their own identities. The main difference here between Beck/Giddens and myself was my addition of the aesthetic (hermeneutic) dimension. In this book all three of us have developed notions of collective reflexivity. Thus my contribution addressed 'reflexive community' and Beck and Giddens have spoken of institutional reflexivity. It is to this that I now turn.

Beck's contribution works from the distinction between 'reflexivity' and 'reflection'. Here reflection is individualistic, conscious and intentional. Reflexivity is like a 'reflex'. It is neither individualistic nor conscious nor intentional. Reflexivity is how the axial principle of reflexive modernity comes into contradiction with the principle of simple modernity. Here reflexive modernity is largely dealing with the side effects, the dangers or 'bads' which stem from simple modernity's production of goods. Further, reflexive modernity's ethos of 'ambivalence' comes into contradiction with simple modernity's imperative of order. Beck states that reflexivity also includes reflection. The latter can be individual, or it can be collective and institutional. Thus the opposition of reflexive and simple modernity as 'reflex' involves the opposition of reflexive modern institutions with simple modern ones. The emergent institutions democratically, responsibly and rationally reflect on the risks and side effects of simple modernity. Though Beck is in principle quite opposed to the instrumental rationality and technocracy of expert-systems, this focus on (alternative and democratic) institutions carries with it a great reliance on competing sources of expertise and competing expert systems. For Beck and Giddens here reflexivity involves as it were 'representative democracy' inside the new institutions with the lay public 'voting' on competing forms of expertise. There is little room in this for the 'participatory democracy' of informal everyday lay politics and social movements.

Beck states that he is neither a 'realist' nor a 'constructivist' but an 'institutionalist'. The most important thing about institutions, for their part, is *responsibility*, a notion which may be the key to the corpus of his work. For Beck, responsibility is involved in the 'insurance principle' of simple modernity. In reflexive modernity the insurance principle no longer holds as responsibility for dangers runs into spatial, temporal and social unpredictability. The subtitle of his book *Gegengifte* (literally translated as 'antidotes' or 'counterpoisons'), published two years after *Risk Society*, is *Organized Irresponsibility*. What Beck means by this is that the coalition of business firms, policy-makers and experts who create the dangers of contemporary society then construct a set of discourses of disavowal of such responsibility. In doing so they convert the 'dangers' that they themselves created into 'risks' of the sort that, say, smokers or gamblers undertake.

The second discursive institutional construction here is also one of *legitimation* of the coalition of firms, policy-makers and experts, on the one hand, to the lay public on the other. What Beck wants in its place is a principle of legitimation based not on disavowal but on avowal of responsibility. There is considerable convergence here with the notion of 'trust' that Giddens has developed in this book. In Giddens's previous work modern trust was invested mainly in expert-systems. Now he wants to develop a notion of 'active trust'. Active trust emerges when institutions become reflexive and the propositions of the experts are opened up for critique and contestation. With such critical activity of the lay public, trust in expert systems becomes not passive but active. What for Beck is understood in terms of responsibility or legitimation would for Giddens then be mediated or abstract trust. The investment of trust in institutions – which is bound up with obligations and responsibility – must be a question of legitimacy. Hence for both theorists institutional reflexivity entails the dialogical avowal of responsibility by institutions or active mediated trust.

Beck and Giddens both have presumed that, with the coming of late or reflexive modernity, for the first time we live in a fully post-traditional society. Until now, however, neither has thematically addressed what is meant by tradition. In this volume Giddens devotes considerable and careful thought to this matter. For him the paradigmatic characteristic of tradition has to do with the nature of *truth*. Here in traditional societies, specialists in knowledge are 'guardians' – whether priests or magicians – and truth is *formulaic*. In modernity in contrast knowledge specialists are 'experts' and truth is *propositional*. 'Formulaic truth' is recognized in its effects. Language in this formulaic truth is not 'referential' but 'performative'. Causal efficacy is attributed for example to true rituals. 'Propositional truth', on the other hand, is valid by virtue of its correspondence with facts and its support by argument.

Tradition, notes Giddens, is not comprised of facts like customs but is a normative structure of binding moral content. Such a normative structure involves 'integrity' and a particular temporal character. Traditions are bound up with 'collective memory', itself a 'framework' for the reconstruction of 'past time' which in turn 'organizes future time'. Giddens uses these concepts to great advantage. Science for example in an earlier modernity is a matter of experts, but the public accepts their truths unquestioningly as formulaic truths. Only in late modernity do scientific statements become treated by the now reflexive public as contestable propositional truths open to 'discursive articulation' and critique.

Reflexive modernity is characterized for Giddens by 'experimental' openness and 'dialogic democracy'. Yet there continue to persist whole sets of phenomena that are quite clearly not reflexive and only dubiously modern. These persisting practices seem on the face of it even to be traditional, though in fact, Giddens contends, they are not. Such phenomena on closer inspection turn out to be *compulsions*. 'Compulsions' look like traditions – they depend on formulaic truths and repetition – but they are shorn of the integrity of the framework of tradition and are unconnected to collective memory. Compulsions are not open to experiment or discursive articulation.

Addictions such as alcoholism, drug addiction and food addictions exemplify such compulsions. Much of conservative political discourse similarly instantiates such 'ritualization without ritual', in depending on formulaic truths while shorn of connection to integral tradition. Traditions, Giddens observes, are spatially particularistic. And so is contemporary nationalism, speaking the language of them and us while bereft once again of enracination in integral collective memory.

This is brilliant stuff. The application of a small and clear battery of concepts to understand a range of social phenomena. Giddens's notion of institutional reflexivity involves (as does Beck's) the transformation of expert-systems into democratically dialogical and political public spheres. The propositional truths from this democratically validated expert knowledge – which is global, that is universal and valid in any place – is then appropriated by social actors in everyday life. Its precepts act effectively to disembed traditional meanings in the most immediate spheres of everyday life, in the local community and in the most intimate of 'pure relationships' – whether love, friendship or parent–child. This institutional reflexivity operates through time-space distanciation by stretching dialogic expert knowledge across time and space.

Democracy of emotions or emotionalization of democracy?

But the problems start just when Giddens starts to apply these notions to the intimacy of pure relationships. The 'pure relationship' is characteristically modern in that it is disembedded from traditional institutions and their normative expectations. That is, paradigmatically premodern relationships are integrated into and regulated by the normative framework and expectations of the community. The pure relationship is disembedded from these normative expectations. Instead it is regulated by symbols drawn from 'abstract systems' on a global spatial scale. At stake in the pure relationship is not the traditional situatedness in and commitment to the community (or polis in for example Aristotle's idea of friendship) but instead intimate mutual disclosure and 'growth'.

In my main contribution to this book I criticized the notion of the pure relationship in Giddens's previous work. I argued that its assumption of chronic intervention by expert-systems would lead to chronic disruption in the achievement of meaning and understanding in the relationship. In the present book he develops his notion in two ways. First, he makes clearer the fact that the expert-systems involved are scientific institutions based on propositional knowledge. Second, he applies the model of public sphere politics to what he calls a 'democracy of the emotions'. This would seem only further to confirm the impersonal, *gesellschaftlich* and abstract nature of this intervention of the expert-systems and the institutions into the intimate. It is likely, it seems to me, that such abstract systems might be destructive of meaning, intimacy, intense semantic interchange and emotional sharing and understanding which are central to late modern emotional relationships.

First, I do not think that contemporary emotional relationships are primarily bound up with propositional truth. Surely democratically contested (expert) propositional truths on sexuality, love, childrearing and gender roles can and do play a positive role in structuring intimate relationships. But another sort of truth that is neither 'formulaic' nor 'propositional' plays, I think, an equally or more important role. This third type of truth might be called *hermeneutic truth*. This 'hermeneutic' or 'narrative' truth is neither *gemeinschaftlich* like formulaic truth nor *gesellschaftlich* like propositional truth. Like propositional truth it is, however, characteristically modern. Such hermeneutic truth is involved in the mutual disclosure of intimate relationships. It is involved in the construction of the intense semantic interchange which such relationships comprise. These affectively charged communications are based on the construction of a web of shared assumptions and pre-understandings, on the construction of a 'semantic horizon'. Hermeneutic or narrative truth is also a property of the symbols involved in the (time-space distanciated) intervention of films, poems, novels, popular music in the pure relationship.

They are also involved in what I have called hermeneutic or aesthetic reflexivity, a concept that Giddens rejects and says 'smacks of post-structuralism'. Although influenced by post-structuralism, like Giddens I oppose the way that such theories assume the deconstruction of meaning, narrative and truth through the play of the difference of the signifier. Giddens prefers to understand meaning in terms of 'indexicality'. In this sense ethnomethodology has thematized the notion of 'indexical particulars'. This presumes shared meanings, as already held presuppositions about routine activities and language use, as necessary for any social relationship to exist. I think the way I have spoken about meaning in this book has a lot more to do with indexicality than it does with post-structuralism.

The problem is, I think, that the chronic intervention of abstract systems often serves to empty out these meanings and tends to make relationships meaningless, or even impossible. I think that hermeneutic truth and narrative knowledge (including the work of Gottfried Benn quoted by Beck and Nicholson Baker quoted by Giddens) serve to crystallize and 'retrieve' these meanings. This third type of truth involved in aesthetic or hermeneutic reflexivity often does act to deconstruct certain utilitarian and impersonal constructs of abstract and expert systems. It does so, however, not in order to destroy meaning but to retrieve it. This notion of hermeneutic or aesthetic reflexivity, I argued in the body of my contribution and shall argue further below, is neither Romantic nor atavistic.

Second, Giddens speaks of a 'democracy of the emotions' based on a newly post-traditional 'principle of autonomy', itself based on a 'capability to represent one's own interests' and 'the possibility of resolving interest clashes through (public) dialogue'. He sees the emotional relationship as a 'sub-political area' whose 'democra-tizing tendencies' are bound up with 'active trust' based on 'reflex-ivity, autonomy and dialogue'. Similar utilitarian assumptions of choice and scientistic assumptions of expertise are built into Beck's understanding of for example the effects of biotechnologies of re-production on pure relationships in the family. The latter are criti-cized to the extent that child development may be potentially displaced from the public provision of education to the private purchase of genetic engineering. Similarly a number of feminist and gay criticisms of genetic technologies argue that the main em-powerment involved is for agencies of social control over the bodies of women and gays. These are indeed important points. Less attention, however, is typically addressed to the disruption of the hermeneutic truths of the care relationship between lovers, between parent and child, by the choices involved in this informationalization of the body.

I spoke above about Giddens's idea of 'active trust'. Here in simple modernity trust is invested in abstract systems and in exper-tise 'based purely on the assumption of technical competence'. In-tellectuals not only manufacture expertise in this context but, as in Beck's legitimating function, they 'manufacture trust'. In late mod-ernity – whose institutional reflexivity entails 'the continuous filter back of expert-theories, concepts and findings to the lay population' – expertise is contested by this population and trust becomes 'active'. That is, there is 'the investment of trust in the light of alternatives'.

The problems come when this sort of active trust becomes integral to the private sphere of the emotions. And the problem lies in the very mediatedness and contractuality which informs Giddens's notion of active trust. Intimate relationships would seem indeed to be based on a different sort of active trust, but it is likely that the presumption of such an implicit contract between autonomous parties with their own interests would not be conducive to it. Active trust as a relationship between autonomous interested individuals would seem also to presume a certain proceduralism not unlike that of courts of law. Intimate relationships are based, hopefully, on trust that is not rule-bound, not procedural. They are based instead on the very most immediate investment. They are based on what Schutz in his description of the life-world calls 'care' (*Sorge*), on what Levinas, and Bauman via Levinas, have attempted to understand as *Mitsein*. Active trust would involve the constant creation of the presuppositions, of the prejudgements of this relatively independent world of intensified semantic interchange. It is the co-creation of a collective habitus, the creation by lovers of the classifications, the unthought categories on which their semantic interchange is based. The language of choice, autonomous interests, expertise seems to be closer to the world of neo-classical economics than to what intimate relationships are about.

I want to insist that this second notion of active trust, like hermeneutic truth, is just as fully post-traditional as the sort of reflexivity promoted by Beck and Giddens. It is post-traditional, first, because the relationships (pure and otherwise) it presumes are also disembedded from traditional or early modern institutions, as affect is cut loose from traditional customs and reinvested in the relationship; second, in its break with doxic truth and morality for a possible heterodoxy of with whom and how to have the relationship; third, in its insistence on the constant *creation* of the semantic background on which communications are grounded; and fourth, in the sense that the very materials that make up this semantic background, the very stuff of its habits, are already preconstructed from the time-space distantiated global world of abstract systems, but as importantly from quintessentially modern myths and narratives, the images of popular culture and the like. This too is aesthetic reflexivity.

It is only fair to say at this point that these criticisms address only one side of Giddens's ideas on intimacy. Although his work for my likes gives too great a role to contractuality, expertise and publicity, he has made I think an important contribution in his treatment of the pure relationship as mutual disclosure and authenticity. Moreover, his notions of time-space distanciation and reflexivity have profoundly influenced my thought. Further, Giddens in his work on intimate relations, his juxtaposition of them and public politics is courageous and is asking all the right questions. Particularly insightful is his attempt to question assumptions on the left of contractuality and proceduralism by looking to conservative political philosophy for forms of obligation and trust that are non-contractual and challenge constitutionalism. Here however one would have to begin to recognize the validity of traditions which are not compulsions. Here moreover one might better speak not so much of the 'democratization of the emotions' but of the emotionalization of democracy.

Culture, hermeneutics and the limits of institutions

I think that Beck's and Giddens's idea of institutional reflexivity has great purchase on contemporary social and political life. But let me suggest three substantial modifications of it.

First, institutions are becoming more *cultural* in character. The 'new institutionalism' in organization theory should be understood in this context. Here analysts have come to see institutions not so much as involving normative consensus and contestation, but as being profoundly cultural in nature. These theorists have claimed that at stake in institutions is the contestation and consensus of cultural values, of fundamental classificatory categories, of the social construction of reality. Social scientists such as Stuart Clegg have introduced 'actor–network theory' into this context to reconstitute a Foucauldian theory of power, in which structures are replaced by actor–networks – where the actors are individuals, groups, technologies, artefacts, symbolic dispositives – forming coalitions in the construction and determination of truth.

But what if we consider this 'new institutionalism' a departure not so much in theory as in social change, that is in how organizations and institutions have in fact changed? Thus Klaus Eder (and Beck) speak of a 'post-corporatist' order in which normative conflict about the distribution of goods in the tripartite employers–unions–

state corporatism of the 1960s and early 1970s is no longer at issue. At stake now instead is the social construction of reality. In this context Eder envisages a struggle in the media between environmental protest actors, business actors and policy-makers around a set of meanings to be disseminated among the lay public and frame their reality. Thus Beck in this book wants a national state as 'self-restrained manager', in the role only of 'constructing realities in which the construction of realities of other systems have some freedom of action'. Analysts like Hermann Schwengel of the Berlin Lebenstil working group understand this as the emergence of *Kulturgesellschaft*. In this Schwengel, drawing on Niklas Luhmann, argues that only in very recent late modernity has a cultural sphere fully and finally differentiated off from social, political and economic life. Only now is there full value pluralism, only now the possibility of genuine multiculturalism. Only now is there the possibility of a self-organizing sub-politics in which the stake is the cultural creation of reality.

At issue here too is institutional reflexivity. But this entails more than the democratic contestation of the ideas of experts in a mini-public sphere, although this too is crucial. For Beck the 'way of seeing' of simple modernity foregrounded the distribution of goods. In reflexive modernity in contrast 'ecological threats create a substantive semantic horizon of avoidance, prevention and helping'. And this starts to come closer to the full significance of institutional reflexivity. That is, institutional reflexivity must be understood to embrace the way in which institutions reflect upon, contest and construct the very 'semantic horizon' on which they are based.

Second, not only have previously predominantly social institutions – including economic firms themselves – become more cultural in character, but more strictly cultural institutions (especially education, the media and science) have become increasingly central to reflexive modernity. If, in simple modernity, cultural institutions mainly reproduced the interests of the dominant class in the society, now the cultural institutions themselves are at centre stage. Though I am not at all sure that ours is fundamentally a postmodern condition, I would say that a substantial measure of the cultural artefacts that are disseminated through these institutions is postmodern. Even postmodern theory must be understood in its institutional context, in universities that were founded in the 1960s – such as University of California Santa Cruz and Irvine, Warwick and Essex in the UK, Vincennes previously in France, Essen and

Siegen in Germany – and contesting both the premodern humanism of the old universities and the professionalised modernism of the universities developing at the beginning of the twentieth century. I think that the institutions of art, including critics, museums, DJs, record shops and cinemas, have been central in the legitimation and distribution of such postmodern cultural artefacts – and that both institutions and artefacts are attuned to the sensibility of the lay population in reflexive modernity.

Third, perhaps most importantly, an increasing proportion of our social interactions and communicative interchanges are going on *external* to institutions. An ever greater measure of our labour time for example is now accounted for by production relations existing not within but between firms. This increase in extra-institutional exchange networks is integral to the 'disorganization' of contemporary capitalism. Thus Helmut Berking, also of the Berlin Lebenstil group, speaks of the disengagement of our affective, cognitive and social competencies from the normative expectations of organizations and their re-engagement in the closest affinity groups of lifestyle communities. At issue here is the *Vergesellschaftung der Natur*, as Klaus Eder would have it, but in a double sense. By *Vergesellschaftung*, Eder means not just that nature is socialized in the sense of the contemporary social creation of risks. He means also that society is naturalized. Naturalization, as Beck notes, here means not any sort of essentialism or naturalist reductionism but the thinking through of social and political relations in categories of the natural. And I think that this is true as the semantic horizon of contemporary politics is structured around metaphors like 'body', 'virus', 'risk', 'nature', 'care', 'desire'.

Berking would not disagree but his lifestyle groups are not a question at all of *Vergesellschaftung* but instead forms of 'nachtraditionelle Ver*gemeinschaft*ungen' (post-traditional communalization). Berking starts from radically individualized agents whose affect, previously spread as it were over a broader social space of traditional institutions, is now concentrated in the tight networks of small 'morally overheated' affinity groups. These lifestyle groupings – which have little to do with the taste 'communities' of Bourdieu's *Distinction* – are nexes of intense semantic interchange. They are reflexive, but not in the sense of self-monitoring or democratic debate on competing sets of experts' propositions. They are not reflective in the first instance on propositions at all, but instead on the semantic background, the web of meaning and classifications which are the basis of their understandings. This is a fully different kind of attunement than Beck and Giddens have in mind, yet its precondition is similar to theirs – that is, a radically individualized, fully post-traditional society. This other attunement is partly captured by the notion of reflexivity explicitly formulated by Bourdieu as the systematic reflection on the unthought categories of our thought. But it is often less than fully conscious, often a matter rather of the *sens practique* or the habitus.

This sort of reflexivity is made possible via the (aesthetic) raw materials of time-space distanciated narratives, images, sounds and the like. But its mode of attunement even to itself in self-reflexivity is one which the monitoring subject cannot be de-situated to obtain the objectivity (or realism) of the 'cognitive' reflexivity analysed by Beck and Giddens. Its attunement is not of the subject–object variety presumed in propositional knowledge, but it is hermeneutic. It deals with the semantic backgrounds, the unthought 'primitive' classifications underpinning relationships and lifestyle affinity groups. In self-reflexivity it addresses our own semantic worlds. This hermeneutic attunement suggests the sort of social and cultural analysis of the reflexive anthropologists, for whom reflexivity (as I think it is for Bourdieu) is precisely the departure from the subject–object forms of knowledge into which we are socialized. It suggests instead a relation to the social world that one is analysing, knowledgeably from our own situated (note: not 'standpointed') positions, from our own semantic background, our own prejudgements. Knowledge becomes then a coproduction, a dialogic (though not in Habermas's but James Clifford's sense) process of creating common universes of meaning.

This is not only the self-attunement of Berking's post-traditional communities but would also characterize their sensibility to nature. Again this is not the old peasant *Gemeinschaft* orientation to nature described for example in Max Weber's sociology of religion in *Economy and Society*. It is already individualized, already set free from traditional and early modern institutions. This sensibility however comprises not just knowledge but affect. It is informed not just by science but by poetry, film, music. It is not so much a matter of 'man' and the environment but the systemic balance of ecology and social ecology. It embraces not just the care, and fear, through which we relate to the nature 'out there' but the metaphors through which we relate to our bodies, to the children and microbes we carry in them, to our deaths. In this sense the hermeneutic sensibility towards nature resembles less the Western traditionalist ideal-type than the Japanese 'subject–subject' understanding of the human relation to nature, so aptly described by Augustin Berque.

For Berking these 'morally overheated', semantically intense life-style affinity groups are the stuff of today's social movements. Their active trust is based on the creation of semantic worlds and an ethics of care. This trust undergoes 'routinization' as social relations become more abstract in the transition from affinity group to social movement to formal organization to institution. With each step upward in this hierarchy, trust becomes more mediated, more abstract, increasingly circumscribed by rules. With each step upward trust becomes more contractual, becomes more and more a question of legitimation. With each step upwards from post-traditional *Gemeinschaft* to late modern *Gesellschaft* the emotive and affective investment involved in trust thins out, as ethics becomes less and less linked to affect and increasingly linked to reason.

Thus one can surely agree with Beck and Giddens (and David Harvey) that environmental politics is in the end about damage limitation – and that when it comes to damage limitation one would surely have a lot more confidence in the experts than in the likes of Murray Bookchin. But the question is, who puts the ecological questions on the agenda? Does this have to do with the more immediate and affective (though also cognitive) responses of the lay populations immediately affected and the equally emotive idiom of the protest movements? Or is it the experts themselves? Empirical work being carried out by the cross-national research project co-ordinated by Klaus Eder would tend to suggest that it is the protest movements. Only it would suggest that they themselves have become institutionalized, their language increasingly isomorphic with those of business and policy actors and experts.

Postmodernism and disorganized capitalism

I hope I have been able in this response to develop a bit more clearly the idea of aesthetic reflexivity. It is hardly a new idea. Its roots are of course in Kant's aesthetics in *The Critique of Judgement*; it is developed in Weber's and Simmel's understandings of life conduct and *Persönlichkeit*; we see it in Habermas as a dimension of communicative action and discourse. It takes its place in Charles Taylor's work as a principal source of the modern self. Its connections with hermeneutics are integral – as shown by Taylor himself or as instantiated in Wolf Lepenies's insightful *Die drei Kulturen*, which is an intellectual history in fact of two cultures – scientific and literary as embodied in scientific social theory on the one hand and hermeneutics on the other. A classical sociological theorist such as Simmel for example is in his later hermeneutic analyses writing from essentially aesthetic assumptions.

In this sense there are paradigmatically not one but two modernities, the first with scientific assumptions traversing a genealogy including Galileo, Hobbes, Descartes, Locke, the Enlightenment, (the mature) Marx, Corbusier, sociological positivism, analytic philosophy and Habermas. The other modernity is aesthetic. Apart from brief surfacings in the baroque, in some Dutch landscapes, it appears with vigour as a critique of the first modernity in nineteenth-century Romanticism and aesthetic modernism. If we are to understand reflexivity in the sense of the sociologists of science (and partly Beck in this book) as the self-reflection of a paradigm, then late nineteenth-century literary and artistic modernism was the first time that modernity became properly reflexive. Well before the post-traditional society of the past two or three decades, the first instantiation of reflexive modernity was through the aesthetic. The lineage of this second modernity, which grew through reflection on and as a reflex in regard to the first is Romanticism, the young Hegel, Baudelaire, Nietzsche, Simmel, surrealism, Benjamin, Adorno, Heidegger, Schutz, Gadamer, Foucault, Derrida, and (in contemporary sociology) Bauman.

The point here is clearly not to chronicle the *parenté* of the giants on whose shoulders we stand. The point is not to plot genealogies of 'high modernity' either as science or as aesthetics. This book, it seems to me, is instead about 'low modernity'. It is about how the sensibility of high modernity, both analytic and hermeneutic, has now for the first time spread to the masses of the population in every nook and cranny of social life. And here I agree with Giddens (and I think Beck) that we do live in a fundamental sense for the first time in a post-traditional society. This book is about how this sensibility – both cognitive and affective competencies – detaches from traditional structures and institutions. In this detachment this sensibility – both analytic and hermeneutic – becomes reflexive in turning its critical gaze and competencies on symbolic output of high modernity itself. Thus the critique of expert-systems, of the excesses and assumptions of order of the Enlightenment project either from the analytic standpoint (which Beck and Giddens underscore) or from a more affective, hermeneutic standpoint is not just the lay public in today's modernity becoming reflexive, it is modernity bringing itself to court in self-critique.

If the pervasion of the analytic–scientific world view to the broad masses of the lay public is what Giddens wants to call late modernity, the pervasion of the sensibility of aesthetic modernism to the broad masses of this same public – recounted by countless commentators – is what many others want to understand as *post*modernity. Reflexive modernity is a question of the latter just as much as it is of the former. Beck and Giddens both contest the assumptions of metanarrative order of the Enlightenment project, of simple modernity. For them reflexive modernity is characterized instead by 'ambivalence' or 'experimentation'. Yet their notions of ambivalence and experiment come largely from scientific ideas of indeterminacy, and the unintended consequences of the interventions of science. This is insufficient. In everyday life I expect that such a sensibility derives a lot more from the aesthetic or hermeneutic sensibility.

Finally by 'economies of signs and space' John Urry and I (in our book of that title published in 1994) are not referring to how meaning is deconstructed through the play of signifiers. We are instead addressing the empirical economy in the contemporary world. We are referring to how it is becoming increasingly a 'sign economy' partly through its thoroughgoing informationalization, both of 'labour process' and of what is produced. We try to understand this in terms of 'information structures', an idea derived less from post-structuralism than from Japanese institutional economists. We extend such an idea of 'information and communication structures' from the level of the firm to entire production systems and then to the flows of information and communications (and immigration and tourism) that are taking place on an increasingly global level. Thus we are also talking about economies of space, which at the same time are extensively globalized and intensively localized. These information and communication structures, which stretch over broad areas of space and compress time, contain not just informational signs but also images, narratives and sounds – that is, aesthetic or hermeneutic signs. These not social but effectively cultural structures are the condition of reflexivity for late modern social agents. They are the condition for highly reflexive production in the workplace and for the sort of aesthetic and hermeneutic sensibility described above. Access to such information and communication structures – which are unequally distributed both spatially and socially – is an increasingly central factor in social inequality of class, race and gender in today's world.

It is also in this context that can be seen the extent to which we live in a literally 'disorganizing' capitalism in the sense, not so much of institutional reflexivity but the 'end' or more modestly the decline of institutions and organizations. This is because both intensive and extensive socio-cultural exchanges are increasingly taking place outside of institutions/organizations. In the private sphere, effectively charged semantic interchange is decoupled from the normative expectations of family and community and de-institutionalized in pure relationships – from love relationships to lifestyle affinity groups. Further, within the household communications are displaced from the institution of the family on to the monologic communications from the broadcasting 'few' to the receiving 'many', or the 'robotic dialogics' of the Nintendo or Game Boy.

In public space more impersonal, less effectively invested exchanges are increasingly extra-institutional. Point-to-point communication networks through the information and communication structures, typified by futures, commodity and currency dealing, are often not within organizations but between individuals or firms. The proliferation of alliances in advanced economic sectors, in micro-electronics and biotechnology, are between organizations (and organizations and individuals), are typically brief in duration. Institutional economists such as Williamson and 'socio-economists' like Etzioni may well argue that markets are institutions and presume embeddedness in moral, legal and trust relations. But if they are institutions at all, markets are very special sorts of institutions. They are the least rule-bound of institutions; they comprise the most limited span of reciprocal normative expectations; their social relationships are much briefer in duration than in other institutions. The law they pre-eminently presume is contract law, though institutions by definition are as characterized by 'status' as by 'contract'. The measure of trust markets presuppose is often limited to the foregoing of 'opportunism'. Finally it has been noted that empirically markets operate as long-term, say supplier–buyer, relationships. But to this extent the functional operation of the economy diverges from the market ideal-type only in the direction of much more status (not contract) relations of subcontracting and networks. In any event the point I'm making is that despite the richness of Beck's and Giddens's notions of institutional reflexivity, social relations in reflexive modernity are increasingly *extra*-institutional.

Cultural theory does 'rule the roost' today. In this Giddens is surely right. This is exemplified in a recent event pitting the ideas of Habermas versus Derrida at Frankfurt University in front of an audience of nearly a thousand, where on Habermas's home ground the Derridians outnumbered Habermasians by about four to one. This is a deplorable state of affairs as cultural theory is often useless in addressing issues of everyday life and of politics. In this context the *social*-theoretical interventions of Beck and Giddens must be warmly greeted. Moreover, these are interventions with which I want to make common cause. But I do not think the answer is just to reject and be 'opposed to' post-structuralism and cultural theory. I do not think the best response is to pay little attention to the cultural dimension in what I have argued is becoming ever more a *Kulturgesellschaft*. I think instead that social theory – drawing selectively also on concepts from cultural analysis – can do a better job in understanding the cultural dimension, in our institutions and the sensibility of our private lives, than can the cultural theorists. Beck's and Giddens's reflexive modernity is one in which the social analysis of not just culture but also economic life is effectively marginalized. If 1968 saw the birth of Marxism in the academy then 1989 surely saw its spluttering collapse. This does not mean, however, that social theory in the 1990s should pay little attention to the economy and social inequality.

In the past few years no idea has influenced my understanding of social relations more than that of reflexive modernity. It has especially helped me to rethink postmodernism – and more generally the critique of the modern – in the cultural sphere and the increasing flexibility and informational nature of our economies. No theorists have in this influenced me more than Ulrich Beck and Anthony Giddens. In this context I hope I can urge participation in the social theoretical (and political) project of reflexive modernization. But I must at the same time urge that such participation be at an oblique, interpretive and very critical distance.

Index

flexible, 119
speech act theory, 150
state, metamorphosis of the, 38–41
stranger, 81–2
Streeck, Wolfgang, 125
structuralism, 167–8
structure
  or agency, 111, 119–35
  Giddens' sense, 114, 153–4
  individuals and, 176–7
  see also information and
    communication structures
structure aesthetics, 110–73, 175
sub-politics, 13–23, 187, 192–4, 198
  development of, 34, 39–41, 44
  distinguished from politics,
    22–3, 36, 37
  and politics, 16–23
  and value pluralism, 208
subcultures, 147–8
subjectivity
  to community from, 146–53
  political, 18–19
surrealism, 212
surveillance, 92–3, 94
systems theory, 19, 24–5

Taylor, Charles, 126, 164, 165, 211
  Sources of the Self, 152
technical colleges, 123–4
technocracy, 48
technology, 60, 75, 79, 190
  development and utilization,
    26–8
  and genetic social change, 47
Tönnies, Ferdinand, 113, 114, 145,
  178
Touraine, Alain, 114–15
tradition, 185, 202–3
  adoption of, 78–9
  changing status of, vi-vii
  compared with expertise, 84–5
  complementary to nature, 76–9
  as contextual, 79–82
  discourse and violence, 104–7
  discursive justification, 100,
    105–6
  emotional cast of, 67–8

evacuation of, 57, 73–4, 95–100
and gender, 105–6
Giddens' definition, 63–5
'invented' (Hobsbawm), 93
as a medium of identity, 80–1,
  95
in modernity, 56–7, 91–5
moral content, 65–6
and ritual, 61–6
traditional society, 104
Giddens' idea, 62–3, 66
training policies, 125–6
Trobriands, the, 100
trust
  active in the risk society, 186–7,
    194
  frozen, 90–1
  Giddens' notion of active, 201–2,
    205–6
  risk and reflexivity, 184–97
trust relations, 116
  between experts and lay
    individuals, 89–91
  and reflexive production, 121–7
  and ritual, 79–82
truth
  formulaic, 63–5, 76, 79, 100,
    103–4, 202–3
  hermeneutic, 204–5
  propositional, 202, 203–4

uncertainty, 8–13, 183
  'manufactured', 184–5
underclass, new with reflexivity,
  127–35
United Kingdom, production
  relations, 121–7
United States of America,
  production relations, 121–7
unthought categories, 154–5, 168,
  210
Urry, John, 213

values, clashes, 105
violence, 100, 105, 106
  racial, 131
  tradition and discourse, 104–7
vocation, as political action, 47–52